es

aries

WHISPERS
ACROSS
CONTINENTS

WHISPERS ACROSS CONTINENTS

IN SEARCH OF THE ROBINSONS

GARETH WINROW

AMBERLEY

First published 2019

Amberley Publishing
The Hill, Stroud
Gloucestershire, GL5 4EP

www.amberley-books.com

British Library Cataloguing in Publication Data.
A catalogue record for this book is available from the British Library.

ISBN 978 1 4456 9139 8 (hardback)
ISBN 978 1 4456 9140 4 (ebook)

Typesetting by Aura Technology and Software Services, India.
Printed in the UK.

Contents

Contents

Abbreviations

AFS	Auxiliary Fire Service
AvD	German Automobile Club (*Automobilclub von Deutschland*)
CHP	Republican People's Party (*Cumhuriyet Halk Partisi*)
CUP	Committee of Union and Progress
DHP	Darjeeling Himalayan Railway
DMV	German Automobile Drivers' Association (*Deutsche Motorradfahrer-Vereinigung*)
EIC	East India Company
Hp	horsepower
INC	Indian National Congress
KAC	Imperial Automobile Club (*Kaiserlicher Automobilclub*)
LMI	Liverpool Muslim Institute
NSU	Sewing and Knitting Union (*Naeh- und Strick Union*)
US	United States
YMCA	Young Men's Christian Association
YWCA	Young Women's Christian Association

Timeline

1835	British acquisition of Darjeeling
1839	*Tanzimat* – Introduction of reforms in the Ottoman Empire
1857	The 'Indian Mutiny'
1869	Opening of the Suez Canal
1875–96	The Great Depression of British Agriculture
1881	Completion of the Darjeeling Himalayan Railway to Darjeeling
1887	Opening of the Liverpool Muslim Institute
1888	Launch of the Sikkim Expedition
1907	First Scout camp organised on Brownsea Island
1908	The Young Turk Revolution
1909	Overthrow of Sultan Abdülhamid II
1912–13	The Balkan Wars
1914–18	First World War
1916 (23 Apr.)	Battle of Katiya
1918 (13 Nov.)	*De facto* Allied occupation of Constantinople/Istanbul
1919	Establishment of the South-West Caucasus Democratic Republic
1920 (20 Mar.)	*De jure* Allied occupation of Constantinople/Istanbul
1923 (2 Oct.)	End of Allied occupation of Constantinople/Istanbul
1923 (29 Oct.)	Founding of the Republic of Turkey
1933 (30 Jan.)	Hitler becomes chancellor of Germany
1938 (9–10 Nov.)	*Kristallnacht* in Nazi Germany
1939–45	Second World War

Family Trees

ROBINSON/PALMER

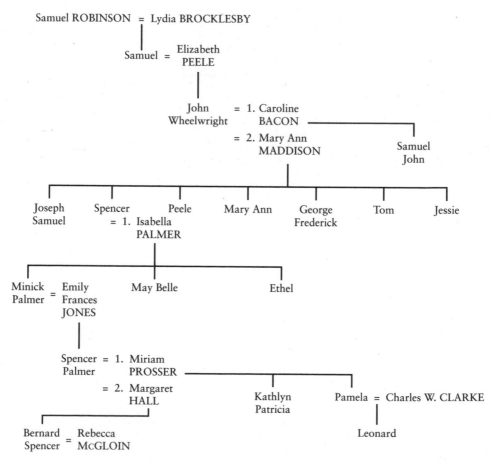

Samuel ROBINSON = Lydia BROCKLESBY

Samuel = Elizabeth PEELE

John Wheelwright = 1. Caroline BACON
= 2. Mary Ann MADDISON

Samuel John

Joseph Samuel   Spencer = 1. Isabella PALMER   Peele   Mary Ann   George Frederick   Tom   Jessie

Minick Palmer = Emily Frances JONES   May Belle   Ethel

Spencer Palmer = 1. Miriam PROSSER
= 2. Margaret HALL

Kathlyn Patricia   Pamela = Charles W. CLARKE

Bernard Spencer = Rebecca McGLOIN

Leonard

RUSSELL/RODDA/ROBINSON

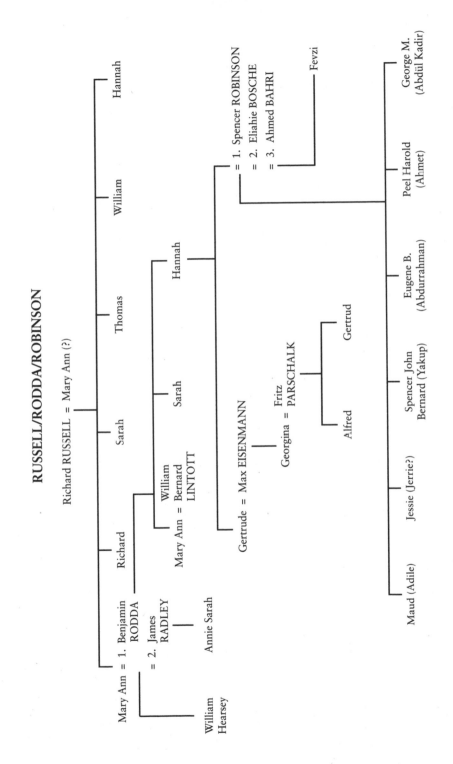

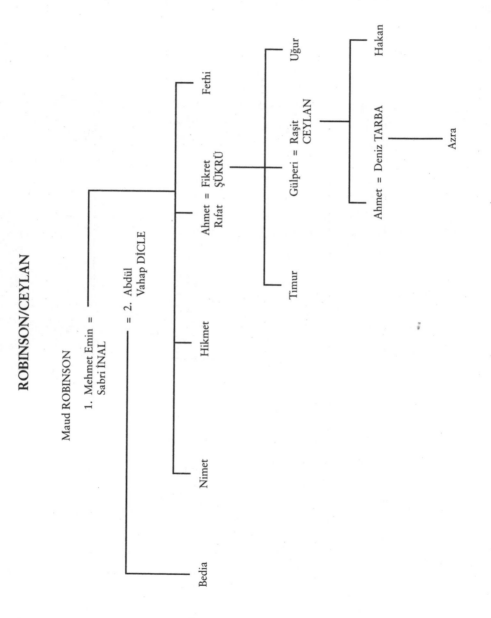

ROBINSON/CEYLAN

Maud ROBINSON

1. Mehmet Emin =
   Sabri İNAL

= 2. Abdül
   Vahap DİCLE

Bedia

Nimet

Hikmet

Ahmet = Fikret
Rıfat   ŞÜKRÜ

Fethi

Timur

Gülperi = Raşit
          CEYLAN

Uğur

Ahmet = Deniz TARBA

Hakan

Azra

List of Illustrations

1. Window, St Helen's Church, Saxby, Lincs.
2. William Henry 'Abdullah' Quilliam
3. Field Marshal Mustafa Zeki Pasha
4. Sultan Abdülhamid II in his youth
5. Fort Graham, Gnatong
6. Darjeeling
7. Ahmed Bahri and the sons of Hannah Robinson (Fatima Bahri)
8. Maud (Adile) Robinson
9. Gertrude Eisenmann
10. Galatasaray football team, 1908–9 season
11. Ahmet Robenson
12. Yakup Robenson and members of 'the camel corps'
13. Hannah Robinson (Fatima Bahri)
14. Ahmet Robenson and members of family at the Lyndhurst estate, Tarrytown, New York
15. Bernard Robinson
16. Ahmet Ceylan

Prefaces

I was unaware that a book on the family was being prepared until I was contacted by the author, Gareth Winrow, early in 2017. It was after my mother, aged 105, had died the previous October. Gareth had spotted an obituary in the press which had references to my father, Spencer Palmer Robinson. He wrote to me to establish that I was indeed the son of Spencer Palmer. This led to a meeting in Leicester where I now live.

Our meeting proved fruitful, with exchanges of photos, letters and documents. My mother had told me many rumours about my father's family history. However, she herself had been unsure of some details. I have found the book to be a revelation. It showed how my family had fitted in the social, political and international history of the time. What I found most surprising was the information about my grandfather, Minick, and how he appeared to turn his hand to anything from working on railways in India and Britain to training in the Royal Engineers in Portsmouth and becoming a submarine miner.

Thanks to Gareth's painstaking research, I have been able to re-establish contact with a member on the Turkish side of the family.

I feel Gareth's book has brought the Robinson family to life and has shown how various individuals in the family were a reflection of Victorian society.

Bernard Robinson
Great-grandson of Spencer Robinson

It is both a great responsibility and a great pleasure to write this piece. The responsibility lies with the balancing act between seeing part of your family history told in such a well-written, well-documented book and the pride and joy of knowing that one of your best friends is behind this whole project. I am lucky enough to have been a witness to how the book was created piece by piece. I always felt extremely comfortable about sharing any part of the family story with Gareth, as it has been told in the family through time, since I knew that it would be in safe hands. When the story caught us by surprise, as it did sometimes, I still did not feel uncomfortable, since I knew that Gareth would handle his material with utmost care and with the highest ethical values. Gareth ended up with many different episodes and details from our family history which were brand new to us. At one point, I felt overwhelmed and a little worried as to how all the pieces would come together in a book that third-party readers could enjoy. When I had the privilege of reading the final draft, I saw for myself that I worried for nothing...

Of all the Robinsons, Ahmet Robenson is the best-known member of the family in Turkey. I had the pleasure of meeting him when I was only seven years old. He gave me and my brother going-away gifts before we left New York on a ship that would take us across the ocean on our way back to Turkey. I still cherish the fond memory of a jar full of coloured candy. I discovered that someone else on the other side of the ocean had also received gifts from Ahmet Robenson when he was a young kid. His name is Bernard Robinson, and he is a distant cousin I found out about when Gareth and Nazan, his wife, met Bernard and his wife to exchange notes and memories.

Last year, several books were published that mentioned Ahmet Robenson due to his role in introducing and developing international sports and Scouting in Turkey. I did something unusual and went to several meetings in Istanbul where those publications were launched and visited exhibitions covering the same topics. It was unusual for me to do this since I have never been a proper sports fan. I enjoyed the events nevertheless, since they gave me the opportunity to meet some very interesting people I would not have otherwise met. Those people knew a lot about Ahmet Robenson, and they were kind enough to share their resources with Gareth. One of them in particular deserves a mention here: Mehmet Yüce. I had a chance to meet him when a panel of experts presented his newly printed book about the first years of soccer in Turkey. His book dedicates one chapter to Ahmet Robenson and one chapter to Abdurrahman Robenson. I would not dare translate the title of his book since it is in Ottoman Turkish and carries tones of subtle humour in it.

Now that I know so much more about one part of my family, I probably ask more questions than ever before. However, I feel so much better connected to my past after reading the adventures of all the individuals mentioned in the book, for the simple reason that I see how life can be a rollercoaster. It gives you strength to deal with life as you go through it one day at a time, knowing that it will sometimes be fun, and sometimes painful. I guess the lesson to be learned is to try to leave behind a story worth telling. All the people chronicled in this book did just that, and Gareth Winrow did an absolutely wonderful job of telling their stories and connecting the dots. As we say in Turkish, '*eline sağlık*', Gareth.

Ahmet Ceylan
Great-great-grandson of Spencer Robinson

Introduction

So it is we often find ourselves, willy-nilly defined by
the very thing we are trying to leave behind.

Glenn Patterson, *Lapsed Protestant*

Raised in the slums of London's East End, Hannah Robinson (born Hannah Rodda) was one of the first women to convert to Islam in late Victorian England. She married a reputedly famous Afghan warlord, known as Gholab Shah, and relocated to Constantinople in late 1891. Six months later the marriage was in tatters. The so-called Gholab Shah was exposed as a charlatan and an inveterate abuser of women. Hannah wrote a letter to the office of the British prime minister, Lord Salisbury, pleading for support. Given the personal involvement of the Ottoman sultan in the case, the issue could have spiralled into a wider diplomatic incident.

This is a snippet of one of the many fascinating stories of a particular family – the Robinsons. This book traces the history of the Robinsons, originally tenant farmers in nineteenth-century rural Lincolnshire, from the hill stations of Bengal to the banks of the Bosphorus, the streets of New York and the halls of Wilhelmine Germany. Tales of success and achievement emerge in the lives of key members of the Robinson family, juxtaposed with accounts of tragedy and humiliation.

Why study a family which is not one's own? The current burgeoning interest in family history is largely based on exploring one's own ancestors to answer the question: 'Who do we think we are?' It does not matter if one's family consists of supposed common folk rather than royalty, celebrities or leading politicians of the day.

Casting our gaze back to the past, we are invariably struck by a feeling of unconditional awe at the struggles and achievements of our ancestors. We are at the same time surprised and delighted if we discover that our past relatives shared similar traits to us and pursued objectives with which we could empathise. These echoes of a past which reverberate in the present both intrigue us and command our willing attention. In seeking to learn more about our ancestors, we are consciously hoping to uncover previously unknown information about ourselves. In this quest, however, we also harbour doubts and concerns that our antecedents may include among their ranks slaveowners, criminals and other figures of disrepute.

How, then, did I become interested in the history of another family – the Robinsons? If truth be told, there was no immediate rush to put pen to paper upon hearing a few of the exploits of 'Ahmet Robenson' from Ahmet Ceylan, a good friend of mine. 'Robenson' is the Turkified form of 'Robinson' and is the name commonly used by Turkish commentators. Meeting the Ceylans in Istanbul in 1988, we were fascinated to hear that Ahmet Ceylan's great-grandmother, Maud (Turkish name Adile), was English. We heard how Maud's brother, known in Turkey as Ahmet Robenson (originally named Peel Harold Robinson), was well known in Turkish sporting circles and had introduced basketball to the country. There was also mention of Ahmet Robenson's mother, Hannah (Turkish name Fatima or Fatma), who had married an officer in the Ottoman Army. The name 'Ahmet Robenson' immediately conjured up disconnected images of Turkey and England. It quickly dawned upon us that our friend, Ahmet, could have long-lost cousins back in England. Family ties between the Robinsons in England and their relatives in Turkey had apparently been severed years before.

In spite of our initial interest, we did not pursue the story further. We picked up the trail again many years later. Living and working at that time in Turkey, and having formed our own bicultural and binational family, tales of the Robinsons increasingly resonated. Ready access to the internet was another bonus. With the encouragement of Ahmet Ceylan and my wife, I decided to investigate the lives of the Robinsons. Given my academic interest in the disciplines of history and international relations, I was already acquainted with the global events in which the Robinsons would become closely involved.

What I unearthed was a veritable treasure trove of hidden and undisclosed family details and facts stranger than fiction. Previously untold tales and adventures surfaced spanning generations and continents. Characters who had only been dimly perceived were suddenly exposed as larger-than-life personalities, while other long-forgotten family members jostled to grab my attention. The Robinsons interacted with a host of individuals who have left their mark on history. These included a Liverpool-based solicitor turned Muslim Sheikh who founded one of England's first mosques, a 'gentleman' and renowned physician working in Queen Victoria's household, and a humble tobacconist who figured prominently in a notorious divorce case. To my surprise, some of the Robinson family were at ease mingling with ministers and aristocrats and even had privileged access to the Ottoman Palace. There were unsubstantiated accounts of political intrigues, reports of suspected espionage and rumours of illicit relationships. These stories were all the more striking given that Ahmet Robenson's mother was born and brought up in poverty. While Ahmet Robenson's father came from a long line of reasonably well-to-do Lincolnshire tenant farmers, the history of the Robinsons would not be complete without taking into account other offshoots of the family. The humble lives of bricklayers, domestic servants, merchant seamen, and those struggling in the workhouse also have their part to play in the unravelling story of the Robinsons.

I could never have imagined that my initial tentative foray into researching the life of Hannah Robinson and her son, Ahmet, would uncover such fascinating details. Here were people who were forced to negotiate their paths through life in times of major political and social unrest. These were individuals who could adapt to rapidly changing circumstances – tragedy would bring opportunity, difficulties might open the door to new achievements. Here were characters whose amazing stories had surprisingly gone almost unnoticed and unrecorded. The more I learned about the Robinsons, the more I realised that their lives should be documented and their tales told. I became increasingly attached to them and started to closely follow and identify with their successes and mistakes, their strengths and shortcomings.

The living Turkish relatives of Hannah Robinson have only vague recollections of parts of the Robinson family narrative. They knew, for example, that Ahmet Robenson's father, Spencer, had lived, worked and died in India, but they were not fully cognisant of Spencer's Lincolnshire roots. Much more familiar to them were some of the stories involving Hannah, Spencer's second wife. In contrast, Spencer's great-grandson living in England was aware of family ties in Germany. An illegitimate daughter of Hannah married a German entrepreneur and settled in Hamburg, where she quickly made a name as a motorbike racing champion and an accomplished automobile racer. However, the English side of the family were much less familiar with the details of Hannah's offspring living in Turkey. As I learned more about the Robinsons, I would be struck by the gulf which emerged over time between branches of the family based in Turkey and England.

Ahmet Ceylan recalls that when he was a young child he saw Ahmet Robenson in New York. The year was 1964. The Ceylans were about to return to Turkey after having lived and worked in the United States (hereafter US) for a period. They drove across the continent from Los Angeles to New York in a black 1958 Chevrolet Bel Air. Ahmet Ceylan remembers that the back seat of the car was filled with cardboard boxes and he and his younger brother were forced to travel seated on top of them. They met Ahmet Robenson in the grounds of a large house. This was the Lyndhurst estate in Tarrytown, New York State – the former home of the original American 'robber baron', Jay Gould. Ahmet Robenson had been employed as a caretaker on the property for several years after having emigrated to the US from the Turkey in the late 1920s. Ahmet Ceylan recollects how this friendly old man brought two jars of colourful candy for him and his brother, and that he seemed to be very comfortable when driving them all in his own car around the neighbourhood next to the estate. Ahmet Ceylan said of his great-uncle: 'My memory of him is of a soft-spoken, nice, old man.'

Thinking back, Ahmet believes that Ahmet Robenson had a very similar presence to that of his grandfather, another Ahmet – Ahmet Rıfat, one of the sons of Maud, sister of Ahmet Robenson. Ironically, Ahmet Rıfat was a dedicated fan of the Fenerbahçe football team. Fenerbahçe were long-time bitter rivals of Galatasaray, the Istanbul sports club with which Ahmet Robenson was very closely associated. Ahmet Rıfat's wife, Fikret, was a graduate of the prestigious Arnavutköy School for Girls in Istanbul. At school, Fikret was a friend of Sabiha Gökçen, the adopted daughter of Atatürk, the founder of the Republic of Turkey. Fluent in English, Fikret was on good terms with Maud and Maud's mother, Hannah. According to Ahmet Ceylan, at one point in her old age Hannah may have contemplated visiting her son in New York and had asked Fikret to accompany her. This plan never materialised. Nonetheless, Fikret visited her husband's grandmother in Izmir several times and had affectionate memories of these trips.

Every family is unique. We may have a clear conception of what a family is or what it should be, but in practice there is no ideal family. All families have interesting stories to tell. Some of these stories may have become distorted or exaggerated through the passage of time and the handing down from generation to generation. Facts become misplaced, truths unconsciously and unknowingly reworked and reshaped. Family tales are more likely to have been remoulded or embellished if the family has spread across continents. Myths could then take hold to be reinforced by later generations. Past events are recalled and reinterpreted in the present. Memories of family members might be constructed or invented, and 'dark truths' ignored and then forgotten.

The historical backdrop for many of the stories recounted here is the turbulent period which heralded the end of the nineteenth and the start of the twentieth centuries. This *fin de siècle* was marked by the questioning of established customs and accepted ways of living and the challenging of traditional norms and values. Entrenched views on race, class and gender were confronted. New political ideologies and social movements became increasingly popular. Technological developments resulted in a globalising but not yet globalised world.

This was an era of change and opportunity. There was a sense that certain previously accepted modes of behaviour were losing their relevance or were at least open to question. Novel means of interpreting thoughts and action were in the process of fermentation. In this time of endings and beginnings it was not clear whether these new ways would lead to a better life. It was a period of transition, and 'a world in which the new and old co-existed'.[1] In practice, it was also an age in which political, social and economic unrest resulted in revolution, and the colliding of empires culminated in war.

The Robinsons, wherever they were situated, were both witnesses and participants in this unfolding chain of events. Those who remained in England contended with the consequences of a major agricultural depression and the impact of a rapidly transforming society. Some family members, for various reasons, emigrated to distant lands and began new lives in unfamiliar surroundings. This urge – or perceived need – to start over again was a reflection of the nature of the times. The world was becoming smaller, but this was still an era when the allure and mystique of what was imagined to be the exotic Orient remained a source of fascination and trepidation for people in the West. Commencing a fresh life in India or in the Ottoman Empire would have been a major undertaking for anyone brought up in the heart of rural Lincolnshire or raised in the slums of London. The Robinsons would also be caught up in the tragedies of the First World War. Alongside this, they personally observed the deaths of empires and the births of republics.

As well as possibly referring to a birthplace or a location in which one spent one's formative years, home is often closely associated with family. It may be remembered as a secure and protective environment, a place of relaxation where one can let one's defences down. In this sense, home might be looked upon as a repository of meaningful recollections, a vessel full of positive memories. A family which has migrated may believe that it has succeeded in establishing new roots and created a home overseas. But others beyond the immediate family may perceive their identity differently, and may not accept them as part of their community. Family members could continue to be regarded as foreigners. This might be the case even if the family adopted the religion of the locals and fully embraced the customs and traditions of their neighbours. Is it possible to feel 'at home' when one's sense of belonging is challenged and one's very presence in a country is questioned by outsiders? In the example of the Robinsons in the Ottoman Empire and Turkey in particular, I could not help wondering at the extent to which others might still define them by that which they were 'trying to leave behind'.

When I started to investigate the Robinsons, two obvious questions sprung to mind: who were they, and what did they do? I did not set out to provide a comprehensive history of all members of the Robinson family from Lincolnshire. This would have been an impossible task.[2] Victorian families tended to be large. I did not want to go through the laborious exercise of simply compiling long lists of names and dates of births, marriages and deaths. This welter of detail presumably would have little attraction to a wider audience. I have therefore endeavoured to keep to a minimum the names of family members. The use of family trees and a timeline will hopefully enable the reader to navigate a path through the labyrinth of key dates, names and events.

I took Spencer Robinson as my starting point. As I began to examine more closely the lives of some of Spencer's immediate relatives, the contours of something much more substantial emerged. It became increasingly clear that here were stories, and stories within stories, which not only chimed with the spirit of the times but also clamoured to be told. I also soon realised, however, that the job I was undertaking would not be easy and would at times be frustrating because of the paucity of family correspondence and the lack of other records. Letters between family members are usually a key source to help one understand the history of a particular family. Unfortunately, few of the Robinsons' letters have been preserved, but those that are available, including a few in the National Archives, do provide revealing insights. They offer windows through which we as outsiders are able to peer in and observe the lives of the Robinsons at a moment frozen in time.

Where possible, I have conducted interviews and exchanged communications with living members of the Robinson family in England, Turkey and Germany. Here, stories partly based on rumour were recounted. Sometimes, these tales were revealing in showing how major events in the family history had been forgotten or were previously known only by select individuals within the family. Family memories, while important, are often incomplete and may be unintentionally distorted.

I attempted to make full use of information available on the internet in various family search engines. Here censuses, birth, marriage and death records, details of wills, workhouse notices, passenger lists, trade directories, electoral rolls, post office records and so on were all valuable. Materials from local archives and old newspaper accounts were especially useful. Documents and texts from the late Ottoman Empire and early Turkish Republic were more difficult to access because of the use of the Ottoman script and less systematic record-keeping. Articles and books were also consulted to gain a better appreciation of the wider social, economic and political context in which the Robinsons lived and worked.

Visits were made to locations in England and India which provided important settings for some of the stories. I am especially grateful to the local historian Kit Lawie for taking me around the farmsteads and graveyards of East Keal and its surrounding hamlets. She and her family had lived and worked in the area for generations. Her ancestors must surely have crossed paths with Spencer Robinson and his contemporaries.

There are still lacunae in the family narrative. Try as I might, in some cases I was unable to discover how certain key individuals met and then married. Occasionally, I was forced to speculate on why major life-changing decisions were made. The answers to some of my questions remained infuriatingly beyond reach. But, as in all history, the history of any family may be reassessed and reinterpreted if fresh evidence is revealed. Perhaps a reader of this book might be motivated to come forward with information which could shed new light on a particular episode. After all, history is a living subject and one which should not be foreclosed.

While processing these various materials, I was struck by certain myths about the Robinsons cultivated by interested outside commentators. Repeated references to the supposed aristocratic background of Spencer and Hannah (who for some inexplicable reason was often referred to as 'Lady Sarah') were made by Turkish analysts. One usually reputable publication referred to Ahmet Robenson's father as 'Sir Rhodes'.[3] Ahmet Robenson himself colluded in the rewriting of his family's history. In an interview he gave shortly before his death, Ahmet boldly claimed that his family was one which had given England prime ministers, and that they were connected to the Rhodes family which had lent its name to the part of the British Empire known as Rhodesia.[4]

Some observers may have deliberately elevated the status of the Robinson family for propaganda purposes. Turkish commentators put much emphasis on the conversion of 'Lady Sarah', and ostensibly Spencer, to Islam. The higher the social status of the Robinsons, the more weight could be given to the voluntary conversion of prominent Christians to Islam. Ahmet Robenson may have intentionally spun a narrative about his family's supposed lofty origins to counter an opposing storyline which cast serious suspicion over the loyalty of the Robenson family to the Ottoman/Turkish cause. As a part of this fabrication, Ahmet appeared to have knowingly played upon the similarity between the 'Rodda' and 'Rhodes' surnames.

Accounts of the Robinson/Robenson family are littered with other errors. The Turkish version of Wikipedia, for example, mentions Liverpool as the birthplace of Ahmet Robenson, and this is then reproduced in almost all Turkish works referring to him. In reality, Ahmet Robenson was born in the foothills of the Himalayas. His mother's second marriage did take place in Liverpool, when Ahmet was a small child, and this perhaps accounts for the continued reference to the port.

In 2018, the Turkish government unexpectedly opened its records to allow the public to access data on their family history. The background details given for the family of Ahmet Ceylan were strewn with errors. There was no reference to the English heritage of the family. The official records did not refer to a 'Sir Rhodes' or a 'Lady Sarah'. Instead, an 'Ahmet Remzi' was listed as the father of 'Ayşe' (i.e. Adile or Maud). The mother of 'Ayşe' was recorded as 'Fatma', who was supposedly born in Istanbul in 1866. Ahmet and Zekiye were listed as Fatma's father and mother. Such basic mistakes lead one to question the value and authenticity of the Turkish/Ottoman family records.

Many questions in the history of the Robinson family remain unanswered, and the narrative is far from complete. In my research on the Robinsons I was led along paths which I could never have envisaged. Some roads turned out to be disappointing cul-de-sacs. Other avenues opened up into expansive networks where previously unknown characters were signposted. Stories had to be repeatedly rewritten and re-evaluated to take into account new findings and revelations. Several of the stories covered universal themes to which all families can relate: the loss of a partner; the birth of a child; the collapse of a much-worked upon project; the success of a business enterprise; movement up the social ladder; the disappointment of failed opportunities.

This book, above all, is an open-ended inquiry into the Robinsons. I attempt to follow members of the family in their particular journeys through history. Observing the lives of individuals and how they deal, or fail to deal, with obstacles and challenges confronting them enables one to explore the past from other angles, and arguably helps make history come more alive.

Writing about a family which is not one's own does automatically entail a certain responsibility. Not wanting to either judge or pre-judge, I was consciously aware of the importance of letting the characters act and speak for themselves as much as possible. I certainly did not intend to make the book a portrayal of the lives of the Robinsons along the lines of a family soap opera. In practice, though, I must confess that I could not help but warm to some of the characters and even find an affinity with them. The more I learned about particular members of the Robinson family, the more difficult it became to separate myself and remain emotionally detached. My hope is that I have done justice to the characters on whom I have focussed.

I dedicate this book to the Robinsons.

1

Spencer Robinson I: Lincolnshire Roots

Doesn't thou 'ear my 'erse's legs, as they canters awaay?
Proputty, proputty, proputty that's what I 'ears 'em say
Lord Alfred Tennyson, 'Northern Farmer: New Style'

Introduction

An account of the lives of Spencer Robinson and his immediate family can only begin in rural Lincolnshire. Direct descendants of Spencer living in England came to believe that his father, also purportedly called Spencer Robinson, was a farmer and landowner who resided at Hagworthingham Hall in the county. This was not the case. Spencer's father, John Wheelwright Robinson, probably never lived in the Lincolnshire village of Hagworthingham. The Old Hall in the village, built in the mid-seventeenth century, was owned and occupied by the Cheales family. The Cheales were local gentry who had lived in the county since at least the thirteenth century. However, John Wheelwright's second wife, Mary Ann Maddison, was born in Hagworthingham, and there were other close family ties between the Robinsons and Maddisons.

The Robinsons were actually a well-established family of Lincolnshire tenant farmers. Scattered in villages throughout the county, by the mid-nineteenth century the Robinsons were in general well-to-do country folk running several of the larger farms in Lincolnshire. Spencer Robinson himself was born in East Keal in Lincolnshire on 22 March 1838 and was baptised in the same village three days later. Spencer's father, grandfather and great-grandfather had all been tenant farmers in the county. They had apparently got on well with their rich landlords, who were the owners of large landed estates. Although 'only' tenant farmers and not major landowners themselves, the Robinsons became significant pillars of the communities in which they lived.

However, times were changing. Spencer and his brothers were the last generation of Robinsons to primarily earn their living from the land. Improvements in transportation with the spread of the railway network meant that Lincolnshire was no longer so isolated from the rest of the country. The journey to London became much easier. New job opportunities further afield beckoned. The mid-1870s saw the beginning of what is known as the Great Depression of British Agriculture, and this had a major negative impact on farming in Lincolnshire. The Robinsons were not saved from its effects; each of Spencer's three brothers involved in farming were casualties of the resulting economic downturn in the 1880s. Personal tragedies also took their toll. Some family members were compelled to abandon farming and leave the county. Others, as in the case of Spencer, opted to seek fresh challenges overseas. Spencer himself encountered further financial difficulties in India.

The sons of the next generation of Robinsons after Spencer were no longer so closely tied to the land. They embarked on new careers beyond the county or abroad. Those remaining in England took up professions such as engineering and law or worked in the civil service. In some cases, the daughters of the next generation of Robinsons married husbands who were not farmers and re-located to live outside Lincolnshire. The Robinsons were therefore typical of other reasonably wealthy rural families in the late nineteenth century who were forced to adapt to the changing times in Victorian England.

Spencer's experience as a farmer in Lincolnshire would help him in his later years. Hard work, discipline and the ability to manage a team of labourers proved to be essential skills which he could tap when working in the tea estates of India. A penchant for taking risks did not always pay off, but his personal energy, social bonhomie and thirst to be an active member of the community would find echoes in the lives of his own children.

*

The family of Spencer Robinson can easily be traced back to the mid-eighteenth century. In this earlier period, the names of certain members of those families with whom the Robinsons intermarried would leave their mark on later generations. Surnames such as 'Spencer', 'Peele', 'Wheelwright', 'Minnick/Minick' and 'Palmer' were used as first and middle names for the sons of future Robinsons.

Spencer Robinson's great-grandfather Samuel of 'Hackthorn' (a parish north of Lincoln) was probably born in 1737 or thereabouts. He married Lydia Brocklesby in the Lincolnshire village of Faldingworth in May 1765. Samuel and Lydia raised a family of eight children. Shortly after their marriage the couple settled in Bishop Norton in the same county where Samuel worked as a farmer. Later, they moved to nearby West Torrington where Samuel died in June 1812, reputedly aged seventy-five. In his will, he left an estate worth approximately £800 – a very tidy sum of money at the time.[1] His wife died at the impressive age of ninety-three, shortly before the birth of Spencer, her great-grandson. Lydia passed away in the Lincolnshire village of Asgarby in the house of her son, also called Samuel, on 8 September 1837.[2]

Spencer's grandfather Samuel Robinson was born in Bishop Norton in 1766. He married Elizabeth Peele in Grayingham in the same county in June 1796. About eight years later, Samuel moved to South Ormsby in Lincolnshire to become the tenant of Campaign Farm. This property was owned by the local Massingberd family. The Massingberds were wealthy landowners who had lived in the county since the fourteenth century and were the occupants of South Ormsby Hall. Two brothers in the family had fought on the side of the Roundheads in the English Civil War but were later pardoned by King Charles II. Campaign Farm may have been named after a camp used by Parliamentarian soldiers when the Battle of Winceby was fought in the area in 1643. Alternatively, the name perhaps originated from a nearby Roman encampment.

In 1832, Samuel relocated again to take up residence at Asgarby House in Asgarby. This property, extending over 480 acres, dated back to at least the sixteenth century and belonged to the Ecclesiastical Commissioners – the corporate body which managed the properties of the Church of England. Samuel eventually moved from Asgarby after his wife's death and by 1841 he was living in East Keal with one of his sons, John Wheelwright, the father of Spencer Robinson. It seems that Samuel's eldest son, William Wheelwright, took over the running of Asgarby House. The Robinson family continued to live at Asgarby House until the late 1920s. Samuel died in 1850, leaving an estate worth over £1,100.

The mother of Elizabeth – the wife of Samuel – was known as Jane Wheelwright of Grantham. Elizabeth's father, William, a grazier from Grayingham, was the son of William and Elizabeth Peele (née Spencer).[3] Samuel and Elizabeth Robinson had in total eight children. The five sons of Samuel and Elizabeth all became farmers earning their living in different villages dotted throughout Lincolnshire.

Clearly, the Robinsons were advancing up the social ladder. They were becoming increasingly prosperous Lincolnshire tenant farmers. Before his death in 1834, Joseph, the youngest son of Samuel and Lydia Robinson, had made his name as a wealthy tenant farmer in East Keal. Joseph farmed land covering over 209 acres for the local landowner and lord of the manor, John Hassard Short.[4] He left an estate valued at over £3,000.[5] Following on from his uncle's success, John Wheelwright Robinson also became an influential farmer in the village and flourished in the period which became known as the golden age of 'High Farming'.

Farming in Nineteenth-century Lincolnshire

The famous English novelist H. Rider Haggard noted, when describing Lincolnshire, that 'to those who are concerned with the land and agriculture this is perhaps the most deeply interesting county in all England'.[6] The second-largest county and one of the least urbanised, Lincolnshire was and remains predominantly agricultural. Well known for its wolds and fenland, parts of the county also included stretches of heath and marsh. Different qualities of soil necessitated the adoption of various types of farming to get the most out of the land. The contrasting topography also encouraged distinct ways of life in communities spread across the county.

In Victorian England, rural society was generally based on a three-tiered hierarchical structure. Wealthy local gentry – often the lords of the manor of particular villages – owned substantial tracts of land. Much of this land was managed by tenant farmers who paid fixed annual rents to their landlords. The tenant farmers, in turn, hired and paid the wages of agricultural labourers to work the fields.

The status of the tenant farmer in nineteenth-century England was complex and ambiguous. They could be the tenants of more than one landowner. The amount of land they farmed varied considerably.

In Britain in the 1870s and 1880s, 70 per cent of tenant farmers maintained holdings of less than 50 acres. Only 18 per cent of tenant farmers managed land of over 100 acres.[7] So-called 'capitalist farmers' controlling property over 300 acres were a small minority.[8] It has been suggested that in Victorian England 'farmers were not gentlemen, but they could live like them'.[9]

Lincolnshire was famous for its system of tenant right. This involved 'the just claim of a farmer to compensation for any unexhausted improvements made by him and remaining on his holding at the end of his tenancy'.[10] In effect, under this system any incoming tenant paid the outgoing tenant for improvements to buildings and land carried out by the latter and in so doing the newcomer purchased the tenant right.[11] If the tenants disagreed over payments to be made, the dispute was resolved by binding arbitration. This system was intended to give the tenant farmer security for any financial investments made during his tenancy. In practice, the landowners also assisted tenant farmers in making investments.[12] Such capital was required to improve land cultivation and management in the era of so-called 'High Farming' in Victorian England.

'High Farming' covered roughly the period from the 1830s to the mid-1870s. This timespan witnessed the start of the mechanisation of farming with the introduction of new types of drills and the application of steam-powered equipment. The increasingly widespread use of fertilisers and feeds such as oilcake also resulted in the more intensive cultivation of crops, while drainage improvements led to the expansion of arable land. These were boom times for farmers as agricultural output increased. Spencer Robinson and his father were clearly beneficiaries of this golden age.

Writing in the mid-nineteenth century, Lord Alfred Tennyson, himself the son of a Lincolnshire clergyman, in his two poems on the 'old' and 'new' style of northern (Lincolnshire?) farmer, had contrasted the values and lives of farmers of different generations. The Old Style Farmer was primarily concerned with satisfying the interests of his landlord. The New Style Farmer – a product, in effect, of 'High Farming' – was more concerned with wealth accumulation and in acquiring 'proputty'. Certainly, 'High Farming' required the business acumen to handle properly investments.

This golden age ended with the onset of the aforementioned Great Depression in British Agriculture. This occurred from around 1875 to

1896, when there was a sharp fall in the prices of agricultural goods due to bad weather and poor harvests, and increasing competition from the imports of wheat and wool. Farmers also struggled to contend with imported meat, as technological developments enabled ships for the first time to transport considerable volumes of produce safely across long distances in refrigerated containers. The price of wheat plummeted by over 50 per cent between 1871 and 1875 and between 1894 and 1898. This had an impact on the farming community in Lincolnshire, where the number of farmers working the land declined from 11,788 in 1871 to 10,048 in 1881.[13]

This depression forced landowners to reduce their annual rents in an attempt to ensure that tenant farmers could continue to farm the land. A number of tenant farmers relinquished their holdings to stave off bankruptcy. In practice, though, in spite of the severity of the depression, bankruptcies were quite rare. Even at their peak in the period between 1881 and 1883, bankruptcies accounted for no more than 0.4 per cent of the rural population.[14] The Robinsons suffered more than most other farming families, which may have been because the extensive holdings they held required substantial capital outlays to be maintained.

Farmers in nineteenth-century Lincolnshire generally followed the practice of 'mixed farming' in which crops were cultivated and livestock maintained. 'High Farming' enabled the extensive use of the four-course rotation of crops over a four-to-five-year period. This typically entailed the cultivation of turnips, barley, oats and wheat. Oats and turnips were largely grown as livestock feed. Wheat was the most profitable crop, although it was also the most soil-demanding and required more intensive cultivation. Sheep farming formed an important component of agricultural life. The long wool of the Lincoln breed of sheep was nationally known. In 1879, Lincoln wool accounted for 17 per cent of the total production of wool in England and Wales. Cattle breeding was less popular in Lincolnshire, although the Lincoln Red short-horn was reared to produce beef. The county was not well known for horse breeding.[15]

The practice in Lincolnshire was for tenant farmers to vacate their property on Lady Day, 5 April. Usually, tenant farmers gave their landowners six months' notice. However, farmers were reluctant to terminate their tenancies because of the complications involved.

They would have to endure the time-consuming process of selling their crops, implements and fixtures. Leaving their farms often resulted in a loss of business and social contacts. If the farmer was to remain in his profession, he needed to have found beforehand a new farm to which he could relocate. Uncertainties over whether incoming tenants would agree, or be able to pay compensation according to the system of tenant right, were additional disincentives to moving.[16] Landowners may be tempted to offer better terms to keep tenant farmers whom they knew they could get along with. Failing that, landlords preferred to let farms to the relatives of tenants with whom they had had previous dealings.[17]

There were a number of possible reasons to explain why successful tenant farmers decided not to renew their tenancies. Perhaps they were seeking to move up the 'agricultural ladder' by becoming owner-occupiers, or by transferring to work on a larger rented farm. They might have decided to vacate their rented farms and in effect move 'sideways' to similar-sized rented properties in order to allow their sons to take over the holding.[18] Other personal issues or a family tragedy could also result in farmers choosing to end their tenancy. In the case of the Robinsons in Lincolnshire in the late nineteenth century, several of these factors were at play.

East Keal: Straddling Wold and Fen

East Keal is a village nestled on the edge of the Lincolnshire Wolds.[19] Situated along several undulating hills, land towards the southern perimeter of the village slopes gently into fenland. The name of the village appears to be derived from the Danish term 'Estrecale', which refers to it being the easterly high point when viewed from the fen. There had been a Roman settlement in the area. The settlement of Estrecale was listed in Domesday Book. In 1851, East Keal had a total population of only 475, spread across eighty-six dwellings.

In the mid-nineteenth century, the village of East Keal was situated on the turnpike road that linked the market towns of Spilsby and Boston. East Keal became better connected with the rest of the country after the opening in May 1868 of the 4½-mile stretch of railway track between Spilsby and the Great Northern Railway at Firsby. From Firsby, passengers could take the train to London on the Scunthorpe–King's Cross line. Five trains each day ran on the single-track branch railway line connecting Spilsby and Firsby. An additional train ran

33

on Mondays from Boston market and on Wednesdays to Boston market. The branch line was opened in the hope of reviving trade which had been lost following the inauguration of the nearby East Lincolnshire Railway in 1848. The line soon carried produce and cattle from Spilsby market.[20] Access to the railway connection to London meant that for the first time it would be feasible for local moneyed people to live and work in the capital on weekdays and spend weekends back at home in Lincolnshire. Families were no longer strictly tied to the land.

East Keal was well known locally for its Anglican Church of St Helen. The church remains a prominent landmark in the village today, jutting above the treeline and visible from a distance across the pastureland. In the mid to late nineteenth century, services at the church were conducted by the Reverend Joseph Spence, who lived in the new rectory at Barley Cliff at the western end of the village. As the local vicar, Spence was a notable and influential figure in East Keal. He was also popular among the villagers. John Hassard Short, the lord of the manor, was another prominent landowner. The title of lord of the manor was a relic of the feudal area. The Short family had been lords of the manor in East Keal since the early seventeenth century and were known as generous supporters of the church. The first lord of the manor for East Keal, Peter Short, was granted a coat of arms by King Charles II in 1666.

In the time of the Reverend Joseph Spence, the village had a local school that was partly supported by subscription. There was also a brick and tile works that extracted potting clay. The brickyard provided materials used for the construction of houses in the community. Families working at the brickyard lived in the adjacent Brickyard House. Much casual labour was employed at the brickyard, including boys, who helped dig clay, and women, who conditioned the clay. According to an account published in 1863, the other inhabitants of East Keal were employed in a range of trades and professions. There was a blacksmith, a tailor, a joiner and wheelwright, an overseer, a baker and grocer, a parish clerk, and a postmaster and grocer. Most notably, there were also ten farmers listed, including Spencer Robinson and his father.[21] The village also benefitted from two much-frequented watering holes – The Saracen's Head and The Duke of Wellington.

One of the distinguishing features of East Keal is that it is a village which straddles both wold and fenland. There are many myths and legends concerning the fens. According to the celebrated nineteenth-century historian Thomas Macaulay, the fens were inhabited by the 'Breedlings' who 'led an amphibious life sometimes wading, and sometimes rowing, from one islet of firm ground to another'.[22] Other accounts somewhat derogatorily refer to the fen-dwellers as 'yellow bellies'. The sickly, amber complexion of the fen people was attributed to their supposed propensity to crawl in the mud in the manner of the eels which they hunted. There are countless stories of mysterious creatures and spirits roaming the fens including boggarts, werewolves and strange dogs. For cxample, the 'Tiddy Mun' was a bog spirit no taller than a three-year-old child with the appearance of a dishevelled old man wearing a grey gown and possessing a laugh which resembled the call of a peewit.[23] Not surprisingly, perhaps, local folklore referred to the wetlands as dangerous places. Even after the draining of much of the fens it is still possible to detect among the inhabitants of the wolds a feeling that the fen-dwellers are somehow distinct from themselves. 'They are different people from us' was the casual remark of a farmer's wife I encountered on a trip to East Keal when discussing the fen people of today.

This perception may now be accounted for, at least in part, by the contrasting practices of farming in the wolds and in the fenland. The poor chalk soils of the wolds meant that large farms were required to enable farmers to produce enough crops to support a living. The 'poor wold' in the district around Spilsby consists of steeper hills which are more difficult to cultivate and less fertile soils than the 'good wold' in the north of the county. The much richer soils of the drained fens allowed farmers to earn a living by growing crops such as potatoes in holdings which were often smaller than 50 acres.[24] Agricultural labourers tended to earn higher wages working on the fenland.

In practice, the distinction between wold and fen was less clear-cut. However, a north–south divide in the use of land over a small area was still discernible in East Keal by the mid-nineteenth century. A lot of rich land had been opened for farming following the drainage of the fens by the Scottish engineer John Rennie in the eighteenth century. Previously, a large area to the immediate south of the village had consisted of watery wasteland which was only suitable for cattle and sheep grazing in the summer months. Land to the north of the parish was sandier, with chalk, and was thus less suitable for crop cultivation.

By the time Spencer Robinson was a farmer in East Keal, sheep and cattle were to be found grazing among the fields and hedgerows in the farms to the north of the village at the very edge of the wolds, while farms in the original fenland concentrated more on crop cultivation, growing barley, wheat, oats, turnips, seeds and beans as well as potatoes. However, those larger 'capitalist' tenant farmers who concentrated on 'mixed farming' – Spencer Robinson among them – managed land in both wold and fen.

The Robinsons of East Keal

Spencer's father, John Wheelwright Robinson, the third son of Samuel and Elizabeth, accumulated wealth and boosted his social standing as a tenant farmer in East Keal. He brought up his family of five sons and two daughters from his second marriage in the Lincolnshire village. However, only Spencer followed in his footsteps to become a significant tenant farmer in East Keal itself.

Born in 1806 in the Lincolnshire village of South Ormsby, John Wheelwright Robinson began farming at Sausthorpe near Spilsby. His first wife, Caroline Bacon from Pinchbeck in Lincolnshire, died in 1833 only two years after they had married. Their infant son, Samuel John, had perished in April 1832 at the age of six months.[25] In January 1835, John Wheelwright married once again. His new wife was Mary Ann Maddison, Spencer's future mother, and the wedding took place in Hagworthingham, near East Keal. Mary Ann's father, Joseph, had worked as the village butcher in Hagworthingham; his death in 1833 was noted by the local press, being 'equally lamented' by the many families 'who employed him as an honest and civil tradesman' and by the local poor who looked upon him 'as a benefactor and friend'.[26]

The Robinson and Maddison families became closely connected, which was perhaps not surprising given their geographic proximity and their similar social standings. A direct descendant of one of John Wheelwright's brothers drew to my attention the extent of the Robinson–Maddison ties. For example, he noted that Thomas Robinson, a younger brother of John Wheelwright, married Elizabeth Maddison, another daughter of Joseph Maddison.

By 1839, John Wheelwright was managing land in East Keal. Estate records reveal that he had taken over 35 acres of fenland in the village from John Hutchings, a tenant farmer working for John Hassard

Short.[27] It seems, though, that John Wheelwright had enemies. In November 1845, a large fire broke out at his fen farm. A substantial crowd congregated to watch the destruction of 'a strawstack containing the produce of 12 acres'. The damage could have been much worse if it were not for the help of labourers who succeeded in saving a sizeable wheatstack and an oatstack. The local press declared: 'No doubt exists that it was the work of an incendiary.'[28]

Apparently no longer restricted to the fens, the census of 1851 noted that John Wheelwright was running a farm which covered an area of over 400 acres and employed nine labourers. Perhaps he was at that time managing land which had previously been rented to his uncle, Joseph Robinson.

John Wheelwright was a supporter of the Conservative Party. In the 1852 North Lincolnshire elections, he used his two votes in the Spilsby polling district to support the two Conservative candidates who were running for office against one Whig/Liberal opponent.[29] The Conservatives ran on a ticket which backed protectionism. They opposed the recent repeal of the Corn Laws, which had ended the imposition of tariffs on imported agricultural produce. The farming community at the time, concerned about the possibility of increased competition from cheap imports and fearing for their livelihoods, tended to criticise the free trade policies of the Liberals.

By 1855, John Wheelwright was the new tenant of East Keal Hall. The property had formerly been the seat of the Short family. John Wheelwright remained in residence at the hall for the next ten years or so. According to a newspaper article of May 1865, advertising the place for let, East Keal Hall was 'very desirable' and 'pleasantly situated'. It had 'ample rooms', a stable and coach house, and an 'excellent walled garden stacked with citrus fruit trees'. The property was 'in every way suitable for the occupation of a genteel family'.[30] East Keal Hall was set back a little from the old turnpike road, which is now the frenetic and noisy A16.

John Wheelwright became a leading figure in the village community. He served as a churchwarden for the Reverend Joseph Spence. Churchwardens played a key role in parish affairs. They were responsible for the upkeep of the parish accounts, which entailed services such as receiving rents and rates from parishioners, distributing charitable aid, and managing the payment of expenses to maintain the church and other ecclesiastical property. One of John Wheelwright's claims to fame was the help he gave to support the renovation of the village church. In March 1853, the old tower of St Helen's Church, built in the fourteenth century, collapsed. Money was collected by voluntary contributions to rebuild the tower. The lord of the manor and Reverend Spence each donated £100. John Wheelwright, 'the largest occupier', and at the time churchwarden, contributed £20.[31] Spencer's father used his acquired wealth to procure land from John Hassard Short. In April 1864, John Wheelwright paid the then considerable sum of £2,450 to acquire property from Short's East Keal estate. This was the largest purchase of land in a sale in which the lord of the manor received about £44,000 in total.[32] Spencer's father seemed to have been in the process of becoming a significant landowner as well as tenant farmer in East Keal.

By 1866, however, John Wheelwright had moved to Saxby near Market Rasen in Lincolnshire. There he rented and managed the 650-acre property of Saxby Manor. The property was owned by the Earl of Scarborough, the lord of the manor, and had a yearly rent of £819. John Wheelwright died in Saxby on 8 December 1869 after suffering kidney failure. A wealthy man at his death, in his will he left effects totalling almost £6,000. In memory of his father, Peele Robinson commissioned work on a stained-glass window at St Helen's Church in Saxby. The window, depicting two scenes of Jesus feeding the hungry and the sick, was completed in 1875.[33] John Wheelwright lies buried in the churchyard at St Helen's.

John Wheelwright's second wife, Mary Ann, led a long life and died over twenty-two years after the passing of her husband. Spencer's mother had moved to Camberwell in London, to live with her daughter Jessie and her son-in-law Robert E. Clitherow. She was registered as residing at the Camberwell address in the censuses of 1881 and 1891 before dying there in her mid-eighties in April 1892. In her will, she left over £60 to her youngest son, Tom. Although Mary Ann spent her last years in London, she had continued to own over 43 acres of land in East Keal. After her death, and according to the will of her husband, this freehold and tithe-free estate was put up for sale. A farmhouse, stables and buildings and 34 acres of land was advertised together with rich feeding land of over 9 acres known as Matthews' Close.[34]

Although there were relatively few bankruptcies resulting from the agricultural depression of the 1880s in England, three of John

Wheelwright's sons did face grave financial difficulties. One of them, Peele Robinson, fled the country as a result of the ignominy following his bankruptcy. In Victorian England, bankruptcies were publicised in the local media and in *The Gazette*. Full details of public examinations, adjudications, the appointment of a trustee and information regarding the size of the debts were made available for all to read. Following the Bankruptcy Act of 1869, bankrupts were no longer necessarily sent to prison, but the public shaming stigmatised them for life.

John Wheelwright's eldest son, Joseph Samuel Robinson (b. 1836), started his working life as a farmer. By 1861, he was running a 317-acre farm, known as Ivy House, in the village of Lusby, not far from East Keal. Ivy House was another property which belonged to the Ecclesiastical Commissioners. Joseph Samuel soon suffered a string of family tragedies. Both his first and second wives passed away relatively young, and a son from the second marriage died in his infancy. At the same time, Joseph also ran into serious financial trouble. Throughout 1881, proceedings were conducted in Lincoln county court to liquidate his estate. His creditors lined up to collect their debts. In December 1881, a final call was made for creditors to prove their debts.[35]

By 1881, Joseph Samuel had abandoned farming and had relocated to London. He was living as a lodger with his sister Jessie and his mother in Camberwell. This must have been a major loss of face for the eldest of the Robinson brothers. In his middle age, Joseph Samuel had to face the indignity of relaunching his career by working as a humble lawyer's clerk. In 1891, still working in a lawyer's office, Joseph Samuel had moved away from his sister's house to take up residence in Great James Street in Bloomsbury. This was a much more upmarket district of the City. Head of the household, Joseph Samuel also had two lodgers – a policeman and his wife – and a boarder. Did this suggest that the fortune of the one-time farmer had improved? Perhaps not. The Bloomsbury accommodation had previously been the main dwelling of Joseph's younger brother, Tom – a very successful medical practitioner. Joseph Samuel died intestate in May 1902, leaving one daughter from his second marriage. Bucking the trend of family members moving away from the land, a cousin, Alfred Robinson, gave up a job in mechanical engineering to manage Ivy House in 1880. Alfred continued to farm at Lusby until his death in 1925.[36]

The life of Peele Robinson (b. 1840) was another cautionary tale. Living with his brother Joseph Samuel in Ivy House in Lusby in 1861, ten years later Peele had taken over the management of Saxby Manor from his father. In 1871 he married Elizabeth Clixby, who came from the village of Willoughton in Lincolnshire.[37] Elizabeth was the daughter of the farmer Joseph Clixby. Ironically, perhaps, given the later fate of his son-in-law, Joseph Clixby was elected as a guardian of the poor in Owmby, Lincolnshire, in April 1878.[38] At the time of the 1871 census, Peele and Elizabeth were 'absent on a wedding tour'. They were spending their honeymoon in the well-known Ridler's Hotel in Holborn in London. Situated at the 'attractive' end of Leather Lane, the popular and respectable hostelry was famous for its particular ambience. Each night, without fail, the candles standing on the hall table in their unforgettable old brass candlesticks were lit. The hotel offered an attractive venue for the holding of business meetings and receptions. The demolition of the hotel just before the turn of the century prompted an outburst of complaints from former satisfied clientele.

Peele Robinson appeared to be the paragon of a country gentleman. He was appointed parish constable of Saxby in March 1879,[39] a position of responsibility connected with the local criminal justice system but with little actual power by that time. Peele was a regular prize-winner in agricultural shows for the quality of his livestock. He also participated in the time-honoured rural practice of judging young hounds that had been 'walked' – i.e. brought up from puppyhood – by local farmers. The Peele Robinsons lived a life of luxury. The very popular Elizabeth Robinson was known to the locals as a 'Lady Bountiful'. Lavish parties were held at Saxby Manor, with many of the guests purportedly 'finishing up under the table'.[40] However, by 1884 Peele was declared bankrupt. He was perhaps a victim of the agricultural depression at that time, but his extravagant expenditure must also have contributed to his demise. According to local newspapers, Peele owed over £5,287 to fifty-five unsecured creditors, and a further sum of £1,937 to partly secured creditors. After deducting from his assets all required payments for rent and wages, Peele only had £3,659 available to pay the substantial number of creditors.[41]

In these circumstances, Peele Robinson took the life-changing decision to flee to the British colony of Natal in southern Africa in early 1885. Newspapers noted how, unwilling to face public shame, he had 'absconded'.[42] Peele was on the passenger list of the *Norham Castle*, which departed from London on 21 January to sail to Cape Town.[43] He had escaped before the completion of the sale of his livestock, farm equipment and household furniture and effects. His wife and four children at the time were initially left behind, the intention being that they should follow after Peele found employment. The story goes that Peele sent a cable to his wife urging them not to come because southern Africa was 'no place' for her and the children. However, the family had already embarked on the long journey before the cable arrived.[44] On 23 April 1885, Elizabeth and the children boarded ship to set sail from Southampton to Natal.[45] There then followed a period of considerable hardship for the Peele Robinsons. In search of employment, reportedly the family had had to travel by ox wagon from Durban to Johannesburg.[46]

It is not clear what jobs Peele initially took up in southern Africa. However, records of the Freemasons' Lodge in Addington, in Durban, reveal that by 1893 Peele was employed as a publican in the small rural settlement at Volksrust. Situated immediately across the border from Natal in the then independent state of Transvaal, Volksrust had been established only five years earlier and did not acquire municipal status until 1904. The isolated settlement was located near the site of the famous Battle of Majuba, where in 1881 the Boers had defeated a British force. Volksrust means 'People's Rest' in Afrikaans. This seems to be a reference to the fighting units recuperating in the area after their clash with the British. In the midst of rich grasses and wetlands, this remote outpost only gradually expanded with the development of trade after a railway line connected the Transvaal with Natal via Volksrust in 1896. As the small town lay some 300 kilometres from the port city of Durban, one would suppose that Peele was not a regular attendee to events organised by the Addington Lodge.

Peele Robinson must have been one of the first inhabitants of Volksrust. As a pioneering family in such a far-removed community, life presumably was not easy. Working as a bar manager to service the needs of the local maize, sheep and dairy farmers would have been in stark contrast to the comforts and worldly pleasures of Saxby Manor. Peele died at Volksrust on 26 September 1895.[47] After his death, Peele's wife and children remained in southern Africa. Only one of the children decided to take up farming.

Peele's brother George Frederick Robinson (b. 1844) had ten children from his two marriages. His first wife, Martha Pattie Robinson, was a cousin. Nine years after their wedding, she died in 1879 at the age of thirty-three. Five years later George Frederick married Annie Glasier. The daughter of a farmer from Kingthorpe in Lincolnshire, Annie had been employed as a governess at the Manor House in East Keal in 1881. Between 1869 and 1887, George Frederick ran a 340-acre farm in the Lincolnshire village of Edlington.[48] He employed quite a large workforce. Ten men and four boys laboured on the farm in 1881. George Frederick was another tenant farmer of John Hassard Short. As the agricultural depression took hold, landlords in the county tended to reduce their rents to encourage farmers whom they trusted to stay on as tenants. George Frederick had paid a half-year's rent of £343 2s 6d in 1883. Four years later this rent had been lowered to £290, but it did not prevent George Frederick from vacating the farm that year.[49] In January 1887, it was announced in the local press that by an indenture he had assigned all his real and personal estate and effects to five Horncastle tradesmen.[50]

Another victim of the worsening economic climate, George Frederick and his family moved first to the Lincolnshire market town of Horncastle and then to Lincoln. Abandoning farming, by the time of the 1901 census George Frederick was working as a 'brewer's traveller'. Presumably, this job entailed obtaining orders from customers for a brewery in the area. Ten years later, George Frederick was employed as a 'seed crusher traveller'. This probably involved procuring orders for a local grain business which was involved in extracting oil from seeds. After retirement, George Frederick and Annie spent their final years together living in Bournemouth.

The youngest son of John Wheelwright Robinson, Tom (b. 1846), chose an alternative career path and became a highly successful general practitioner. Tom originally worked as an apprentice for John Elsey, a chemist, druggist and artificial manure agent who ran a lucrative business on the High Street in Horncastle. A much-respected member of the Pharmaceutical Society, Elsey may have provided useful contacts for the ambitious young Tom. By the time of the 1871 census, Tom was listed working as a reserve medical officer at the London Hospital in Whitechapel. After qualifying as a physician and becoming a member of the Royal College of Surgeons, he took up residence in London and eventually found accommodation in fashionable Marylebone. An acclaimed public speaker, Tom was also the author of several books on the diagnosis and treatment of syphilis, eczema, baldness and greyness. He became a consulting physician to St John's Hospital for Skin Diseases.

Tom also pursued other interests and hobbies. He wrote articles on the local history of Lincolnshire. In February 1899, at the annual meeting of the Revesby Cycling Association, Tom was chosen one of the club's vice presidents. At the meeting, it was decided that ladies could be admitted as members to the association.[51] As will be seen, this was at the time when another member of the extended Robinson family was making an international name for herself as a competitive female cyclist.

The doctor also frequented literary and artistic circles in London. An avid socialite, he was a member of the Garrick Club, the Author's Club and the Green Room. Tom was a good friend of the artists Frank Brangwyn and Edward Burne-Jones. He collected a number of works by Brangwyn, who later became an official War Artist of the First World War. Before commencing on his religious painting *The Miraculous Draught of Fishes*, Brangwyn consulted with Tom. The doctor suggested that a robust Christ should be depicted physically drawing a net. After some consideration, Brangwyn dismissed Tom's recommendation and instead portrayed Christ as a distant spectator of his miracle.[52]

Stanley Maidens Robinson, the doctor's only son, became a solicitor specialising in work for theatre companies. Continuing the links with the stage, Tom's grandson 'Tommy' Maidens Robinson worked as a stage director in London's West End theatres.[53]

In spite of his busy professional and social life, Tom preserved links with Lincolnshire and with farming. In 1871, he married Mary Roberta Maidens. Mary was the daughter of Robert Maidens, who had been the lord of the manor in the village of East Kirkby before his death in 1865. As the new lord of the manor, Tom was the owner of East Kirkby Manor House, which was connected to a farm of over 300 acres. In contrast to his brothers, Tom thus acquired a title and became a landowner rather than a tenant farmer. Exploiting the railway connection, Tom spent the remainder of his life maintaining his medical practice in London and returning to Lincolnshire at weekends to oversee the running of the farm.

Clearly an amiable character, 'Dr Tom' was regarded with considerable affection in the East Kirkby community. Known locally as a 'great croquet player', he was also fond of good company on a day's shooting. A favourite with the youngsters, when in the village he often sat on the stile opposite the local school. He played games with the children when they came out from school, told stories, and handed out money and sweets. Villagers recounted how he would take time to gossip with them in carpenter Robert Spikin's shop next to the school. Tom made calls on those in the village who were sick. According to the doctor, the villagers would remain healthy if they kept to the Lincolnshire diet of 'Beef, Bread, Beer and Butter'. His famous cough mixture continued to be used by locals well after his death. In the late 1930s, it could still be bought from 'Mrs Ironmonger', on whom he had bestowed the privilege of selling it. Regarded as a 'generous man', he marked Christmas by gifting the nine workmen employed at East Kirkby Manor 'a new pipe, 4 lb of tobacco, 9 gallons of beer, 1 stone of beef, 1 bottle of whisky and a £1 note'.[54] The stained-glass window in the local church, depicting Jesus healing the sick, was erected in his honour three years after his death in 1919. He left effects of over £13,000 to his widow.

The two sisters of Spencer Robinson both found husbands and abandoned Lincolnshire. Jessie (b. 1852) married the surgeon Robert Edward Clitherow in Camden in 1879. The Clitherows were a well-established family of Lincolnshire solicitors based in Horncastle. Robert established a practice at Peckham Rye in Camberwell. There, the couple lived at Lancaster House. This was previously the home of the poet Marian Richardson, who had invited the Italian revolutionary Garibaldi to stay with her in Peckham Rye on a visit to London. Jessie died in London in November 1902. A pulpit was named in her memory at the mission church in Nunhead.[55] This suggested that Jessie had been a regular churchgoer. She did not have any children. Robert Edward remained a widower for almost forty years until his death in July 1939.

The elder sister, Mary Ann (known as 'Polly', b. 1842), married William Greeves, a successful fruit farmer from Elm near Wisbech in Cambridgeshire. The ceremony took place in East Keal in April 1872. William's father, Emmanuel, had farmed at Strawberry Hall in Tydd St Mary in Lincolnshire. The couple had nine children. Polly passed away in Wisbech in January 1922. Her husband died eight years later and left in his will effects totalling over £35,000.

Spencer Robinson – Farmer, Volunteer and Pillar of the Community
Little is known of Spencer's early years. Surprisingly, in the 1841 census he and his older brother, Joseph Samuel, were not living with their parents and grandfather in East Keal, but were listed as 'boarders' in a house in Vicarage Lane in the village of Sibsey in the same county. The head of the household was Maria Hobson, a forty-year-old local schoolmistress, who presumably taught at the Sibsey Free School, which was situated on Vicarage Lane. Maria lived alone with her three children. It is not clear why the three-year-old Spencer and his brother were staying with the schoolteacher. Perhaps, on the day of the census, they were there receiving some pre-school education? The schoolmistress may have recently moved to the neighbourhood. In the 1841 census, her two daughters and one son (the youngest child aged nine) were noted as being born 'in Scotland, Ireland or in foreign parts', although Maria herself was listed as born in Lincolnshire. In Victorian England, impoverished children – and especially those from the workhouse – were 'boarded out' to local families for a 'better' upbringing. Clearly, though, in the case of the Robinsons, poverty would not have been a factor in accounting for Spencer and Joseph Samuel boarding in the household of Maria Hobson.

Ten years later, Spencer and Joseph Samuel were living with their family in East Keal. Like his elder brother, Spencer took up the responsibility of farming at an early age. In the 1861 census, the young and unmarried Spencer Robinson was listed as head of household and farmer at Top End in East Keal. The four other residents at the farm were identified as a housekeeper, groom, housemaid and pupil.

It seems that Spencer inherited much of his father's enthusiasm for local civic duty. As in the case of John Wheelwright, Spencer appeared to have a special interest in the work of the parish church. In particular, he seems to have enjoyed a warm relationship with the church's rector.

The Reverend Joseph Spence took up residence in the rectory at Barley Cliff in East Keal in 1860 and lived there until his death in 1893. His father, John, also had been rector in the village. Joseph Spence was apparently a much-liked member of the local community. Chairman of the school's committee, he took an active part in the running of the local school, including teaching classes on religious education. Joseph Spence had first lived as a bachelor at Barley Cliff with his aging mother. In November 1865, he eventually married Maria Maulkinson, who was the niece of Henry Gildon, a prominent local farmer of East Keal. The ceremony took place in Clerkenwell in Middlesex.

Spencer was responsible for the extensive celebrations which were held in East Keal when the Reverend Joseph Spence returned from his marriage tour accompanied by his bride. The newlyweds were welcomed in the afternoon by a large party of over 230 villagers. A 'capital repast' was organised in a large barn decorated with flowers, evergreens and mottoes for the occasion. The barn was situated in the grounds of Barley Cliff. The principal inhabitants of the village officiated as carvers while the local labourers and their wives sat down for the feast. In the evening, when dinner was served, a band played for some hours with 'unflagging zest' and there was much dancing. Ale and tobacco were available for those who preferred not to dance. The next day, the children of the school were entertained with games and were served plum cake and tea. The local newspaper reported, 'The whole of the arrangements were made by Mr Spencer Robinson and did him great credit.' The account added, 'A day more thoroughly enjoyed is not remembered to have taken place in East Keal.'[56]

The young Spencer Robinson was also actively involved in the activities of the Seventh Spilsby Rifle Volunteers Corps, which was formed in 1860.

In January 1858, the Italian nationalist and revolutionary Felice Orsini had attempted to assassinate Emperor Napoleon III of France and his wife on their way to the opera in Paris by throwing three bombs at their carriage. This plot had been hatched in London by French political refugees, and the bombs used in the attack had been manufactured in England. This prompted serious concerns that France could use the botched assassination attempt as an excuse to invade England. In England at that time, memories of the Napoleonic Wars waged half a century earlier against Napoleon III's uncle were still fresh. The shortcomings of the British military had recently been exposed in the Crimean War and in the crushing of the 'Indian Mutiny'. The militia was perceived as a ramshackle body which was not up to the task of defending the country in the event of the regular army fighting on the continent. The Franco-Austrian

War of 1859 stirred further fears that British forces could become embroiled in a new European war. In these circumstances, there was concerted lobbying for the establishment of a properly organised volunteer local defence force. Even Tennyson, with his impassioned appeal in the 1859 poem 'The War' for 'riflemen, riflemen, riflemen form', became engaged in the campaign to press for the setting up of such a force. Yielding to these demands, Secretary of State for War Jonathan Peel issued a circular on 12 May 1859 which called for the creation of a nationwide Volunteer Force. The Volunteer Act of 1859 rapidly led to the formation of companies of rifle volunteers throughout the country. Artillery and engineer corps were also formed. The origins of the modern Territorial Army may be traced back to the 1859 Act.

The national mood of the country at the time fully supported the swift establishment of the volunteer units. The National Rifle Association was also founded in 1859 to support the volunteer rifle corps and to promote rifle shooting. The association held its first competition to find a champion marksman on Wimbledon Common in July 1860. Queen Victoria herself fired the opening shot in the competition.

The volunteer units were to be supervised by the lords lieutenant, the queen's personal representatives in each county who had previously been responsible for organising the militia. Members of the voluntary corps had to pay for their arms, uniform and other equipment. They also had to cover all other costs except when assembled for actual service. Volunteers were required to purchase the increasingly outdated muzzle-loading Enfield rifle together with bayonet and rounds of live and blank ammunition. Certainly, poorer groups in society could not afford to pay up and join the volunteer rifle corps. Membership of the corps therefore tended to be confined to the supposedly more trusted and reasonably well-to-do middle classes. The Volunteer Act of 1863 did provide some pay and relief for the volunteers and their families. However, raising additional funds for the corps through organised dinners and other social functions, often attended by prominent members of the community, remained an important aspect of work for the volunteer rifle corps.

In April 1860, the Seventh Spilsby Rifle Volunteer Corps held elections to choose non-commissioned officers. The local press noted how Spencer Robinson had collected and paid into the corps fund the sum of two pounds, five shillings and sixpence. According to the news report, 'It is suggested that other members of the corps might benefit the fund by imitating so good an example.'[57]

As a member of the corps, Spencer presumably attended the inauguration of the volunteer unit, which took place in Spilsby in July 1860 with an impressive sequence of marches and other ceremonies. The two-hour demonstration on the parade ground turned out to be popular with the ladies. A long and detailed account in the local newspaper declared, 'It is long since such an assembly of the fair and beautiful of marsh and wold was witnessed in this town as that which graced and animated the exercises of the Rifle Corps.' An 'excellent dinner' followed in the town hall, attended by local dignitaries who offered various toasts and well-wishes. In his speech, the venerable General Rawnsley, who had held Her Majesty's Commission for more than fifty years, noted that observing the drill together with him earlier in the day was Lady Franklin, 'a lady of heroic distinction'. Lady Franklin had made a donation to the rifle corps.[58]

The lady in question was the widow of none other than Sir John Franklin, he of Northwest Passage fame. Born in Spilsby, Sir John had fought at the Battle of Trafalgar and had become governor of Tasmania before embarking in 1845 on his ill-fated voyage to discover the Northwest Passage between Canada and the Arctic. His body would only be found in 1859 on Beechey Island, in the Canadian Arctic Archipelago of Nunavut. Jane Griffin, the future Lady Franklin, was the daughter of John Griffin, the governor of Goldsmiths, the London-based banking and commodity trading business. She had come to take a great interest in Spilsby's affairs after her marriage to one of the town's greatest scions. A statue of Sir John Franklin now graces the central square in Spilsby.

In September 1860, after conducting their usual drill on a Friday evening, the Spilsby volunteers were entertained in a marquee pitched in the front of the village on the Cowgate Farm of Mr Kirkham of the White Hart Hotel. There, in the presence of the commanding officer of the corps, 'a capital spread was provided for their refection'. It was hoped that the meeting would become an annual one. Responding to the 'ladies', in his toast Spencer Robinson invited the corps to take refreshment at his father's on the next Friday evening, 'and the invitation was cordially accepted'.[59]

Spencer also attended the Spilsby Rifle Corps ball held in January 1862. This was a popular and lively event. Taking place in the local town hall, dancing commenced shortly after eight in the evening and 'was maintained with the greatest spirit until four the next morning'.[60]

The young Spencer Robinson appears to have been a much-liked and energetic member of the local community. It seems that he was also the opening batsman for the East Keal cricket club. In July 1862, a return match was played between East Keal and the neighbouring Horncastle Victoria Club. In a rather low-scoring match, an S. Robinson could only muster two and five runs in his two innings. Lower down the batting order a G. Robinson (George?) struggled to score two runs and then was out for a duck. After the game, the players retired to dine at the Greyhound Inn, where a 'first rate repast was provided'.[61] If this was indeed Spencer Robinson who batted as opener, it appears that he did not quite attain the level of sporting proficiency which some of his sons would later display.

Spencer Robinson was also looked upon as someone who could be trusted to manage local business affairs. For example, in January 1866, those interested in purchasing lots of land in the auction of the property of the late Henry Gildon were advised to apply to Spencer Robinson to view the holdings.[62] A couple of years later, Spencer was one of two appointed trustees for the sale of shares held in the local Alford Corn Exchange Company.[63] The exchange handled takings from the market in Alford. Registered in 1856, the company had a nominal capital of £1,400, and by 1864 there were seventy-six shareholders.[64]

On 15 October 1868, Spencer Robinson married Isabella Ann Palmer at a ceremony in Burnham, Buckinghamshire. Baptised in the village of Gooderstone in Norfolk in 1842, Isabella was the eldest daughter of Thomas and Isabella Palmer. Spencer's father-in-law, referred to as a 'gentleman' on the marriage certificate, came from Hockham in Norfolk. He had worked as a farmer and then cattle dealer in the county before moving to Barking in Essex by the time of the 1861 census. Thomas Palmer was still alive in 1891, aged seventy-six, retired and widowed and living in St Dunstan, Kent, with another of his daughters. He died the following year.

Within a short period, Spencer and Isabella had three children. A daughter, Ethel May, was baptised in East Keal on 21 August 1871, but she then passed away in the same month. The couple's first child, a son named Minick Palmer, was born in July 1869 in East Keal. Minick (also spelt Minnick) was an unusual choice of name. However, Isabella's youngest brother had been baptised Graseley (or Grayley?) Minnick Palmer. Isabella's parents had also named another daughter Mary Minnick Palmer, but she had died at a young age in 1848. The origins of the name appear to have come from the wife of Isabella's grandfather, who was called Mary Minnick before her marriage. In his later years, Minick Palmer preferred to be called Palmer. Spencer and Isabella also had another daughter, May Belle Robinson, born in 1870 in East Keal.

According to the 1871 census, Spencer Robinson and his family lived in a farm by the turnpike road in East Keal. It was noted that the farm covered 335 acres. Much more detail of the farm can be gleaned from the local press. Through late 1870 until at least March 1872, several auctions were held to sell different items of property of the farm after the Robinsons had decided to leave the area and move south.

The auction that took place on 21 November 1870 covered freehold estate belonging to Spencer Robinson. This indicated that while a tenant farmer Spencer also owned some portion of land. Indeed, in the sale of part of John Hassard Short's estate in 1864, Spencer had purchased a small plot of land for £20.[65] The lot up for sale in 1870 involved an expanse of pastureland called Home Close. This land was bounded on the north by other property belonging to Spencer Robinson and on the south by lands belonging to a Mr J. F. Sharpe. The eastern end of the lot was marked by the turnpike road running from Spilsby to Boston and to the west was bounded by lands belonging to a Mr John Thompson and by more property owned by Spencer Robinson. The land tax on this lot amounted to six shillings and three and a half pence.[66] It seems that Home Close had earlier been rented by the same tenant farmer, John Hutchings, from whom Spencer's father had acquired land in the fens.[67] This suggests that other sections of Spencer Robinson's farm may have been previously rented by John Hutchings.

News of further auctions revealed more information about the land and property managed by Spencer Robinson. Part of the premises was known as Home Yard. What was offered for sale covered items such as 'rich grass, turnip, mangolds and yard keeping with hay and seeds'.[68] With regard to livestock, there were at least 702 long-wool sheep, forty-eight 'short-horned beasts' (presumably Lincoln Red short-horn cattle), three horses and twenty-five pigs.[69] Another newspaper account referred to a milch cow, three bulling heifers, 'eight he and she lambs' and a nine-year-old black cart mare. A vast array of equipment was also offered for sale including a wheelbarrow, trays, sheep troughs, water tubs, brackets, hen coops, a cut box, a tumbril bottom, and 'sundry wood, iron etc'. Further implements included a superior Whitechapel dog cart, a shepherd's pony cart, three sets of harness, three gardener's turnip cutters, nets and stakes etc.[70]

A range of items of furniture for sale were also listed such as two iron bedsteads, two mattresses, a wash stand, a large sponge bath, Windsor stools, two dressing tables, a bacon bin, a hat stand, three clothes horses, a scraper, a salting tub, four mahogany chairs, an easy chair, six kitchen chairs, three kitchen tables, a bureau, two wash tubs, three fenders, five irons, a pancheon rack, an eight-day clock and various other articles.[71]

Advertised 'to let' was a 'good house' with six bedrooms, dining and drawing rooms and all other offices. This was accompanied by about 8 acres of garden and grassland, a carriage-house, a two-stall stable, a granary, a cowshed, piggeries, etc. The advertisement concluded that together with the livestock and implements on sale, 'the above would be a desirable occupation for a genteel family'. To further promote the sale and letting, the advertisement added that the property was located about 2 miles from Spilsby, 'where there is a first-class railway station'.[72]

Clearly, Spencer Robinson had become a prominent tenant farmer in East Keal who was engaged in 'mixed farming'. A capitalist tenant farmer, he owned a variety of livestock and managed a considerable expanse of land. The sale and letting of property, livestock and equipment may have attracted much interest. The family's move to another part of the country with very young children must have required careful planning. Presumably, it would not have been easy for Spencer to decide to relocate given his longstanding ties to Lincolnshire and his highly visible role in the local community. Agreements would have had to be made with the incoming tenant over issues such as tenant right, and the landlord himself would have needed to give his stamp of approval. However, it seems that the move south by the

Robinsons to a farm on the outskirts of the village of West Firle in Sussex may well have been prompted, at least in part, by the failing health of Spencer's wife, Isabella.

The Robinsons may have relocated to West Firle by September 1871 or shortly thereafter. Unlike in Lincolnshire, in most other parts of the country Michaelmas (29 September) as well as Lady Day were dates in the calendar when tenancies commenced. Although the sale of some of Spencer's land had been publicised as early as the autumn of 1870, the auctions for equipment and livestock had only really gathered pace from September 1871 onwards. According to the census of April 1871, the Robinsons were still resident in East Keal.

West Firle: Neighbours to the Gages

The Anglo-Saxon word *firle* referred to oak woodland. The village of West Firle, on the South Downs, was mentioned in Domesday Book. According to Kelly's Post Office Directory of 1867, the village and parish of West Firle lay a half-mile south of the turnpike road connecting Lewes and Eastbourne. The village accommodated the Church of St Peter (referred to as an ancient Gothic building), a national school, a post office and a workhouse. With a population of 631 in 1861, the inhabitants of West Firle included a boot and shoe maker, a wheelwright and blacksmith, a butcher, and a grocer, draper and corn miller. There were also several farmers. The 'principal point of attraction' was Firle Place, the grand seat of Viscount Gage. As lord of the manor, the viscount was owner of much of the land in the parish.

The Robinsons took up residence at the farm known as Bushy Lodge, which was located about 1½ miles north-east of the village.[73] The previous occupant there, James Walker, was a tenant of the lord of the manor. Walker had managed a 480-acre farm employing eight men and four boys. In addition to the farmhouse, the property included a gatehouse where the gatekeeper and his family lived. There were four other housings on the site for agricultural labourers and their families. It would appear that Spencer had moved to a farm larger than the one he had managed at East Keal.

By the time of Spencer Robinson's relocation to West Firle, Henry Hall Gage, 4th Viscount Gage of Castle Island (Co. Kerry), was in residence at Firle Place. The viscount was well known as a fierce conservative who had attempted to derail the Great Reform Act of

1832, which had introduced a measure of electoral reform in the country. He was also the author of various papers on mathematics and mechanical science delivered at the Royal Institute and at other learned societies.[74] Sitting in the House of Lords for over fifty years, he became known as 'the father of the House'. The viscount was a close friend of Sir Humphry Davy, the distinguished Cornish chemist and inventor.

Firle Place had been designed as a great Tudor manor house by Sir John Gage, a soldier and courtier who had served as lord chamberlain in the years 1553–56. Around 1725, another prominent member of the Gage family, Sir William Gage of Hengrave, 2nd Baronet, is said to have introduced to England the plum which would come to be known as the Greengage plum.[75]

Several well-known figures came to reside in West Firle. The famous economist John Maynard Keynes lived in the village for twenty-six years. He was closely connected with members of the Bloomsbury Set who also lived nearby. The artists Duncan Grant and Vanessa Bell lived at Charleston farmhouse at the edge of the parish, while Virginia Woolf spent 1911 in the property she named Little Talland House, opposite the village hall. Grant, Bell and Woolf all found their final resting place in the West Firle churchyard. The English literary critic Cyril Connolly later rented accommodation at Bushy Lodge itself in the late 1950s and early 1960s.

By 1843, the Gages owned 3,320 of the 3,392 acres in the parish of West Firle.[76] The village was a classic example of a so-called 'estate village' and 'close parish'. A number of these communities were clustered in the area of the South Downs. In contrast to the 'open' parishes, where landownership was dispersed and more trades and services were available, West Firle was in effect governed from above by the Gage family. The Gages had a significant influence over 'the tone and tempo of village life'.[77] Even local leisure activities were controlled by the Gages. In estate villages and close parishes, powerful landowners often placed restrictions on the building of small cottages, discouraging the poor from living in the neighbourhood.[78] However, West Firle did have a workhouse able to accommodate up to 180 inmates. Apparently, in the time of the fourth viscount, the Gages went so far as to dictate the seating arrangements in church. The front row was reserved for the Gages, for any guests of the lord of the manor, and for the largest tenant farmers, the Wadmans. Lesser tenant farmers, followed by tradesmen and then farm workers occupied the pews behind the Gages.[79] The Wadmans took over Bushy Lodge immediately after the Robinsons. Presumably, therefore, Spencer and his wife had graced the same pew as the lord of the manor.

Spencer was soon fully embraced as part of West Firle's high society. In mid-December 1871, Viscount Gage celebrated his eightieth birthday in lavish style. His 'principal tenants' were invited to attend a grand dinner at the historic Ram Inn in West Firle. The hostelry dated back to the sixteenth century and its name derived from the ram which was emblazoned on the coat of arms of the Gage family. Thirty or so guests, including an S. Robinson of Bushy Lodge, enjoyed an 'elegant repast'. After dinner, the attendees withdrew to the drawing room to have dessert and drink numerous toasts. One toast was 'to the health of the new tenants'. The toasts were interspersed with rounds of singing.[80] It seemed that Spencer had little problem in adjusting to social life among the community of prosperous West Sussex farmers.

Poor health had probably forced the Robinsons to relocate to an ostensibly more salubrious climate by the sea in the south of England, for Isabella was seriously suffering from tuberculosis. Living in West Firle would have also enabled her to have close contact with her spinster aunts Mary Ann, Sarah, and Elizabeth Palmer – all three were then resident in separate lodgings in nearby Brighton. The three aunts would later be buried by Isabella's side in the cemetery of the Church of St Peter in West Firle. Isabella tragically died on 12 March 1872 at Bushy Lodge. She had passed away before her thirtieth birthday. According to the death certificate, Spencer was not present at the time of her passing.

It seems that Spencer Robinson stayed in the county only for a brief period after his wife's death. Records indicate that on 28 April 1873 he was invited to become a member of the Freemasons' Tyrian Lodge no. 1110 in Eastbourne. According to data provided by the Lodge, Spencer was a farmer residing in West Lewes. There does not appear to be any earlier record of Spencer Robinson as a member of a Masonic lodge in Lincolnshire. A listing in the *Commercial Gazette* in late August 1873 referred to bills of sale and the property managed by Spencer at Bushy Lodge.[81]

The misfortune of losing his young wife may have prompted Spencer to vacate Bushy Lodge and seek out fresh challenges overseas.

Before leaving, Spencer seems to have entrusted his two small children to relatives in England. They were certainly both resident in the country at the time of the 1881 census. Masonic records reveal that by November 1874 Spencer had likely been settled for some time in the tea-growing district of Darjeeling in India.

Although Lincolnshire had been the long-established home of Spencer Robinson and his farming ancestors, current members of the extended Robinson family living in Turkey were not fully informed about the English roots of their family. Generations of Robinsons had worked on the land in Lincolnshire, but by the late nineteenth century the combination of economic pressures, technological developments and new opportunities led to some family members abandoning the county. A new world was emerging, one which Spencer's grandfather would have probably struggled to recognise.

Career openings and failings, or marriage, resulted in some of the Robinsons choosing to vacate the neighbourhood. However, ties with the home county were never completely severed. For example, Spencer's brother Tom and his brother-in-law Robert Edward Clitherow were both prominent members of the London Lincolnshire Society. When family members passed away, they were often buried in some leafy Lincolnshire village graveyard – even if they had lived and worked outside of the county for decades. Ultimately, home may be where one's parents and other family members are buried. For these Robinsons, the rituals of death incorporated the rites of a final homecoming.

From our vantage point, how may we assess what turned out to be only the first stage of Spencer Robinson's life? It seems that he had endeavoured to follow in the footsteps of his father and become a respected and influential tenant farmer in East Keal. A genial host, Spencer Robinson was a well-liked and much-admired figure who had energetically thrown himself into affairs of the community. In his youth, he comes across as 'one of the boys' who was at the same time generous in spirit and full of animation. If it had not been for his wife's illness, perhaps Spencer may have been destined to spend his last years in rural Lincolnshire. Perhaps Spencer would have proven himself more adept than his brothers in negotiating a course through the economic storms that battered and afflicted rural lives in the 1880s. Perhaps, unlike his brothers, he might have had the business acumen and financial nous to surf safely through the agricultural depression.

Instead, Spencer was forced to struggle to adapt to the impact of economic and technological change when living and working in the hill stations of India.

Perhaps perversely, tragedy and misfortune can often be the harbingers of rebirth and fresh opportunities. This would seem to apply to Spencer Robinson's life, although one can never be sure that it was the premature death of Isabella which compelled him to leave behind his two young children and forsake life in England. Presumably, the decision to emigrate must have been a difficult one. Unfortunately, I was unable to discover surviving personal correspondence of Spencer Robinson referring to his life in Lincolnshire and West Firle. What is known, though, is that Spencer, like some of his brothers, remarried and embarked on a new career.

2

Spencer Robinson II:
A Life in India

The one land that all men desire to see, and having seen once,
by even a glimpse, would not give that away for the
shows of the rest of the world combined.

Mark Twain, *Following the Equator*

Introduction

According to Bernard Spencer Robinson, the story was that his great-grandfather had purchased a tea plantation in Darjeeling and had helped build the Darjeeling Himalayan Railway (DHR). He added that Spencer Robinson may have sold some land he owned to enable the construction of the railway. Bernard then handed over a package of photocopied materials related to India that had been passed down in the family. These included a few railway tickets, part of an Indian telegraph, photographs of natives posing for the camera, some press clippings, news of entertainment in Darjeeling, and several faded images with written text relating to the British expeditionary force to Sikkim. A closer investigation revealed that here were hidden gems.

The tickets for travel on the DHR included a free pass, third class, dated 24 April 1887, for two apprentices for the journey from Tindharia to Kurseong. It was issued by the resident engineers at Tindharia. I knew that Spencer's son, Minick, had worked as an apprentice at the DHR's locomotive repair yard situated at Tindharia. There was also a second-class free pass issued by the DHR in December 1889 for the downhill journey from Darjeeling to Siliguri. The ticket was made out for 'Mr P. Robinson with sister'. Were the passengers Minick (Palmer) and his then eight-year-old half-sister, Maud? Perhaps Minick was accompanied by his half-sister, Gertrude? Or had May Belle come to visit her brother? The telegraph was posted from Pedong to P. Robinson in Kalimpong with the cryptic message, 'Sorry white away regrets his aid useless now.'

There were a few pages from a magazine or newspaper describing in some detail the histories of assorted Tibetan dances – including the lion, bison, mask and lama dances. In bold handwriting in black ink at the bottom of one of the pages was a note indicating that these dances were performed at Queen Victoria's Jubilee celebration in Darjeeling on 17 February 1887. The author noted, 'I was present at all these dances.'

Several copies of photographs depicting various staging posts for the British expeditionary force to Sikkim in 1888 were accompanied by brief descriptions in the same handwriting. The images were of military camps in scenic mountain landscapes. There was a photograph of the settlement at Sedonchin, with its telegraph and post office, situated 8 miles below the strategically important outpost at Gnatong. A few huts were clustered in front of a bank of trees. Here, it was noted, all sheep and cattle were slaughtered to feed the troops stationed at Gnatong. Another photograph showed a *dak* bungalow or rest house in densely wooded terrain which lay 'on the way to Gnatong'. There were two images of the encampment at Gnatong itself. One was of a tented site which appeared precariously perched on a mountaintop. Another was of a much more secure-looking group of huts, composed of white deal, thatched with bamboo, and protected by a wooden stockade. Titled 'Fort Graham, Gnatong', at the end of a brief description of the camp the author added, 'The hut that I now occupy I have marked.' Unfortunately, though, the marking was no longer visible.

Initially, I assumed that the handwriting in these messages was that of Spencer Robinson; I was aware that Spencer had played a role in helping to supply provisions to the British expeditionary force in Sikkim. However, attached to the papers were the words, in the same script, of a famous epitaph which was slightly adapted:

My Mother – She was – But words are wanting to say what: Think what a woman ought (underlined) to be, and she was that.

The text was followed by the initials M. P. R. Above the text was a note:

My Mother – Died 12-3-1872. Aged 29 Years.

Clearly, then, the handwriting in the various notes was that of Spencer's son, Minick. It was Minick, at the time a young railway engine fitter, who had personally accompanied the troops on what was referred to by the press at the time as the 'campaign in the clouds' where 'to advance is to brave unknown perils'.[1] It is quite likely that he accompanied his father on the Sikkim expedition.

In contrast to Lincolnshire, India was also a significant point of reference for the Turkish descendants of Spencer Robinson. For example, I heard rumours circulating among the family that Spencer was at one time a governor in India. This story turned out to be false. I was also informed that Spencer's daughter Maud (Adile) apparently travelled to India from Istanbul, although this could not be corroborated. Certainly, Maud, unlike some of her younger brothers, would have had clearer memories of life in the British Raj, and she evidently passed them on to her children. Bedia Hanım, Maud's daughter from her second marriage, had always wanted to explore the Indian sub-continent. In her high school yearbook of 1947, Bedia wrote how she wished to travel to India and Baghdad (her father originated from today's Iraq). Her dream was never realised.

India also played an important role in the narrative of Turkish commentators in their accounts of how Spencer's second wife, Hannah, and, indeed supposedly Spencer himself, converted to Islam. According to one error-strewn account, in 1890 Spencer and his wife, referred to as Sarah, were shocked at the harsh treatment of Muslims in India. The story goes that the couple clashed with the British governor, 'Andrew'. In reaction, Spencer and Sarah converted to Islam, renamed themselves Abdullah and Fatma, and relocated to the Ottoman Empire.[2] Another widely used source described how Spencer served in India as a military officer. Converting to Islam, and at the invitation of the sultan, Spencer left India to serve as an officer in the Ottoman armed forces.[3] These stories bore little correspondence with reality. Turkish descendants of the extended Robinson family noted how they heard that before his death Spencer repeated the word of God and became a Muslim. Again, though, this cannot be confirmed. It was also extremely unlikely. Spencer was buried in a Christian cemetery in the district of Kalimpong in India in 1889. Hannah only converted to Islam in 1891, after having returned to England.

Darjeeling was known as the 'Queen of the Hill Stations' in India. In a well-known book about the settlement written early in the last century by the historian E. C. Dozey, it was stated that in Victoria Terrace, on Mount Pleasant Road, 'Conductor' Spencer Robinson was the manager of the Carrying Company and Tonga Service. Started by 'Lloyd, the Banker', the company's office was on a road on an elevated ridge in the settlement where the European quarter was located. Other businesses, administrative offices and social facilities and amenities used by the British and other Europeans were to be found there. The book, first published in 1917, added that the premises used by Spencer Robinson were then occupied by Robert and Company (details of which are not known) and Master's Curio Shop.[4] The curio shop, with branches in Simla and Lucknow, specialised in selling photo-type post-cards, including ones with panoramic views of Darjeeling and its neighbourhood. No date was given for when Spencer managed the office. The company mentioned was likely also known as the Calcutta and Darjeeling Carrying Company and Tonga-Dak Carriers, whose Calcutta agents were Lloyd and Company. Spencer Robinson worked for this company between 1880 and 1882. He also ran an office in this period for the firm in Kurseong, a smaller town downhill from Darjeeling.[5]

Spencer Robinson had been employed in other occupations in the Darjeeling district prior to taking up work for Lloyd and Company. The first record I could find of his presence in India came from the invitation for him to join the United Grand Lodge of England Freemasons at the Mount Everest Lodge, which was situated in Darjeeling. The invitation was dated 28 November 1874. The lodge had only been constituted the previous month. In its initial years, the Freemasons assembled in the Lodge Room in Darjeeling. They moved to the local town hall in 1880 before finally finding a home one year later in Masonic Rooms in the town. Gatherings of Freemasons were welcome opportunities for the scattered expatriate community to come together. Spencer Robinson was registered in the lodge as a tea planter.

The family letters available indicate that upon moving to India, Spencer commenced work in the tea sector. He may have been appointed as an assistant to a manager of one of the many tea gardens which had recently been established. By 1876, he had taken up a desk job working for a Calcutta-based firm which became one of India's foremost managing agents. But Spencer maintained an interest in tea. He rented land to enable his second wife to operate a small tea venture. After a few years engaged in other professions, Spencer concentrated more attention on the tea industry and he became a joint owner of three tea estates in the Darjeeling district. However, he was not always successful in his various enterprises. Having accumulated substantial debts, Spencer was imprisoned for five months in the Presidency Jail in Calcutta in 1885.

Why did Spencer Robinson decide to embark on a new life in India in particular? Much has been written about the sons of established families in Victorian England journeying to India to make their fortune and a name for themselves while serving as senior officers in the military or high-level colonial officials. Others, with a spirit of adventure, may have chosen to make a fresh start by cutting ties with the homeland and seeking out new challenges abroad. Tea planters, for example, were often depicted as opportunists and fortune hunters. The maintenance and development of the British Raj to further Britain's colonial interests depended on the skills and expertise of a whole range of professions. The services of engineers, technicians, lower-level civil servants, tradesmen, policemen, teachers, barristers, missionaries and so on were all valued, and incentives were offered to encourage men from various walks of life to make the passage to India.

The ongoing industrialisation and increased exploitation of India in the 1870s, with the expansion of the railway network and the cultivation and export of commercial crops, such as tea, led the government in London to seek to recruit a new workforce for the British Raj. At a time when agriculture in England started to suffer from the consequences of a prolonged recession, the last decades of the nineteenth century in India were a period of unprecedented growth and prosperity for the colonial administration and its capitalist backers. The shock of local uprisings in 1857 – the failed 'Mutiny of 1857' – had also prompted London, for security reasons, to encourage more settlers to arrive in India. With the opening of the Suez Canal in 1869, the sailing time between England and India was reduced to a matter of weeks rather than months. This increased the attraction of living and working in India. Improved transportation links provided more opportunity for families to spend time together in India, and allowed the possibility for frequent trips to be made back to the homeland.

Just why Spencer Robinson opted to relocate to India may never be known. However, he had experienced the trauma of losing his young wife only months after uprooting himself from the familiar surroundings of the Lincolnshire fens and wolds. The prospect of returning to the East Keal neighbourhood with its recent memories may not have been so welcoming for Spencer, particularly after the drawn-out procedures over the sale and letting of his property there.

The Hill Stations of India

The uprisings that commenced in 1857, and which took over one year to brutally crush, had a major impact on British rule in India. There had been occasional unrest before, triggered by things like the raising of taxes, but the events of 1857 were far more serious. Indian soldiers in the British East India Company (EIC), the sepoys, rebelled following rumours that pig and cow fat – forbidden by the Muslim and Hindu religions – had been used as ingredients for the pre-greased paper cartridges used for new rifles. To load the rifle, the sepoy had to bite the cartridge, thereby releasing the powder. The eventual failure of this rebellion led to the demise of the increasingly enfeebled Mughal Empire, and the British Crown effectively assumed full control of India. Under the British Raj, the EIC was dissolved in 1874. Many local princes nominally maintained control over large swathes of Indian territory, but these native rulers pledged allegiance to the British Crown as colonial rule was further consolidated.

Prior to 1857, there had been a degree of intermingling between the British occupiers and the indigenous communities. It was not uncommon for settlers to live among the locals, marry the natives and adopt some of the customs and traditions of the territories in which they lived. Such behaviour was much less commonplace in the wake of the uprisings. The increasing popularity of hill stations in British-controlled India reflected the mounting concern and desire among the colonial rulers to remain separate and distinct from the natives. A total of eighty hill stations would serve as settlements, often guarded by a detachment of troops, which offered the British and other Europeans a measure of security with the Indian population mostly removed and centred on the distant plains below. These hill stations provided a number of other important political, social and economic functions.

According to historian Dane Kennedy, 'in the hill stations the British could replicate the bourgeois civic culture that characterised the social world they left behind in England'.[6] The hill stations took as their model the English village. They were seen as closed communities where the English could relax, play and feel at home. As schools and other amenities were rapidly established, the settlements became increasingly attractive places for women and children to reside. It was believed that families could be brought up safely in the hillside communities. Those who could not afford to send their children back to boarding schools in England had the opportunity to provide their offspring with a decent education in the hill stations. In the words of Kennedy, the hill stations became, in effect, the 'nurseries of the ruling race'.[7]

High above what were perceived to be the disease-ridden plains, the hill stations were regarded as places where one could escape from the stifling heat, grime and poverty. The English were convinced that breathing the crisper mountain air led to longer and healthier lives. The still widely held 'medieval belief' in the hazards of 'miasmic airs', and the views at the time on the supposed relationship between climate, race and health, boosted the popularity and attractiveness of the hill stations.[8] In the summer months, heads of local governments with their panoply of bureaucrats, secretaries and servants physically relocated *en masse* from the sweltering plains to the cooler climes of the hill stations.

Hill stations also served as important strategic bases and key trading centres. This was particularly the case for those settlements situated near the border or located along or not far from established trading routes. The economic value of hill stations further increased if they were situated, for example, close to significant tea-producing areas.

In reality, the English and other Europeans, perched in their alpine-like settlements, could not remain completely cut off from the natives. The hill stations required local labour to maintain the running of basic services. This workforce tended to inhabit the less salubrious parts of the hill station, located several tiers below the residences of the English and other Europeans. Wealthier locals would in time find accommodation which encroached on those parts of the settlement which had been the preserves of the non-native occupiers. The supposed health benefits of the hill stations were also somewhat exaggerated given the cold and damp conditions which were experienced in certain seasons. A clinging and persistent mist often enshrouded the settlements. Descending wisps of cloud were often the harbingers of what would become a steady and prolonged thin drizzle. The vagaries of the weather notwithstanding, the hill stations remained favoured locations for the English and the Europeans well into the twentieth century.

The District of Darjeeling

The British under the EIC had established control of the territory around Darjeeling (in today's West Bengal in north-eastern India) in 1835. The area was acquired from the local ruler, the chogyal of Sikkim. The district had been the subject of dispute between the Kingdom of Sikkim and the Nepalese Ghorka Empire. A whiff of controversy surrounds the British acquisition of the strip of land. According to some commentators, the territory was handed to the British by the chogyal as a gift of friendship. Others indicate that the ruler of Sikkim was duped into agreeing to the 'dubious deed of grant' without receiving other territories which had supposedly been proffered by the EIC.[9] The British authorities quickly recognised the strategic importance of the location. Troops could be quartered at a hill station which was ideally located on the trading routes connecting India with Sikkim, Nepal, Bhutan and Tibet. The less oppressive climate up in the hills also meant that a sanatorium could be built there to enable troops to convalesce. With the later development of the tea industry, Darjeeling assumed greater importance and became the summer headquarters for the lieutenant-governor of Bengal and his administration.

Communications with the outside world were improved by the construction of a military road – also known as the Pankhabari Road – connecting the hill station with the plains. Completed by 1842, this was replaced by the flatter, wider and more easily negotiable Hill Cart Road, which was built in the period 1861–69. Transportation links further improved with the opening of the DHR in 1881. The security of the area had been reinforced in 1849 with the EIC's acquisition of the strip of land known as the Tarai, which had previously belonged to Sikkim. A densely forested and malaria-ridden area, its possession enabled a direct connection between Darjeeling and the British-controlled plains. Before this, the Darjeeling area was an enclave surrounded by territory ruled by the chogyal of Sikkim.

Situated in the foothills of the Himalayas, with the majestic Kanchenjunga ('The Five Treasures of Snow'), the world's third-tallest peak, visible on a clear day, the town of Darjeeling rapidly expanded. This was largely due to the enthusiasm of the Scottish civil servant Dr Archibald Campbell, who arrived in the area in 1839 to take up the newly created post of Superintendent of Darjeeling. A member of the Indian Medical Service, Campbell had previously served as British Resident in Nepal. It was he who first experimented with the planting of tea from Chinese leaf varieties in the garden of his residence.

In 1835, Darjeeling was merely a collection of twenty or so scattered humble dwellings with a population of about one hundred. The indigenous inhabitants were the Lepchas, a people of Mongolian origin who practised Buddhism. Becoming a municipality in 1850, by 1852 the township had expanded to accommodate around seventy houses.[10] Nine years later, Darjeeling had 3,000 inhabitants, and the population increased fourfold over the following twenty years. Cottages built in the Swiss style with manicured gardens sprang up along the ridge in the European quarter of town. The Anglican church of St Andrew was built as early as 1843. The much-respected Church of England's St Paul's School, based in Calcutta, opened a branch in the town in 1864. Banks, government buildings, a postal and telegraph office and a library were also established, among others. The town's famous botanic gardens first received visitors in 1878. Ten years earlier, the Darjeeling Planters' Club had opened its doors and had quickly become a key social hub for the British and European community.[11] With employment on offer, especially with the expansion of tea gardens in the area, Nepalese, Tibetans, Punjabis and Bengalis were also attracted to settle in the Darjeeling district. The Europeans constituted only a small minority of the population living in the neighbourhood of Darjeeling.[12]

As the hill station at Darjeeling extended and transportation links improved, other satellite communities were established in the neighbourhood such as at Kurseong and Kalimpong. Roughly 20 miles from Darjeeling and located at a height of 1,500 metres on the Hill Cart Road as it climbed up from the hot plains, Kurseong – the land of the White Orchid – grew in size and was recognised as a municipality in 1879. The British had secured control of the area around Kurseong back in 1835 with the acquisition of Darjeeling. Enjoying a milder climate than Darjeeling with less harsh winters,

Kurseong was a favourite of those settlers who were reluctant to live at higher altitudes. A number of tea estates were established around the hill station. The headquarters of the DHR would be based at Kurseong. The town expanded in size as rail traffic along the DHR increased. Originally serving as a co-educational school for the children of the railway workers, the Victoria School opened just outside Kurseong on Dow Hill in 1879. According to Dozey, writing in 1917, the town, with its two churches – the Anglican Christ Church and a Roman Catholic church – plus library and town hall, had a population of about 5,000.[13] Kurseong became well known for the Clarendon Hotel there, which until 1894 also served, in practice, as a station for the DHR. The grand hotel was forced to close in 1938. The railway station still provides a focal point for the town. Kurseong itself commands an impressive view of the rivers that shimmer as silver ribbons in the plains far below. In recent years the town has become famous for its ghost stories. The Victoria School is reputedly the haunt of a headless boy.

About 29 miles east of Darjeeling, Kalimpong was only acquired by the British Raj after the successful conclusion of the Anglo-Bhutan War (1863–65), when the foothills and plains known as the Dooars were also annexed. This squashed the potential threat posed by the Bhutanese to the security of Darjeeling. While much less developed than Darjeeling, Kalimpong eventually became another important outpost with its bazaar. Kalimpong was of strategic value, situated on the trade route between Tibet and India. Access to Kalimpong from Darjeeling was via the leech-infested valley of the River Teesta. Dozey noted that the population of Kalimpong was about 1,200.[14] The much smaller British community was deprived of much of the thrills and frills of the social life that Darjeeling could offer.

Settlers residing in Kalimpong had to be of a much tougher disposition. The first schools in the area were only established in the early 1870s by hardy Scottish missionaries. Educational opportunities expanded following the opening of the Scottish Universities Mission Institute in Kalimpong in 1886 under the guidance of the Scottish missionary William Macfarlane. An imposing Gothic church erected to commemorate the work of Macfarlane still towers over the hill station and is visible for miles around. Kalimpong's strategic significance grew further following Francis Younghusband's expedition to Tibet in 1903 and 1904. This was part of a manoeuvre by Britain to thwart

Russia's ambitions in Central Asia. The town is now well known for its flower markets, nurseries and panoramic views.

I found evidence that Spencer Robinson lived at various times in Darjeeling, Kurseong and Kalimpong.

Managing Agents and Bullock Carts

Until the early nineteenth century, the EIC had largely maintained control over trade and business in British-controlled India. The position of the EIC, though, was increasingly challenged by agency houses. These were private partnerships that made use of capital from the savings of former civil and military employees of the EIC. The agency houses began trading in commodities such as opium, sugar, cotton, indigo and later tea. The managing agency system was introduced when agency houses first promoted and then later secured the management of joint stock companies.[15] The agency houses were, in effect, vehicles through which the colonial rulers could further exploit local resources.

Through so-called agency contracts, managing agents in effect obtained control of companies which they administered.[16] The managing agents provided these companies with a range of services such as marketing and the provision of equipment and accounting. They also perhaps held shares in companies. Managing agents occasionally assisted in helping establish new businesses. These agents played an instrumental role in supplying the necessary expertise and capital to develop the economic infrastructure of the British Raj in India. Most managing agents had their headquarters in Calcutta, the capital.

According to the *Bengal Directory*, in the years 1876–79 Spencer Robinson was employed by Bird and Company, a firm which at that time was listed as railway contractors and forwarding agents. The business had its main office in Calcutta, but Spencer was initially engaged as an assistant at the firm's Kurseong branch. By 1879 he had been promoted to the position of manager at the Kurseong office. His work involved handling the company's bullock train and tonga (a horse-drawn light carriage) *dak* carriers which transported goods, people and the post from the plains to the hill station at Darjeeling. It seems that Spencer lived as well as worked in Kurseong in this period and in the first half of the 1880s.

Bird and Company became a leading managing agent. Unlike many of its competitors, it first acquired its reputation not in trading but in providing labour services. The firm was established in 1864 by Sam Bird, a former ship's captain and the agent for the India General Steam Navigation Company, which was located in Allahabad. The business originally served as a labour contractor supplying manpower to East Indian Railways, starting as a family business with Sam's brother Paul also playing a key role. By 1870 the company started renting offices in Calcutta. Other handling contracts were secured from steam navigation companies and from the Eastern Bengal Railway. The year 1873 was a landmark one for Bird and Company. A contract was secured from the provincial government of Bengal to handle rice deliveries to help relieve a local famine. Able to unload huge volumes of rice, the company quickly acquired a reputation for professionalism. Operating as a managing agent, Bird and Company soon reacted to intense competition in transportation by moving into other interests such as coal, jute, paper, cement and cotton.[17]

Connected with their work for East Indian Railways, Bird and Company operated the 'bullock train service' which ran between Caragola and Darjeeling.[18] This presumably commenced working after the company won the handling contract at Sahibganj rail station in 1869. Goods and passengers from Calcutta were transported by rail northwards to Sahibganj and then carried by ferry across the River Ganges to Bhavanipur. The next 2 miles were negotiated by foot along a wide sandy bank to Caragola. From there, a bullock cart proceeded along a new road, broad and metalled, to Siliguri and then embarked on the climb along the Hill Cart Road to Kurseong and finally to Darjeeling. This was a time-consuming journey. According to W. B. Gladstone, the Chairman of the Board of Directors of the DHR, it could take five to six days to travel from Calcutta to Darjeeling in 1878. He noted that this 'was about as exhausting and uncomfortable a journey as can well be imagined'.[19]

Kurseong was thus an important station along the winding route negotiated by the bullock train. By 1879, it seems that Spencer Robinson was responsible for the Siliguri–Darjeeling leg of this journey. The connection of Siliguri to Calcutta by rail and ferry following the further development of the East Indian Railway network, and the extension of the Northern Bengal Railway line in 1878, would have made the Caragola–Siliguri stretch of the bullock train route much less commercially attractive.

A bullock 'train' consisted of two-wheeled box-shaped carts provided with tarpaulin hoods which were driven by two bullocks. Additional bullocks were used to negotiate steeper gradients, and sometimes even elephants were employed to cross streams swollen by heavy rains.[20] In practice, bullocks could only travel 20 to 30 kilometres in a day in good weather when using one of the few well-surfaced roads.[21] Bullock trains could only be used to carry goods and passengers to Darjeeling once the Hill Cart Road was completed in 1869. Previously, passengers may have been transported to Darjeeling along the old military road using a *palki*. This was, in effect, the Indian equivalent of the sedan chair, but in contrast to the relatively straightforward task of negotiating the streets of seventeenth-century London, the Indian coolies toiled to carry their passengers up the hillside.[22]

With the opening of the Hill Cart Road, a daily service of bullock cart trains operated in each direction. Bird and Company competed with the Darjeeling Bullock Cart Train Company to transport goods to the hill station. However, the two companies often ran bullock trains together on grounds of security. Each company had a train of ten to twelve bullock carts.[23] Armed guards, equipped with armour and spikes, were employed to protect the bullock trains, but the trains made very slow progress and took three days to complete the original journey from Caragola to Darjeeling. Departing Caragola at 4 p.m., the bullock train reached Siliguri at 11 a.m. on the second morning and Kurseong would be passed during the middle of the third day.[24]

Tonga services usually consisted of two horses pulling a light carriage. Occasionally, oxen might be employed. A system of relays was used with horses stationed at certain intervals along the route. Mail (*dak*) was delivered by means of the tonga services.

The arduous journey using the bullock train from Caragola to Darjeeling was vividly depicted by an intrepid and self-styled 'lady pioneer' who was travelling with her husband.[25] The train was described as a 'hackery' covered by a right tilt in a sort of gypsy arrangement which was yoked to two small bullocks. The 'whole thing' appeared as if it must have been 'in use in the time of the Pharaohs'. The almost solid wood wheels rolled 'round with a reluctance and squeak that is positively maddening'. The train moved at around one and a half miles per hour. One train carried the wife and husband, while another was loaded with luggage. The journey was punctuated with stops at staging bungalows which were like 'roadside inns' providing rest and replenishment. Travel by a bone-rattling bullock train was thus quite an experience, but for several years it was one of the few ways to reach Darjeeling by the Hill Cart Road.

By 1880, Spencer Robinson had left Bird and Company and had started to work as an inspecting agent and manager for the Calcutta and Darjeeling Carrying Company and Tonga-*Dak* Carriers. It is not clear if Spencer's new employer was a business rival or a partner to Bird and Company. The headquarters of the Calcutta and Darjeeling Carrying Company was at 35 Strand Road North in Calcutta, just a couple of doors away from Bird and Company, and both firms shared other premises in the capital at 25 Mangoe Lane. Strand Road was one of the main avenues of the bustling metropolis, stretching along the banks of the Hooghly River, a tributary of the Ganges – although the locals today refer to the waterway as the Ganges River. The many godowns (warehouses) which lined the side of the road by the river now lie derelict. Only a few grand houses of the late Victorian period remain intact along the congested tree-clad highway. For his part, Spencer Robinson continued to work from Kurseong, where in 1881 and 1882 he was listed as superintendent for the Calcutta and Darjeeling Carrying Company.

Interestingly, in 1883 Spencer formed his own company, together with a John Henry Rose Harley, to continue the bullock train business. This company may have replaced the Calcutta and Darjeeling Carrying Company as Robinson, Harley and Company was also run from 35 Strand Road North. The next year the company was renamed Harley, Robinson and Company and had moved to 41 Strand Road North. The establishment of this business proved to be costly for Spencer. With the completion of the DHR in 1881, the days of the bullock train and tonga *dak* carriers to deliver goods from the plains to Darjeeling were clearly numbered. It would be much quicker, safer and easier to transport materials and passengers from Siliguri to Darjeeling by rail. By 1883, the godowns, depots and much of the infrastructure connected with the bullock trains had been sold to the DHR for 20,000 rupees.[26]

The Darjeeling Himalayan Railway
The expansion of the railway network was important for the British Raj for several reasons. Railways could be used as a means to control and pacify the local population. Troops could be speedily

despatched to trouble spots or could be quickly relocated to border areas. Railways also facilitated a substantial increase in trade as commodities such as salt and coal, and later cotton and tea, could be transferred for much less cost to markets internally and externally via seaports. The acceleration of the development of the rail grid after the 1876–78 famine, to ensure that in future provisions could be swiftly delivered to districts suffering drought, suggested that railways could also have important welfare benefits.[27]

The first railway track in India was laid in 1853. The British government had initially refused to build the railroads themselves; instead, private investors were encouraged to provide capital in exchange for land and assurances of future profits. The second spurt of railway construction commencing in the 1870s was due to more direct involvement by the British Raj. There then followed in the 1880s the start of a public-private partnership, with both the government and companies cooperating in the running of the rail network. In practice, taxes were raised on the local population to help fund railway building while British shareholders made huge profits from their initial investments.

After Siliguri had been connected to Calcutta by rail in 1878, pressure mounted for work to begin to link Siliguri with Darjeeling by steam tramway or rail. This made sense both strategically and economically. Troops could be deployed more quickly to Darjeeling and to other stations en route, while the booming tea industry would have a swifter outlet to external markets. Larger volumes of rice and other provisions could also be transported uphill to service the growing army of tea plantation workers. Originally the brainchild of Franklin Prestage, an agent of the Eastern Bengal Railway, work on what became known as the DHR started in 1879 after the project had gained the backing of Sir Ashley Eden, lieutenant-governor of Bengal, who had set up a committee to assess the feasibility of the project. Managing agents Gillanders Arbuthnot and Company were commissioned to undertake the construction of the railway along the approximately 50-mile route. This company later owned and managed the railway from its Calcutta office. The section between Siliguri and Kurseong was opened on 23 August 1880 and the official inauguration of the line's operation to Darjeeling took place on 4 July 1881.[28]

In its first year, the DHR carried 8,000 passengers and 380 tons of goods.[29] According to the then sixty-years-old Mark Twain, commenting in 1896 after an exhilarating descent from Darjeeling in a small canopied handcar, a trip on the DHR 'was the most enjoyable day I have spent on earth'.[30] A train carriage used on the line was later named after him. The spectacular rail journey, climbing from Siliguri at 120 metres above sea level to Darjeeling at over 2,000 metres, took originally around ten hours. This was much quicker than by bullock train or tonga. Much of the narrow gauge (2 feet or 610 millimetres) line, which was only suitable for small-sized locomotives, was laid alongside and often criss-crossed the Hill Cart Road. The line ascended to its summit at the station at Ghum above 2,500 metres before gently descending to Darjeeling. The first versions of the so-called 'Toy Train' laboured to climb the steeper parts of the route. For this reason, in 1882 four loops and four reverses (zig-zags) were added between stations lower down the line to ease the gradient. Using the DHR, tea could thus be carried much quicker and safer downhill from Darjeeling. Previously, tea chests carried by bullock carts were often damaged due to moisture.[31]

Although local workers were hired to construct the railway, in the initial years of its operation the DHR was run and maintained largely by staff imported from England. Below the top level of management, no 'trained subordinate staff' existed and hence train drivers, station managers, guards and traffic inspectors had to be recruited from England or from English communities in India.[32]

Spencer Robinson worked in various periods as a traffic manager/ traffic superintendent for the DHR from the station at Tindharia ('Three Ridges'). Correspondence from Spencer (discussed in more detail below) revealed that he had taken up this post with the inauguration of the DHR. He then held the position of traffic manager in 1884 and again between 1886 and 1888. With Siliguri as the first station, Tindharia was the fifth station encountered on the climb up to Darjeeling. Tindharia became the site of the DHR's workshop, with the first locomotive built there on site in 1919. Employed together with Spencer at Tindharia in 1884 were an inspector, a station manager and two guards.

Traffic control was essential for the maintenance of the DHR. The 'Up' service covered traffic climbing towards Darjeeling, and the 'Down' service involved those trains descending to Siliguri. Given the single narrow-gauge line, trains could not always pass at stations and so sidings and twelve intermediate passing points were constructed along the route. Communication between stations was by Morse telegraph. The 'Down' service was given priority with the exception of the 'Mail', which was allowed to pass first in either direction. Goods trains were obliged to give way to services carrying passengers. Speed restrictions were also in place – 16 mph along the plains and 10 mph for the ascent and descent.[33] Accidents often occurred as a result of drivers not adhering to the speed limits. In Kurseong, the train proceeded at walking pace as the rail line ran through the centre of the town's main market. Locals often nonchalantly hopped on and off the train as it wound its way through the narrow streets.

Traffic inspectors also needed to check for landslides. Heavy rainfalls in the monsoon season could lead to torrents of water gushing down the hill slopes. Occasionally, snow could accumulate and block the tracks in winter. Elephants and Bengal tigers prowling along the tracks were another occupational hazard. According to one particularly eye-catching account, in the 1920s the authorities in Calcutta received the following message of panic from Tindharia: 'Tiger eating station master on platform. Rush instructions by telegraph!'[34]

The Presidency Jail of Calcutta

The three main commercial centres of the British Raj – Calcutta, Bombay and Madras – were known as Presidency towns, and each was equipped with jails to house unfortunate bankrupts. The 'Presidencies' originally referred to those territories of India which came under the direct rule of the EIC. In the late nineteenth century, the Presidency Jail of Calcutta was located on the Calcutta Maidan in the heart of the capital – now the site of the grounds and gardens of the famous Victoria Memorial. Newspaper reports in early 1885 referred to 'serious charges of cruel treatment' in the Presidency Jail. Prisoners found smoking were apparently placed in irons for one month. Others were punished for various misdemeanours by spending forty-eight hours in solitary confinement 'in a dark cell'. There were harrowing stories of inmates made to grind wheat from six in the morning till three in the morning the following day. Beatings, reduced dietary feedings and torture were evidently not uncommon. Prisons in India were notoriously disease-ridden, with cholera and tuberculosis being especially prevalent. An official commission into the running of the Presidency Jail in Calcutta exonerated the superintendent of the institution of most of the allegations levelled against him, but he was nevertheless found guilty of some 'grave and serious' charges.[35]

Conditions in the civil section of the Presidency Jail were more tolerable than those in the criminal division of the prison, and it was in the civil section that insolvents were held. The law on bankruptcy in India did not mirror that in Britain; contrary to the Bankruptcy Act of 1869 approved by the House of Commons, general opinion in the British Raj favoured the continued imprisonment of debtors to deter individuals from seeking to make a quick profit through rash speculation and extravagant spending.

According to his second wife, Hannah (of whom more later), Spencer Robinson was admitted to the civil section of the Presidency Jail in Calcutta on 11 July 1885.[36] This was around the same time that several of his brothers were becoming victims of lavish spending and the agricultural depression in England. Apparently, Spencer was 44,000 rupees in debt as a result of the collapse of Robinson, Harley and Company. Over the next seven months, Spencer desperately sought to secure funds from colleagues to secure his release. He also attempted to obtain additional money by manoeuvring to sub-lease land for which he was paying rent to a local Indian dignitary. This land, which included a small tea garden and factory, was under the management of Spencer's wife.

In her letter referring to Spencer's incarceration, Hannah noted that Robinson, Harley and Company, involved in the bullock train business, had been struggling financially for two years. In correspondence with G. M. Reily, the Calcutta-based manager of the Land Mortgage Bank of India, Spencer Robinson described how he had made provision for the company's debt payments to be made to the Oriental Bank. However, one of the partners had absconded with the money.[37] No name was specified by Spencer. According to the *Bengal Directory*, one of the partners was John Henry Rose Harley, and a G. M. Harvey was listed as the company's agent.

Harley was a Calcutta-born merchant who was involved directly or indirectly in other bankruptcy cases. A previous business partner of his, Diethelm Freck, was declared insolvent and languished in prison in Calcutta in 1885. Freck and Harley had run a business in the capital between 1879 and 1880 before the two clashed and parted ways, and Freck eventually became manager of a tannery.[38] Harley himself was made bankrupt in 1891 after the collapse of his business in Calcutta as a tarpaulin manufacturer and paint dealer.[39] A George Montgomery Harvey lived and worked in Calcutta in this period. According to his marriage certificates of 1891 and 1894, Harvey was listed as a 'broker'. I have not been able to learn about other possible partners in Robinson, Harley and Company.

When in prison, Spencer expressed alarm over what might happen to his wife, who was heavily pregnant, and to the infants in his family. This forced him to compose a series of pleading letters to Reily of the Land Mortgage Bank of India. The bank owned several tea estates in India. Spencer sought to persuade Reily to pay him money for the sub-lease of land for which Spencer was paying rent to a local Indian landowner, the maharaja of Burdwan. Because of his grave financial difficulties, Spencer was behind in rent payments to the Burdwan estate. If the land could not be sub-leased to the Land Mortgage Bank of India, Spencer feared that he would lose all rights to the rented land, which was being managed by his wife.

The land in question was referred to by the Robinsons as the 'Rajbaree estate'. Spencer Robinson was, in practice, a tenant of the estate, and, as a wedding present, in 1880 he had handed over the property to his wife.[40] The estate appeared to lie immediately to the south-west of Kurseong. It was bounded by the Pankhabari Road, the Korbia tea garden, and by other property owned by the maharaja of Burdwan. The maharaja's residence on the southern outskirts of Kurseong was also known as 'Rajbari' ('Rajbaree'), or 'The Retreat'. This indicates that the Robinsons were based primarily in Kurseong in the first half of the 1880s. In one of his letters, Spencer noted that his wife intended to build a house on the Pankhabari Road.[41]

The Burdwan estate extended over a vast territory in Bengal. The Indian dynasty which ruled over the estate enjoyed close links with the British Raj. In effect, the Mehtab family collected rents and then transferred much of this revenue to the British authorities. Non-payment of rents to the Mehtab family thus meant less money ending up in the coffers of the British Raj. In the mid-1880s, the Burdwan estate was managed by Thomas de Burgh Miller and a Punjabi, Lalla Bun Behari Kapur (Kapoor). It will be seen that Spencer Robinson had a close business relationship with Bun Behari Kapur and possibly Miller over the management of other tea estates, and this may have worked to Spencer's advantage at the time of his imprisonment. In one of her letters to the Calcutta agent of the

Land Mortgage Bank of India, Hannah Robinson remarked that Mr Miller was 'most kindly, making every possible concession'.[42]

In his communications from prison to Reily, Spencer Robinson became increasingly desperate. Noting how his wife and children were suffering, he implored the manager of the Land Mortgage Bank of India to send some money to Hannah, saying it was 'a matter of life and death'.[43] In another letter, he exclaimed that his wife was about to send her children to the magistrate and that she was threatening to commit suicide.[44] Fortunately, though, some time in December 1885, Spencer was finally released from his confinement. Reily had provided Hannah with some money to meet immediate needs, and then Spencer's friends and a local church raised the 500 rupees required to enable the Oriental Bank to agree to allow Spencer to be set free.[45]

Following Spencer's release, a contract was drawn up allowing the sub-lease of land at the 'Rajbaree' estate to the Land Mortgage Bank of India. But, at the last minute, objections were raised by the Planters Stores and Agency Company Limited.[46] It seems that Spencer also owed money to this managing agency, which was involved in the running of numerous tea companies. Eventually, a deal was struck with the agency and terms for the sub-lease of land were agreed. According to the contract signed on 27 January 1886 between Spencer Robinson and the Land Mortgage Bank of India, two parcels of land were sub-leased to the bank for a period of three years at a rent of 100 rupees per month and one hundred pounds of Pekoe tea. Presumably after having secured guarantees that the contract would be signed, thirteen days earlier Spencer had written out a cheque for the payment of 1,200 rupees to the Burdwan estate to help pay for rent previously owed.[47]

The Planters Stores and Agency Company Limited finally agreed to drop all proceedings against Spencer Robinson on the condition that they would receive monthly payments from Spencer's employment at the DHR.[48] While Spencer lingered in the Presidency Jail, Franklin Prestage, who was still employed with the DHR, had intervened and personally offered Spencer his old job as traffic superintendent at Tindharia, which was located downhill, not far from Kurseong.[49] This action on the part of Prestage may also have facilitated Spencer's release from prison.

To his credit, Spencer Robinson swiftly recovered from what was undoubtedly a traumatic experience for himself and his family.

The sub-lease of land may have compelled the Robinsons to abandon Kurseong. Spencer was soon employed in a new business enterprise in Kalimpong. Work in the Kalimpong district would somehow have to be juggled with employment for the DHR at Tindharia. Contacts and previous work in the tea business could have helped Spencer secure an early release from the Presidency Jail in Calcutta. However, these ties had not saved him from his initial incarceration.

Working with Tea

Spencer Robinson did play a role in the development of the tea industry in the Darjeeling district. This industry depended on bullock cart trains and then railways to deliver tea to the plains and from there to ports for transportation to England. Presumably, given his agricultural background, Spencer would have been more familiar with the workings of the tea business compared to other novice tea planters fresh from Britain.

Although he was registered as a tea planter in 1874, it was not until 1883 that Spencer Robinson was mentioned in the *Bengal Directory* as one of the proprietors of the Dhundibree tea garden. Spencer was listed as a co-proprietor of this tea garden in 1884 and 1885, and, between 1884 and 1888, he was also a co-owner of other tea plantations in the Darjeeling district at Dilaram and Pronub Bun.[50] Prior to 1883, in most cases the *Bengal Directory* only referred to the name of one proprietor who may have owned the tea garden along with unspecified 'others'. Spencer, therefore, may have been a co-proprietor of one or more tea gardens before 1883. Certainly, he was closely connected to the small 'Rajbaree' tea estate.

The significance of the development of the tea industry for the growth of Darjeeling and the other settlements nearby should not be underestimated. The EIC had begun exporting tea from the Assam region in north-eastern India in the 1820s, but it was only in 1852 that the first commercial tea gardens were established in the Darjeeling area after the earlier experiments in planting tea by Superintendent Campbell. The first tea 'factory' in the district entered operation in 1859. The expansion of the tea industry in the Darjeeling district was phenomenal as customers in England became eager to taste the high-quality black tea. Soon, many experts were claiming that Darjeeling produced the world's greatest tea.

Although less abundant than other brands, Darjeeling tea became a prized commodity. By 1866 there were thirty-nine tea gardens in operation around Darjeeling. Eight years later there were 113 tea gardens in the vicinity.[51] Tea cultivation was encouraged by state-assisted development of the commercial crop. Land was leased on favourable terms, but initial capital and investment were still required. For example, in 1864 the government introduced leases in Darjeeling for the cultivation of tea which covered a thirty-year period. The land was rent-free for the initial five years and then an annual rate of six annas per acres was charged.[52] An anna was equal to one-sixth of a rupee. The growth of the tea industry in the Darjeeling district was one of the main reasons why the colonial administration pressed ahead with the construction of the DHR in the late 1870s.

Would-be tea planters were hired by large businesses connected to managing agents in India. These agents were able to offer initial capital. 'Tea planters' were first employed as assistants to the manager of a tea estate. Many of these tea planters were bachelors coming from working- or middle-class backgrounds, or even members of the minor gentry. Often, they had little or no knowledge of working on the land, but they were confident that they could do the job. Certainly, they had no experience of employment in the tea industry. Many could not identify a tea bush and had no grasp of how to process the tea leaves. According to one account, in the early days of tea cultivation in India, 'only those Englishmen who failed to make it as soldiers, sailors, clerks and by default, with nothing else to lose and nowhere else to go took up life as a "tea planter"'.[53]

The managers of tea gardens have also been scathingly attacked. One commentator noted that with the dramatic expansion of the tea business in India in the 1860s there was a feeling at the time that 'any fool could run a tea garden'. People who had failed in all other tasks were often recruited as managers of tea gardens.[54] Purportedly, those tea planters who had started on the estates as bachelors had to work for several years before they could marry. Even then, permission to marry had apparently to be first granted by the *burra sahib* (the head manager at the tea garden), who might also decide to first vet the proposed wife in question.[55] The seemingly omnipotent *burra sahib* was at the apex of a tight hierarchical structure within a typical tea estate.

The tea planter's job was a strenuous one. Starting from scratch, it would take five or so years before the first tea could be manufactured.

A 40-40-20 scheme was adopted in the nineteenth-century tea estates: 40 per cent of land was reserved for the tea crop, 40 per cent was left wild as a natural buffer and soil anchor, and the remaining 20 per cent housed the substantial number of workers and their families.[56] Tea planters were required to oversee the work of hundreds of labourers (mainly imported Nepalese in the case of Darjeeling) rather than engage as farmers tending the crops themselves. Tea planters supervised the various stages of cultivation – clearing away trees and shrubs, planting the seedling, pruning and later plucking the bush – and then oversaw the processes involved in the manufacture of the tea in the factory – the weighing, withering, rolling, fermenting, drying, sifting and, finally, packing of the leaves. Their role was more that of manager and accountant. Living in their bungalow separate from the workforce, they were also required to provide housing for the plantation workers and their families. Tea planters were responsible for the laying of roads to connect the tea gardens, for example to the Hill Cart Road or the nearest train station.[57]

Given what the life and work of a tea planter entailed, it is extremely difficult to imagine that Spencer Robinson could have both worked as a planter and been employed full-time for Bird and Company and other agencies. It is therefore more feasible that Spencer may have started work in India as a tea planter, contracted by a large agency on account of his farming experience, before being hired by Bird and Company. Several years later, and given his ties to the 'Rajbaree' tea garden, Spencer may have decided to return to the tea industry by becoming a full- or part-time co-proprietor of at least three tea gardens.

The Darjeeling Planters' Club was the centre of social life for tea planters and tea owners in the neighbourhood, and Spencer Robinson was most probably one of its members given his enthusiasm for fully participating in the activities of the local community. Established in 1868 on land donated by the local maharaja of Cooch Behar, the club was famous as a venue where tea planters and other Englishmen and Europeans in the district could gather to socialise, play billiards, drink, party and gamble. The only rickshaw allowed to be parked at the entrance to the club was that owned by the maharaja.[58] The club was well-known in particular for its sale of pink gin which was consumed in prodigious quantities. It had four billiard tables, a reading room and library above the dining room, stables, and a three-storied building next-door to accommodate the servants.

Tea planters had to change into formal attire before they could order refreshment. After much drink, in order to be ready for starting work at daybreak, planters then had to embark on the perilous journey home by night on horseback.[59]

A visit to Darjeeling in May 2018 revealed that the club was undergoing another of its renovations. The building had become a rather forlorn-looking empty shell. Only one small room had escaped demolition and was preserved for use. 'Strictly for members only', the room contained a small table atop a carpet surrounded by a cluster of what appeared to be leather chairs. A balcony beyond hosted another row of chairs. It is to be hoped that after its restoration the club will be able to reclaim some of its former ambience and grandeur.

The Dhundibree tea garden was located at Punkaberry in the district of Darjeeling and covered 175 acres according to the listing in 1885. The estate at Pronub Bun was slightly smaller, extending over 150 acres, and was situated near Kurseong. The tea garden at Dilaram – which has since become an important tourist attraction – was located along the banks of the River Rinchentong, not far from Kurseong. Established in 1870 by a certain Mr Bell, by 1885 the estate covered some 250 acres. Controlled by the same colonial agents, Begg, Dunlop & Co., and sharing the Dilaram logo, the Dilaram and Pronub Bun estates were obviously closely connected. A Calcutta-based managing agency, Begg, Dunlop & Co. was formed in March 1856 and had acquired extensive interests in tea, indigo, coffee, sugar, tobacco and coal-mining. From 1883 onwards, the Dhundibree tea garden came under the control of the managing agents Williamson, Magor & Co. Established in 1868, these agents eventually acquired huge stakes in the global tea industry.

Spencer Robinson was listed as one of several co-proprietors who owned each of the three tea gardens. A. B. Miller and J. B. Miller and Lalla Bun Behari Kapur were listed as co-proprietors. Given Bun Behari Kapur's involvement, the 'J. B. Miller' in question was perhaps actually Thomas de Burgh Miller. A co-proprietor of three large tea businesses together with the two managers of the Burdwan estate could therefore have worked to Spencer's advantage when he sought to sub-lease the 'Rajbaree' tea garden.

A Hindu by birth, Bun Behari Kapur was closely connected with the Mehtab dynasty of Burdwan. Born in the mid-1850s, Bun Behari Kapur was appointed vice president of the Burdwan Raj Council in 1879 and became a member of the Bengal Legislative Council in January 1885. Known as Lalla to his friends, Bun Behari Kapur was also an honorary magistrate and a member of the District Board of Burdwan. In 1879, he became joint manager of the extensive Burdwan Raj estates; twelve years later he became sole manager. For services rendered, he was granted the title of 'Raja' in 1893. Six years previously his son, Banbehari Kapur, had been adopted by the wife of the late maharaja, who had not produced an heir. Banbehari Kapur later became the Maharaja Kumar Bijai Chand Mehtab of Burdwan.[60]

Bun Behari Kapur was implicated in the so-called Burdwan affair of 1886. He was accused of the 'criminal misappropriation' of estate funds by Robert Knight, an outspoken British journalist and founder of the broadsheet *The Statesman*, which had its offices in Calcutta. In April 1886, Knight ran a series of articles which alleged that Kapur and Thomas de Burgh Miller were guilty of the financial mismanagement of the Burdwan properties. The accusations were not substantiated and Knight was put on trial for libel. Knight had acquired a reputation as a fierce critic of colonial rule in India. The libel case was dropped after *The Statesman* printed a retraction and an apology. Miller, meanwhile, had died of a fever in July 1886.[61] Perhaps because of Knight's unorthodox and controversial views at the time, his accusations did not seem to have a major detrimental impact on the career of 'Lalla'. They also did not appear to affect Spencer Robinson or his interests in the tea business.

Given his background as a Lincolnshire tenant farmer, Spencer Robinson could scarcely have been compared with those 'tea planters' who had arrived in India with little real interest or experience of working on the land. Spencer's knowledge of how to handle farm workers would have probably worked to his advantage as a tea planter or co-proprietor, even though work on tea estates was far more labour intensive than mixed farming in Lincolnshire. Clearly, in spite of being employed in different periods by various companies and by the DHR, Spencer had maintained a close interest in working with the land.

Teesta Valley and the Sikkim Expedition

Apparently not discouraged by his previous experience with Robinson, Harley and Company, in 1889 Spencer Robinson was listed as manager of the Teesta Valley Bullock Carrying Company. He may have been employed with this company for a period before 1889 while also working with the DHR. The proprietors of the Teesta Valley Bullock Carrying Company were the Calcutta-based managing agency Davenport & Company, a large group with extensive involvement in the growth of the tea industry in India. There was no railway to connect hill stations with the Teesta Valley and the Kalimpong Road station (at Giella Khola, near the Kalimpong settlement) until 1915. Kalimpong could only be reached via the Teesta Valley by the Old Public Works Department Road. Notorious for its flooding, the leech-infested Teesta Valley was known as the Valley of the Shadow of Death in the rainy season. This long-used trade route had been improved in 1888 when sappers from Madras laid girder bridges along the road as part of a strategy to deter and drive back a Tibetan invasion of Sikkim.[62] Despite their efforts, though, it was still prone to flooding.

Given its location, Kalimpong straddled trade routes between India, Tibet and Sikkim. From Darjeeling, goods such as cotton, wool, medicines, tea, rice, salt and tobacco were transported northwards and eastwards. In return, from Tibet came produce such as unrefined lamb wool, hand-woven Tibetan carpets, Chinese silk and precious and semi-precious stones. From Sikkim came spices, fruits, vegetables, cotton, sheep, goats, pulses and yak tails.[63] The Teesta Valley Bullock Carrying Company could have been heavily involved in carrying cargoes to and from Kalimpong. It appears that Spencer Robinson and his family had relocated to Kalimpong, with its flourishing bazaar, to undertake this new business.

One may argue that, in his involvement here, Spencer Robinson played a not insignificant role in the so-called Great Game in Central Asia. The British were eager to offset Russian influence in the region by opening up trade routes with Tibet, thereby hoping to secure access to the much larger Chinese market. Commentators have tended to focus on the importance of the much popularised 'Silk Road',[64] but the comparably obscure 'wool route' was another key component of the British strategy to open up markets and expand political control in the area. The development of a wool route necessitated the establishment of a trade corridor linking Siliguri with Kalimpong and then with Tibet's Chumbi Valley via Sikkim. The Teesta Valley Bullock Carrying Company worked on the Indian stretch of this corridor.

In a letter addressed to a local official in July 1887, Spencer Robinson stressed that the wool trade with Tibet could become a 'large business'. He noted that a merchant trading with Tibet had offered to deliver to him in Darjeeling 10,000 maunds (one maund was the equivalent of about 80 pounds in weight) of Tibetan wool at 16 rupees per maund. Spencer noted that samples of this wool had already been received and would sell for six and a half to seven pence per pound if sold in England according to a recent evaluation. The merchant had given assurances to Spencer that the Tibetans would not place obstacles in the development of this trade.[65]

This letter was written at a time when relations between Britain and the local Tibetan authorities (which were nominally under the control of the Chinese government) had seriously deteriorated. Believing that British overtures to expanding commercial ties were a pretext to a planned invasion, the Tibetans had occupied parts of Sikkim in 1886.

Spencer Robinson's letter about the potential significance of the wool trade was criticised by officials and traders. The manager of the Egerton Woollen Mills Company, based at Dhariwal in Amritsar, was convinced that no single part of Tibet 'could possibly produce' 10,000 maunds of wool in one year as that would require the fleeces of over 200,000 sheep. Others pointed to the continuing trade restrictions imposed by the Tibetans or suggested that wool of almost the same quality could be imported by European manufacturers from places such as America or Australia at a cheaper rate.[66]

In the longer term, Spencer Robinson was vindicated. Trade restrictions were lifted after the Younghusband expedition to Tibet in 1903 and 1904, and Kalimpong became a key entrepot for trade between India and Tibet. Between 1 April 1946 and 31 March 1947, the export of Tibetan wool to Kalimpong amounted to over 106,000 maunds.[67]

Spencer Robinson also played an instrumental role in procuring provisions for the British expeditionary force that ousted the occupying Tibetan forces from Sikkim in 1888. (His important support work for the Sikkim Expedition was later acknowledged in an obituary.) The British were determined to send strong signals to the Chinese that they were not prepared to countenance any threat to British rule in Bengal. According to the *Englishman's Overland Mail*, the Tibetans were swiftly routed in March 1888: 'A few shells from the beautiful little mountain guns settled the whole business in a few minutes.'[68] The truth was far less straightforward.

After diplomatic efforts failed, in February 1888 a force of around 1,300 men under the command of Brigadier-General Thomas Graham had been despatched with the initial aim of expelling the Tibetans from Lingtu in Sikkim.[69] Following the capture of the fort at Lingtu, which had been hastily constructed by the Tibetans, Graham's forces advanced to the exposed peaks of Gnatong to prevent the enemy from launching a renewed assault on Sikkim. Amid heavy April snows, tents were speedily pitched at Gnatong on an exposed ridge at an altitude of over 12,000 feet. Conditions in the tented facilities were appalling. Cattle were lost due to the severe cold, and the camp became 'a slough of despond'.[70] By mid-June, the weather had greatly improved and the encampment was reinforced and made more habitable with the building of a stockade around a clutch of huts. After reinforcements arrived in August, the expeditionary force drove the Tibetans back from the Sikkim frontier and briefly occupied parts of Tibet itself before withdrawing again to Gnatong.

The Sikkim expedition was the first major military operation mounted by a European force in the eastern Himalayas. It was also the first time that the Tibetans had directly clashed with a modern European army. Equipped with bows and arrows, slingshots and seventeenth-century muskets, the Tibetans unsurprisingly proved no match for Graham's forces. Nevertheless, supplying provisions for troops in such elevated and inhospitable terrain was a significant logistical feat. One serious problem was the shortage of mules. Spencer Robinson would have been heavily involved in working to ensure that goods and materials were supplied to the expeditionary force. His close knowledge of the region, organisational know-how and management skills would have been invaluable assets. Initially, provisions were despatched to a base depot at Siliguri, on the junction of the Eastern Bengal and Darjeeling railways. Officers and troops, though, complained of the unhealthy and torrid conditions at Siliguri. More advanced stations were then established with goods transported via the Teesta Valley and Kalimpong using country carts and whatever mules were available.

It was clear from the copies of photographs which Bernard Robinson had in his possession that his grandfather, Minick, perhaps together with Minick's father, Spencer himself, had accompanied the force to Gnatong. I do not know why the young railway apprentice would have participated in the Sikkim expedition. Possibly, he undertook the trek to be of help to his father. The campaign would have been a gruelling one for a civilian who was approaching fifty years of age, as Spencer was. Minick (and Spencer?) may have remained at Gnatong for several weeks given that Minick appeared to have been there when the troops were initially sheltering under canvass. Alternatively, they could have made repeated trips between Gnatong and other camps downhill, although this would have been an extremely arduous exercise. It is not known if father and son also participated in the incursion into Tibet by Graham's troops.

Minick's presence in Gnatong may also explain the telegraph sent to him from Pedong. The telegraph, addressed to Minick in Kalimpong, seems to have been despatched at the time of the Sikkim expedition. Pedong, a settlement lying 20 kilometres to the east of Kalimpong, became the base headquarters of the expeditionary force. Jean Claude White was the assistant political officer with Graham's troops. White had served in the Indian Public Works Department since 1876, and later became Britain's political officer in Sikkim. Was the 'White' mentioned in the telegraph referring to the assistant political officer? If so, the telegraph could be taken as further evidence that Minick was somehow involved in assisting his father in the expedition.

Spencer Robinson's active and important role in the Sikkim Expedition would have fully restored his reputation, which must have been seriously damaged as a result of his temporary and enforced residency in the Presidency Jail of Calcutta.

Family Matters

Spencer Robinson had left for India as a widower, apparently leaving his young children to live with relatives for the time being. In 1881, his daughter, May Belle, was a ten-year-old living with her sixty-four-year-old uncle Frederick Morley Maddison, and his wife Elizabeth, in Hagworthingham. Frederick ran a 68-acre farm in the Lincolnshire village. Spencer's son, Minick Palmer, appears to have left Lincolnshire while still in his childhood. He was living with his grandmother Mary and auntie Jessie in Camberwell in London in 1881 (the census seems to have mistakenly referred to a Minnie P. Robinson as an eleven-year-old boarder).

We have seen that Minick Palmer did live and work in India for a period. He most probably arrived in India in 1885. While in prison in early November of that year, Spencer Robinson had inquired as to whether G. M. Reily of the Land Mortgage Bank of India could find employment for his son. According to Spencer, his son was 'a big boy' in his seventeenth year 'not long out from home'. Any job which could provide 'enough pay to help him at first' would be appreciated, with Spencer adding that his son knew 'a little of the language'.[71]

Perhaps with Reily's help, and given Spencer Robinson's close ties with Prestage at the DHR, Minick soon found employment in the DHR's workshop. According to Minick's army service record, between 1886 and 1889 he had served as an apprentice fitter and turner with the Prestage company in Bengal. The *Indian Directory* for 1887 and 1888 recorded that Minick Palmer was one of several apprentices working as fitters at the locomotive depot at Tindharia. The famous railway works there were only opened in 1914, but the station had been the site of a miniature railway repair and workshop since 1881. Here, locomotives and wagons were maintained. It would have been more convenient logistically for the workshop to be located further downhill. However, Tindharia was chosen because it was regarded as the lowest point on the railway where British employees could comfortably work all year.[72] Tindharia had the advantage of being situated above the 'fever level' of the forested area of the Tarai, where jungle fever was rife. Today, the village's dwellings still cling to the hillside and the workshop, together with a museum, is located a little lower down from the station.

As the previous mentions of a second wife would suggest, Spencer Robinson eventually remarried and brought up a new family in India. Newspaper accounts show that on 24 January 1880, Spencer had boarded the SS *Peshawar* in Bombay; it was due to arrive at Southampton on 19 February. He returned to Bombay on 20 April 1880 aboard the SS *Verona*.[73] While in England, on 27 March, Spencer had married a young woman at St Pancras registry office. Her name was Hannah Rodda. It is not clear where and when Spencer had met his bride-to-be. Given Hannah's background, they definitely would not have been introduced to one another in India. The Roddas were a family struggling to make ends meet in London's East End. In contrast to Spencer's first wife, Hannah's father had been a merchant seaman and her grandfather a bricklayer.

The 1871 census recorded a sixteen-year-old Hannah Rodda working as a housemaid for Dr Geoffrey Pearl, a member of the London College of Physicians. Dr Pearl was living at the time with his wife in the Sussex village of Ripe, which was situated close to West Firle. This was the same neighbourhood to which Spencer Robinson and his wife Isabella had relocated from East Keal by late 1871.

While in India, Hannah gave birth to at least six children. The first child of Spencer and Hannah Robinson, Ida Maud Mary, was born in Darjeeling in November 1881 and was baptised in March 1882 at St Andrew's Church in the same town. The church still stands on the western slope of Observatory Hill close to the famous Windermere Hotel. Its well-known clocktower was added a couple of years after Maud's baptism. On Maud's birth certificate, it was noted that Spencer Robinson was a tea planter based in Darjeeling. A second girl, Jessie (or 'Jerrie'?), was born in February 1883 at Darjeeling and baptised at St Andrew's Church in July. Again, Spencer was recorded as a tea planter. It is highly likely that Jessie/Jerrie died as a young child as she is not mentioned in later census records. Clearly, then, Spencer lived in Darjeeling, as well as in Kurseong, in the period between 1881 and 1883. A first son, Spencer John Bernard, was born in Kurseong in February 1884 and baptised at Christ Church in the same town in August. On the birth certificate, it was recorded that Spencer Robinson was employed as a traffic manager for the DHR and lived in Kurseong.

Spencer's wife returned to England from India either in 1890 or 1891. The 1891 census for England listed three other children who were born in Bengal to the Robinsons. Eugene B. was reportedly born in 1887, and his two younger brothers, Peel (also spelt 'Peele') Harold and George M., in 1889 and 1890 respectively. According to a newspaper report, Peel Harold was born in Kalimpong in May 1889.[74] In his communications with Reily of the Land Mortgage Bank of India, Spencer Robinson noted in October 1885 that 'we have another little baby'.[75] This may actually have been Eugene. On a piece of paper preserved by the family, Spencer's wife had scribbled that Eugene was born in 1885 – rather than in 1887.

However, here our tale meets an abrupt end. Spencer Robinson 'of Kalimpong' died on 12 November 1889 at the age of fifty-one. I have not been able to learn the cause of death. No death certificate is available. He was buried in the Kalimpong K. D. Pradhan Road Cemetery. The cemetery lies off a nondescript road, hemmed in amid a clump of housing in quite a poor neighbourhood. A winding pedestrian path connecting the highway with the small burial ground runs between a clutch of small dwellings. Some of the graves in the cemetery are lost in the undergrowth. Others have tombstones whose inscriptions have become virtually indecipherable. In contrast, the memorial stone of the Reverend William Macfarlane remains well-tended and lies almost in pristine condition. The graveyard stands as a peaceful oasis amid the clatter and bustle of the busy hill town. In Kalimpong, I was struck by how very little has been preserved from the time of Spencer Robinson. Observing the cemetery, it seemed that even the dead of Spencer's generation were gradually fading as the tombstones became silent victims of the ravages of nature.

To my intense disappointment, I could not locate Spencer's grave. Apparently, on his memorial stone, it was mistakenly noted that Spencer had lived in Bengal for eighteen years. Also, inscribed on the stone are the much-quoted words of Jesus as cited in the Gospel of Matthew: 'Come unto me all ye that labour and are heavy laden and I will give you rest.' The stone was erected 'in loving memory by his sorrowing widow and children'.[76] In Spencer's last will and testament, dated 9 May 1888, it was stated that all estates and effects were to be left to his wife for her benefit and that of her children and his. After her death, all estates and effects were to be sold and divided equally among the surviving children of Hannah and Spencer. These clauses were inserted because, as will be seen, Hannah had given birth to a child before marrying Spencer.

An obituary of Spencer Robinson in one of the local newspapers was full of praise for the considerable work he had carried out in India. It was noted that he had 'extensive and practical knowledge of agriculture' and was consulted by the government on various projects. The article acknowledged his impressive services rendered for the tonga system between Siliguri and Darjeeling and for the DHR. It added that commissariat work for the Sikkim force had 'imposed upon him a heavy responsibility', and the 'excessive strain' and 'exposure' to the climate of the Teesta Valley had 'undermined his strength'. In a final tribute, the article explained how he had not only known how to manage many workers but had also succeeded 'in winning their affectionate regard', as was 'testified to in a very touching manner on the news of his death'.[77]

Clearly, in spite of his temporary financial problems, Spencer Robinson had been a valued and much-admired member of the

English community in India. According to the obituary, he had also earned the respect and support of those who had worked under him. Ultimately, the seemingly indefatigable Spencer Robinson died from sheer exhaustion.

*

Spencer Robinson had lived a relatively short but very full life. Contrary to some of the myths about him that have been propagated by Turkish sources, Spencer did not come from an aristocratic background. He had not held prominent positions working for the government of the British Raj, although his activities had certainly contributed to the economic and political development of British rule in Bengal. His life was a fascinating one, covering a period in Indian history when the colony was undergoing a revolution in communications and industrial development. He was present at the moment when the use of cumbersome and slow-moving bullock carts was giving way to the much faster and more reliable railway.

The India that Spencer Robinson knew in the 1880s was one in which the British Raj appeared to be in effective control. In 1886, the spectacular Colonial and Indian Exhibition was held in South Kensington. The Prince of Wales spoke of how the exhibition was an 'imperial object lesson' in the power and grandeur of the British Empire. One of the principal aims of the exhibition was to depict the lives of Britain's Indian 'fellow subjects'.[78] Six months earlier, the Indian National Congress (INC) had been established by a retired British member of the Indian Civil Service to facilitate dialogue between local elites and the British colonial authorities. Other colonial representatives were among its founders. The INC was at the time an apparent misnomer. The circumstances were not ripe to contemplate seriously the emergence of an embryonic Indian nation. Political stirrings would only gather pace after the foolish decision of Lord Curzon, the then Viceroy of India, to announce the partition of Bengal in 1905, which simultaneously alienated the Hindus in the west and the Muslims in the east.

Commentators and scholars in recent years have tended to re-evaluate Britain's role in colonial India with a much more critical eye.[79] Attention has focused on how the colonialists, through a policy of divide and rule, ransacked India's natural resources and prevented the emergence of an indigenous industry. A local landowning class may have benefitted from cooperating with the colonial rulers, but the vast majority of the native population remained poor and were heavily taxed. On the tea estates, most of the indentured labourers received desperately low wages, lived in squalid housing and were tied to work for particular tea planters on lifelong contracts. For most of the locals, hope and signs of positive change came in the first decades of the twentieth century when nationalist leaders in the INC started to attract more popular attention. Unlike in *fin de siècle* Europe, 'progressive' social and political movements in the British Raj were slowly incubated and only gathered momentum in the inter-war period.

Certainly, Spencer was involved in working directly with influential managing agencies of the British Raj, and he also played a role in helping the colonial administration to open up trade routes. However, this scarcely counts as an indictment which can be levelled against him. There is no evidence that he, or, indeed, his wife, exploited the workforce. The obituary, and his earlier life as a tenant farmer in Lincolnshire, suggest that Spencer was essentially an honest man who had a sense of fair play as well as a thirst for enterprise. His second marriage to a woman of humble origin suggested that he chose to ignore the stultifying views of class which prevailed in late Victorian England.

One should not forget that Spencer Robinson was a family man, although the details of his family life remain obscure. He had fathered at least nine children – three from his first wife, Isabella, and six with his second wife, Hannah. Unfortunately, many of his children would have little or no recollection of him. It is not clear to what extent Spencer had been able to maintain close contact with May Belle, his daughter from his first marriage. However, as we have seen, in his later years Spencer was able to spend time in India with Minick Palmer, the son from his first marriage. Spencer Robinson may have returned to England on more than one occasion to see May Belle and Minick Palmer. Certainly, he was present in London in early 1880 for his marriage to Hannah Rodda.

Spencer Robinson left a legacy for his family. Until 1895, the Dhundibree tea garden listed as one of its co-proprietors the 'estate of the late S. Robinson'. However, there is no further reference to this tea estate after 1895. Perhaps the tea garden then amalgamated with another plantation, or maybe it was taken over by new owners and renamed. It is not clear exactly what happened to the 'Rajbaree' tea garden. The deal concluded with the Land Mortgage Bank of India in January 1886 provided for the sub-lease of land over a three-year period. I have not been able to discover what happened to 'Rajbaree' after 1889.

In contrast to many of his relatives, Spencer Robinson did not complete the final journey back home to Lincolnshire. He remains buried in a rundown cemetery in a distant land. One wonders to what extent Spencer regarded his residence in the foothills of the Himalayas as a home from home. He had spent almost one third of his life in Bengal and had chosen to bring up a family there with his second wife. What is known is that Hannah did not choose to linger in Kalimpong. Shortly after the birth of the last of Spencer's sons, Hannah made the long return journey to England together with her young family. What she could not have known at the time was that her own life story would soon whisk her away from England again, and to distant shores once more.

3

Hannah Rodda: From Bethnal Green to Constantinople

Anything may happen when womanhood
has ceased to be a protected occupation.
Virginia Woolf, *A Room of One's Own*

Introduction

Who was Hannah Rodda? My impression of her is that she was a bold, enterprising and determined woman. Here was a woman who, apparently with little formal education, could rise above the poverty and grind of Victorian England, hold her own amid the tiresome rituals and social etiquette of the British Raj, and eventually prosper in the totally unfamiliar surroundings of the late Ottoman Empire and early Turkish Republic. All this she accomplished while raising a family. Peering through a lens which has admittedly become somewhat clouded by the passing years, one can perceive a woman who maintained her dignity and commanded a certain presence. Apparently prone to exaggeration, and in her later years perhaps overly enjoying her matriarchal status, Hannah Rodda was also a woman who excelled in making the most of the opportunities provided to her. Reading the few family letters which have been handed down, in spite of changing her name, religion, and country of residence, Hannah still seemed to have retained a part of her English identity. Browsing through her correspondence and that of her son Ahmet Robenson, I could see how Christmas was still wholeheartedly celebrated, with cards exchanged between family members in Turkey and abroad. Ahmet's letters were written in impeccable English. Hannah must have ensured that her children, growing up in the Ottoman Empire, did not forget their native language.

While not quite a rags-to-riches story, the life of Hannah Rodda was nevertheless an extraordinary one. No Turkish commentator, nor any member of the extended Robinson family in Turkey, was aware of the lowly origins of Spencer Robinson's second wife. As in the case of Spencer Robinson, some Turkish writers interested in the family have somewhat embroidered Hannah's background. Rıfat Bali, for example, perpetuated the myth that Spencer Robinson's second wife was known as 'Lady Sarah'.[1] With stories circulating of the supposedly elevated status of Spencer Robinson, it is perhaps not surprising that there was an assumption that his wife must also have come from a family of a certain pedigree. However, Hannah's son Ahmet was also guilty of exaggerating the origins and background of his mother. In the interview he gave shortly before his death, Ahmet Robenson alleged that his mother came from a family that had become renowned in the fields of art, education and literature.[2] Amazingly, though, accounts peddled among Hannah's descendants in Turkey about her possible connections with royalty have more substance. It will be seen that rumours about Hannah being engaged at one time to Queen Victoria's private doctor are not as ridiculous as they might first seem.

Spencer Robinson's relatives in England believed that Hannah was formerly the wife of a German baron, who was also a doctor, and that the couple had a daughter named Gertrude. This story looks to have mistakenly conflated Hannah's life with that of one of her offspring who became engaged to a German entrepreneur and resided in Hamburg.

From the slums of London's East End and the drudgery of domestic service, Hannah's ascent up the social ladder was both dizzying and spectacular. A decade's sojourn in the hill stations of India was followed by residence in Constantinople and close ties with the Ottoman court. After the death of her first husband, Spencer Robinson, Hannah married twice more and was the mother of at least eight children. She was one of the first female converts to Islam in Victorian England.

Hannah emigrated first to India and then to the Ottoman Empire with her partners. The provision of a third husband – by the sultan himself, according to the family narrative – ensured that Hannah, or rather Fatima or Fatma by that time, remained in Constantinople. To what extent Hannah was able to maintain close contact with all her children and extended members of her family is open to question given the distances involved and the difficulties in communication at that time. Indeed, one wonders how contacts could have continued with her struggling relatives in London.

As in the case of Spencer Robinson, the story of Hannah Rodda had its share of tragedy. The actual account of Hannah's life demonstrates that there is no need to exaggerate or distort what happened to the simple girl from Bethnal Green. Making the most of unforeseen circumstances, the tale of Hannah Rodda from the East End was truly a remarkable one.

Bethnal Green and Marazion

Hannah Rodda was born in Stepney in Middlesex in the last quarter of 1854. According to the census for 1861, Hannah lived with her grandparents at 8 Primrose Street in Bethnal Green. Her grandfather Richard Russell, born in the village of Benenden in the Weald of Kent, was a bricklayer. His wife, her grandmother Mary Ann Russell, originally came from Bexhill in Sussex. Also present in the household were one of Hannah's sisters, Sarah, and her twenty-nine-year-old aunt, Hannah Russell. The Russells had been occupants of Primrose Street since at least the mid-1830s. It is not known why Richard Russell had chosen to move to the capital from rural Kent. However, Benenden, a quintessential English village with a green overlooked by a medieval church, had suffered in the immediate aftermath of the Napoleonic Wars. The return of demobilised soldiers together with the introduction of threshing machinery had led to a shortage of work in the agricultural sector. Many people were also forced to leave the parish because of falling wages, rising rents and climbing food prices.[3]

Once a fashionable neighbourhood with substantial houses and large gardens, by the mid-nineteenth century parts of Bethnal Green had become slums. The district was previously famous for its silk-weaving trade, carried out by Irish and Huguenot workers. This trade was in decline by the time Hannah was born, and Bethnal Green was populated by poorer Jews and others struggling to survive in occupations such as tailoring and furniture making. Bethnal Green was the most impoverished parish in London by 1871. Life expectancy was very low. Of 1,632 deaths in the parish in 1839, 77 per cent were of 'mechanics, servants and labourers' who had a life expectancy of only sixteen years. Tradesmen could expect to live on average only to the age of twenty-six. The district was one of unpaved roads, overcrowding, and a lack of proper sewerage. Disease was rife and the parish was known to be frequented by thieves and prostitutes. By the late 1880s, 44.6 per cent of the population of Bethnal Green were classified as poor or very poor.[4] According to the 1861 census, other occupants of Primrose Street included a porter working at the famous fish market at Billingsgate, a char woman, a painter and glazier, a warehouseman, a wine cellar man, and a cork cutter.

Details of the lives of many of Hannah's immediate relatives are vague. It is not clear when her grandparents died. We know that they fell victim to poverty as both were admitted for a period to the workhouse in Bethnal Green in March 1869. This followed an order of removal from the workhouse in nearby Mile End Old Town. As the responsibility for the upkeep of inmates in the workhouse fell to the local parish, officials were eager to ensure that workhouse residents originated from their parish. If this was not the case, inmates were returned to the parish that was adjudged to be their rightful place of settlement. By the time of the 1871 census, Richard Russell was back in the workhouse at Bethnal Green while his wife was living with her daughter, Mary Ann (Hannah Rodda's mother), in Bow. A Richard Russell, aged seventy-four, died in the Bethnal Green workhouse five years later. This was presumably Hannah's grandfather.

Richard and Mary Ann Russell had six children. Two of the three boys also became bricklayers. One, William, died at the age of seventeen. The other, Richard, was periodically admitted to the workhouse in Mile End Old Town in the 1890s. The third son, Thomas, may have succeeded in escaping from the squalor and hardship of life in the slums. According to the 1851 census, Thomas was employed as a merchant's clerk. Of the three girls, Sarah married a worker in the General Post Office and went to live in Islington, while Hannah wed a bootmaker and took up residence in nearby Shoreditch. Hannah Rodda's mother, Mary Ann, the eldest of the six children, was born in Stepney in 1826. She married Benjamin Rodda (Rodder), a mariner, at St Matthew's Church in Bethnal Green in April 1848. Benjamin was registered as the son of another Benjamin Rodda (Rodder) who was listed as a carpenter. At the time of the marriage, the couple were living at 8 Primrose Street.

It is not easy to trace the background of Hannah Rodda's father. The records of merchant seamen note that a Benjamin Rodda was born either in 1818 or in November 1819 in Marazion in Cornwall. However, according to the database of the Cornwall Online Parish Clerks, a Benjamin Rodda, the son of a carpenter of the same name, was baptised in Marazion in November 1816.

The seaside settlement of Marazion, a deeply historic town, is located immediately opposite the well-known landmark of St Michael's Mount near Penzance. Handling coastal trade, Marazion became famous for its markets. Legend has it that Joseph of Arimathea – he who is reputed to have buried the body of Jesus after the crucifixion – was one of many Jewish traders who exported tin and copper from Marazion and other settlements in Cornwall to the eastern Mediterranean. Noting the spelling of the market town, various accounts have suggested that Marazion was so named because of the activities of Jewish tradesmen in the area. However, the name appears to have originated from a corruption of the Cornish terms '*Marghas byghan*' and '*Marghas Yow*', meaning 'little market' and 'Thursday market' respectively.[5] The settlement was known for its nearby tin and copper mines, and it was heavily populated in the nineteenth century by fishermen and mariners as well as miners. The Rodda family name was quite popular in the county. Rodda could have originated from the Cornish version of the English surname Rodd, referring to someone who lived in a woodland clearing.[6]

There is a possibility that Benjamin's father was the Benjamin Rodda who was baptised at St Hilary in the parish of Marazion in 1783. This particular Benjamin Rodda (let us call him Benjamin Rodda senior) was married twice and fathered many children. A Benjamin Rodda junior was the son of Mary (Harris), the first wife of Benjamin Rodda senior. Having lived most of his life in Cornwall, Benjamin Rodda senior moved to London and was listed in the 1851 census as a journeyman joiner living on King Street in the district of St George in the East. He died in September 1855 at Mile End Old Town in London.

More details of Benjamin Rodda, the father of Hannah, can be ascertained from the merchant seamen records. He first went to sea as a boy in 1831. Just over 5 feet 4 inches in height, and illiterate, the blue-eyed Benjamin Rodda had black hair and a dark complexion. The 1841 census noted that able seaman Benjamin Rodda was staying at the Greenwich Dreadnought Hospital, a special floating hospital for merchant seamen which could accommodate up to 400 patients.

The reason for his hospitalisation is not known. Originally launched in 1801 as a ninety-nine-gun warship, HMS *Dreadnought* had taken an active role in the Battle of Trafalgar in 1805. The famous ship was later converted to a hospital after being decommissioned. Benjamin was a patient at the floating hospital on at least three other occasions – later in 1841, in 1842 and again in 1847. He was admitted in August 1842 suffering from periostitis – a type of inflammation often associated with carrying heavy weights. Five years later he had contracted syphilis.

As a merchant seaman, Benjamin had the opportunity to travel around the world. There is proof that he sailed to Jamaica. Between 1844 and 1854 the government had introduced a system whereby each merchant seaman was listed by having in his possession a registered ticket number. The authorities were attempting to monitor merchant seamen, who were looked upon as a potential reserve for the Royal Navy to be called up in times of war. The system proved unpopular and was eventually scrapped. Records show that merchant seaman Benjamin Rodda had a ticket issued in London in December 1844. However, his ticket was cancelled in 1846 because he had mistakenly left (lost?) the ticket in Jamaica. In order to continue to work as a merchant seaman, Benjamin had to plead his case to the registrar of seamen in London. He may have been fined as a penalty for losing his ticket. He was successful in pressing his case, though, as another ticket was issued in London under his name on 1 July 1846.

Hannah's father died of tuberculosis at sea in March 1856. Shortly after Benjamin's death, Mary Ann Rodda together with her three children at the time, including Hannah, returned to stay with her parents at Primrose Street. It was reported that Benjamin Rodda's parents and other relatives had all passed away and that Mary Ann Rodda was not aware if her husband had made a settlement before his death. In this period, Mary Ann Rodda and her children had also spent some time in the local workhouse.

In 1851, before moving to the workhouse, Mary Ann Rodda lived at 4 Three Colt Lane with her first child, also called Mary Ann (born in Bethnal Green in June 1849). Located close to Primrose Street, Three Colt Lane was an area especially notorious for its unhygienic conditions. An official report from 1848, prepared by an expert on forensic medicine and public health, had noted that a sewer had just been laid down by the road after a public outcry over the filth. In lurid terms the report stated that there had been a ditch in which 'dead cats and dogs were profusedly scattered, exhibiting every stage of disgusting decomposition' The report added, 'There is a great deal of fever in this lane.'[7]

In September 1857, a newspaper reported that at the half-yearly meeting of the governors and friends of the Merchant Seamen's Orphan Asylum, a Mary Ann Rodda had secured enough votes to enter the asylum. Hannah's sister was one of ten candidates from an original list of thirty-seven children deemed eligible to join the asylum. Only three girls were admitted, including Mary Ann, who was voted in with the backing of 169 governors and friends.[8]

The Merchant Seamen's Orphan Asylum was founded in London in 1827 'to afford relief' to orphans of seamen in the merchant service by providing clothing, education and maintenance to help them to secure 'an honest livelihood' after they left the asylum. Able to accommodate up to 120 children in its Bow Road premises, admission was usually by a twice-yearly ballot of those who subscribed or donated money to the charity. To qualify to be admitted, the child's father must have died at sea during active service. No more than two children from one family could reside in the asylum at the same time.[9] Mary Ann was still attending the asylum as an eleven-year-old pupil in 1861, but it seems that neither of Mary Ann's younger sisters, Hannah and Sarah, attended the asylum. It is quite possible that neither sister secured enough votes to enter the asylum. A Sarah Rodda died in London in 1866 aged fourteen. This was most probably Hannah's sister.

After the death of her first husband, Hannah's mother had two further children. A son, William Hearsey Rodda, was born in 1859 in St George in the East in Middlesex. The father of the child is not known. In the 1861 census, it was noted that the one-year-old William was living with a cousin, Sarah A. Ford, a waistcoat maker. Again, details are scarce with regard to William's later life. In 1881, a twenty-two-year-old William Rodda, born in Middlesex, was serving as a 'driver' for the Royal Artillery in the barracks at Woolwich. Drivers were responsible for the management of the six horses employed to draw the gun or wagon. However, this William Rodda was discharged from the Royal Artillery in November 1881 on the grounds of 'ignominy'. Released from the military in disgrace, it was also noted in his record that he had a character which was 'very bad'. In 1891, a thirty-year-old William Rodda, born in Middlesex and employed as a bricklayer's labourer, was living in West Ham with his Irish-born wife, Catherine. Ten years later, according to the census, a married forty-two-year-old Londoner named William Rodda was registered as a boarder (no profession was given) in the lodgings of a beer-house keeper in Plymouth.

In 1867, Hannah's mother married James Radley, who was employed as a cow keeper. The couple lived in Bow. Two years later she had her fifth child, Annie Sarah. It seems that Mary Ann was James Radley's third wife. Cow keepers in London were not uncommon at the time as the capital was in need of readily available fresh milk for the city's residents. In line with many of her relatives, Annie Sarah struggled in her later life. Not having married, and with no children, by 1911 the unemployed Annie Sarah was living off parish relief in a one-room dwelling in Bromley by Bow in London. The census noted that she was 'disabled through rheumatism'. A seventy-eight-year-old Annie S. Radley died in Poplar in Essex in December 1946.

It appears that Hannah's mother died quite soon after her second marriage. In the 1881 census, James Radley was again listed as a widower. A Mary Ann Radley had died in Poplar in October 1879. A James Radley died in the same district in the first quarter of 1886.

Contrary to the views of Turkish writers, from what information can be gathered it is clear that Hannah Rodda came from a very humble and quite troubled background. Several of her close relatives spent periods of time in the workhouse or were dependent on other forms of parish relief. Those members of her family who were employed worked in low-skilled and poorly paid professions. Given these circumstances, it is surprising that Hannah herself did not encounter a similar fate.

A Puzzle: The Roddas and the Lintotts

There is a need to digress a little from the life of Hannah Rodda to attempt to understand the relationship which developed between the Rodda and Lintott families. This connection has some bearing on the life of Hannah's daughter Gertrude. It is an intriguing puzzle which I invite the reader to help to solve. In spite of an extensive trawling of the public records available on the internet, I have been unable to comprehend what exactly transpired between the two families as a result of the questionable activities of a certain William Bernard Lintott.

Nothing is known of the later life of Hannah's elder sister, Mary Ann, apart from her marriage on 11 June 1884 to the thirty-five-year-old William Bernard Lintott at Saint Anne's Church in Soho. Here the story of the Rodda–Lintott connection becomes especially confusing, as it is quite possible that William Bernard Lintott had two wives at the same time. This puzzle becomes more interesting and complicated after we discover that Ida Lintott, William Bernard's wife in 1881, later developed a close relationship with Hannah's daughter Gertrude.

In contrast to the Russells and the Roddas, the Lintotts had been a well-to-do family based in Romsey in Hampshire. William Henry Lintott, the grandfather of William Bernard, had established himself as a successful coal and wine merchant, with offices and depots in Southampton. Mayor of Romsey in 1822, William Henry Lintott had also owned a local flax mill.[10] The Lintott family were so prosperous that a silver shilling was issued in 1812 which bore the crest of the family business – two ships sailing towards a rising or setting sun – and was headed 'William Lintott & Sons'. The death of William Henry was listed in *The Gentleman's Magazine* of 1831. William Henry's son, Bernard, continued to work in the wine industry but ran into serious financial trouble. Accumulating substantial debts, Bernard Lintott served time in prison in 1855 and in 1862.[11] At his death in 1874, Bernard left effects of under £100 to his widow.

Bernard's son William Bernard Lintott, born in Camberwell around 1849, was listed as a clerk living in West Ham in the 1871 census. Before the holding of the next census, William Bernard married a woman named Ida (original surname unknown). In 1881, the couple were living in central London with no children. William Bernard had changed occupation and had become the manager of a billiard room. The thirty-year-old Ida, born in London, had no listed occupation.

In 1884, William Bernard appears again in the marriage records as he weds Mary Ann Rodda. The couple appear to have struggled to find witnesses to their marriage. No members of the Lintott or Rodda families were listed as witnesses. One witness, Alexis Soyer Phillips, was in his mid-twenties and working as a draughtsman. He may have been a friend of the groom's given that he was also born in Camberwell. The second witness, Susan Spindlelow, was the sextoness at the church in which the wedding took place. Did this smack of a rushed marriage, or was this perhaps a ceremony which did not have the approval of the two families concerned? On the marriage certificate, both bride and groom provided the same address for their place of residence – 28 Gerrard Street, London.

The story becomes more intriguing. On the certificate, it was noted that William Bernard Lintott, son of wine merchant Bernard Lintott, was an 'actor' and not a billiard hall manager. Records indicate that this was indeed the case. A William Bernard Lintott was a member of the troupe which worked with the famous young American actress Miss Mary Antoinette Anderson in the years between 1883 and 1889. Although not cast in major starring roles, he nevertheless played known characters in popular productions of the time. Thus, on Miss Anderson's UK tour of 1884 and 1885, Lintott enacted the role of Major Desmoulins in Lord Edward Bulwer Lytton's play *The Lady of Lyons* at the Lyceum theatre in London.[12] Lintott toured the US twice with Miss Anderson, in 1885–86 and 1888–89, when he was ostensibly married to Mary Ann, and performed in various productions including Shakespeare's *The Winter's Tale* and W. S. Gilbert's *Pygmalion and Galatea* and *Comedy and Tragedy*. On the second American tour, Lintott was a member of Henry E. Abbey's Dramatic Company. An American producer and theatre manager, Abbey was known as 'the Napoleon of Managers' because he booked the best European performers for work in the US.

Ida Lintott was also an actor. She accompanied William Bernard on the 1885–86 US tour of Miss Anderson's troupe. After performing in Dublin, the two sailed together with several other members of the company from Queenstown to New York on board the *Gallia*. The ship was scheduled to arrive in the US on 6 October 1885. Thus, the Lintott couple travelled together to New York a little over one year after William Bernard's marriage to Mary Ann Rodda. I was unable to discover if Ida was also a member of the cast for the second tour of the US a few years later.

The address given on the marriage certificate of William Bernard and Mary Ann – 28 Gerrard Street – was the London office of Edmund Gerson, a 'General Agent for French and Foreign Plays'. Gerson had close links with Thomas Holmes, a dramatic, musical and variety agent. While on tour in the US in May 1884, Holmes had given power of attorney to Gerson to transact all his business.[13] We will later see that the same Thomas Holmes had a previous connection with Hannah Rodda.

I have no further information on Mary Ann after her marriage to William Bernard Lintott in 1884. What happened to William Bernard, after the US tour abruptly ended in March 1889 when Miss Anderson collapsed on stage with exhaustion, is also a mystery. The weekly newspaper *The Stage*, which covered developments in the theatre, did note that a William Bernard Lintott passed away in 1903. This William Bernard Lintott, who was a stage manager, died in Croydon in Surrey.[14] This may have been the same William Bernard who had toured with Miss Anderson's troupe. Perhaps he had turned to stage management after retiring from acting. It would seem to be quite unusual for there to be two William Bernard Lintotts closely connected with the theatrical profession in the late nineteenth century. However, the unfortunate William Bernard Lintott who passed away in 1903 had spent the last days of his life in a lunatic asylum after he had earlier attempted to commit suicide.

I do know that Edward Stephen Lintott, the brother-in-law of Ida Lintott, continued the family's wine business until his death in 1889. Edward's son, Edward Barnard Lintott, became a famous landscape and portrait artist and lived in Paris and the US. More significantly, as discussed in a later chapter, I also know that an Ida Mary Lintott, who was a married woman in 1899, was a witness to the marriage of Hannah's daughter Gertrude in 1901.

The evidence indicates that William Bernard Lintott was the same individual who married both Ida and Mary Ann, and that William Bernard was still the husband of Ida when he married Mary Ann Rodda in 1884. If this was indeed the case, it was very surprising that in these circumstances Ida could maintain friendly ties with close relatives of Mary Ann. Perhaps a relative of Ida, Mary Ann or William Bernard may read this book and shed light on what actually happened between the Rodda and Lintott families in the late nineteenth century.

Dr Geoffrey Pearl: 'Gentleman' and Surgeon

In contrast to most of her immediate family, Hannah Rodda chose not to remain in the neighbourhood of Bethnal Green. According to the 1871 census, the sixteen-year-old Hannah was employed as a housemaid for the sixty-four-year-old Dr Geoffrey Pearl and his seventy-four-year-old wife Elizabeth Charlotte (née Rodgers). Also present in the household were a cook, a groom and another domestic servant. The Pearls had rented an accommodation in Ripe in Sussex known as Hall Court. Geoffrey Pearl lived at Hall Court periodically throughout the 1870s. According to the local post office directory for 1880, he was still in residence at the property. When Hall Court was advertised to be let in April 1881, it was noted that this was a 'capital house' with three sitting rooms and five bedrooms/offices, together with stables, a coach-house, a garden, 6 acres of meadowland and also 500 acres of shooting that could be hired.[15]

Dr Geoffrey Pearl was a well-known surgeon who spent most of his working life in Windsor. In 1835, he was appointed house surgeon of the Windsor Royal Dispensary. He held this post for eleven years before working in private practice. He nonetheless remained an honorary surgeon of the dispensary and one of its vice presidents. The dispensary had been founded in 1818 as a charity offering medical treatment to the sick poor of the neighbourhood. When Dr Pearl became house surgeon, the dispensary had recently moved to larger premises which could accommodate up to 400 patients. The resident surgeon and consultant honorary surgeons were illustrious members of their profession and often attended to the health needs of members of the royal family. It is quite possible, then, that Dr Pearl would have on occasion provided medical counselling to Queen Victoria. Certainly, records reveal that in February 1844 the queen had instructed Dr Pearl – the 'resident medical officer' – to organise the distribution of all 'unconsumed wine at the Royal Table' at Windsor Castle for the benefit of 'the sick and poor' in the neighbourhood in the hope of restoring their strength.[16] At the time of the later cholera epidemic in Windsor in 1849, Dr Pearl had 'distinguished himself by the fearless discharge of his professional duties'.[17] The queen, however, decided not to return to the castle at Windsor until the disease abated.[18]

An infirmary was attached to the dispensary in 1858, allowing patients to be treated overnight. Dr Pearl played an instrumental role in establishing the infirmary, initially donating the hefty sum of £100. Queen Victoria, with another £100 donation, and the prince consort, with a £50 contribution, were also on the first subscription list. Dr Pearl later allocated a further £100 to the running of the infirmary.[19] Upon his death, the surgeon left a bequest of £2,000 to the Windsor Royal Dispensary and Infirmary.[20]

In a distinguished career of public service, Dr Pearl had also served as mayor of Windsor in 1856 and had worked as a magistrate in the same borough. When he died in August 1884 in Brighton, he left behind a personal estate of over £38,000. The public notice of his will referred to Dr Pearl as a 'gentleman'. It seems that he and his wife had no children. They had married in July 1840 when Elizabeth Charlotte was about forty-two-years-old. Dr Pearl's wife died at Hall Court in August 1871.

One blemish on what looks like a spotless *curriculum vitae* was gossip circulating in the press in 1845 concerning an incident involving the housekeeper of Prince Albert and a certain Mrs Wells. The housekeeper had set his dog upon Mrs Wells when she was discovered trespassing in a property of the prince consort. Following the attack, Dr Pearl examined Mrs Wells, who was apparently seven months pregnant. Mrs Wells argued that she had not consented to the physical examination. One newspaper account, titled 'Prince Albert and Mr Pearl', was scathing in its criticism of the doctor for performing the examination in the absence of the husband. Sarcastically referring to Dr Pearl as 'that paragon of Apothecaries', the article went on to warn that 'Mr Pearl had better take care what he is about'.[21]

As an investor, Dr Pearl was also caught up with the scandal of the Great Northern Copper Mining Company of South Australia. In the hope of securing a handsome profit from copper mining in Australia, in the early 1860s a number of London-based speculators pumped tens of thousands of pounds into financing what would become an abandoned mining shaft.[22] A 'contributor' to the company, on 15 November 1865 Dr Pearl presented a petition for its winding up to the Master of the Rolls.[23] The business was eventually wound up in March 1869. It seems that Dr Pearl was not seriously adversely affected by the scandal; he would die a rich man.

It is not known how Hannah came to be employed by the Pearls. Dr Pearl owned a number of properties, and in 1865, according to the electoral register, his place of abode was on Victoria Street in Westminster. Four years earlier he was registered as living at High Street in New Windsor. Presumably, Hannah was originally employed as a housemaid for one of Dr Pearl's properties in or near the capital.

What is definite is that on 21 December 1875 Hannah gave birth to a daughter, Gertrude Eveline Mary. The birth certificate was registered late on 15 March 1876. According to the Births and Deaths Act of 1874, births had to be registered within six weeks at the district or sub-district office. This was usually done by the father of the child. Failure to meet these conditions could result in penalties. It was still possible, though, for registration to be completed within three months of the birth. A superintendent registrar would have to be present in such circumstances and a declaration would usually be given by one of the parents to account for the delay in registering. According to the birth certificate for Gertrude Eveline Mary, Hannah submitted her declaration on 13 March 1876. The registration process was thus completed just within the three-month period.

No father was mentioned on the birth certificate. The birth had taken place at the Arun View Hotel in Littlehampton in Sussex. At the time, this small, unpretentious hotel had twelve rooms and offices.[24] Hannah Rodda was listed on the birth certificate as a housekeeper residing at 169 Stamford Street, Lambeth. It appeared that the birth was 'illegitimate'. Arrangements appear to have been made for the child to be born discreetly. There do not seem to be any baptism records. One may not be sure as to the actual identity of Gertrude's father. As will be seen, though, the records do indicate that Geoffrey Pearl played an important role in the upbringing of Gertrude, and it is likely, therefore, that the doctor was the father of the child. The rumour that Hannah may have at one time been engaged to the doctor of Queen Victoria, or at least believed that this was the case, does not seem so preposterous after all. One should recall that Dr Pearl had been widowed back in 1871.

It is not known if Hannah took her child with her to Lambeth, but records show that Gertrude did not travel initially with her mother to India. The 1881 census reveals that the widowed Geoffrey Pearl was living at 18 Park Crescent, Brighton, with his nineteen-year-old grand-niece, Mary Pearl Watkins, a 'companion servant', together with a cook and two domestic servants. Also, present in the household was the five-year-old 'scholar' 'Gertrude Rhodds', born in Littlehampton. There seems little doubt that this child was actually Hannah's daughter, who appears to have been left in the safe keeping of the Pearl household.

What became of Gertrude immediately after Dr Pearl's death in 1884 is not clear. Gertrude could have spent some time in India, although it would have been difficult to arrange travel for the youngster. As will be seen, Dr Pearl had made generous financial provisions for Gertrude in his will and so it is quite possible that he had also made arrangements with regard to her care in addition to her upkeep. Gertrude was living with her mother in Brighton in 1891 after Hannah returned from India. In the 1891 census, Gertrude was referred to as 'Gertrude Robinson'.

As for Hannah, it is not clear how long she remained as a housekeeper in Lambeth. In the 1870s, her address there, Stamford Street, was known as a place where stage artists and music hall entertainers and their agents lived and worked. Mr Thomas Holmes, the celebrated stage agent, lived or worked at 169 Stamford Street in 1877.[25] Among the acts he was responsible for promoting were the popular Moore and Burgess Minstrels, an established blackface minstrel troupe.[26] This was the same Thomas Holmes who had close contacts with the agent Edmund Gerson, who appeared to have ties with William Bernard and Ida Lintott in the mid-1880s. This begs the question whether Hannah, via her prior connection with Holmes, played any role in introducing her sister Mary Ann to William Bernard. The Lambeth address was used as a place of contact for other music hall agents as well as a residence for families.

At the time, Stamford Street was also notorious for its prostitution, petty crime and squalid and disreputable accommodation. Near to the terminus of the London and South Western Railway, the area was known as 'Whorelerloo'.[27] Each morning next to the York Hotel, out-of-work stage performers gathered in the so-called 'Poverty Corner' in the hope of securing last-minute bookings from the stage agents as they passed by to go to their offices. By the early 1890s, the district had become even more infamous as it became the stalking ground for Dr Thomas Neill Cream – the serial killer known as 'the Lambeth poisoner'. Some of his unfortunate victims lived in the dingy dwellings along Stamford Street. But this was also a neighbourhood where honest, hard-working families lived. For example, William Lawson, a railway booking clerk, together with his wife and children, were occupants at 169 Stamford Street in 1871 and 1881. As housekeeper, Hannah would have certainly known William and his partner, Mary.

*

Hannah Rodda and Spencer Robinson were married in St Pancras, London, in late March 1880. Immediately prior to the wedding,

Hannah stayed in the ironically named Spencer's Hotel on Euston Road. Situated opposite the railway terminus at King's Cross, this commercial and family hotel had been established in the 1860s by a native of Lincolnshire. On the marriage certificate, it was noted that Hannah's father had been 'Captain in the Merchant Service'. However, Benjamin Rodda had been a humble seaman who did not rise to the rank of captain. Marrying a man of quite an elevated social status, Hannah here was possibly seeking to aggrandise the stature of her own family.

The wedding was witnessed by A. J. (or A. G.) Davis and Francis Healey. I have not been able to identify A. J. (A. G.) Davis, but Healey was most probably the Francis William Healey who at the time lived in Lambeth on York Road, close to Stamford Road where Hannah had been housekeeper. His father, John Healey, a printer, had lived in Bethnal Green in the 1840s and 1850s. At the time of Hannah's marriage, Francis Healey worked as a 'messenger', delivering copies of *The Observer*. He later worked as a greengrocer in Chester Street, Kennington. Charlie Chaplin would later recall how as a twelve-year-old in 1901 he lived in Chester Street opposite Healey the greengrocer.[28] Later, Healey became a publisher's agent before his death in 1913.

Frustratingly, I do not know the details of when, where and how Hannah and Spencer first met, and I can only speculate if their paths had crossed earlier when Spencer had lived briefly in West Firle, near Ripe, in the early 1870s. What is known is that Hannah had stayed in East Keal before the April 1881 census. It was recorded that Mrs Robinson had 'just gone' and a Mr Charles Wright had yet to take possession of the farm house in East Keal next to the Saracen's Head public house in the village. This property may have been the 'good house' which Spencer Robinson had advertised to let out in 1871 when moving to West Firle. However, Hannah's departure from East Keal seems to have occurred some months prior to the 1881 census. Newspaper records indicate that the unaccompanied Mrs Spencer Robinson set sail from London to Calcutta on 16 November 1880 on board the SS *Eldorado*.[29] Her husband had returned to India several months earlier. I do not know why the newly wed couple had not made the long voyage to India together.

India: An 'Incorporated Wife'?
Although the years living in various Indian hill stations left an indelible mark on the later narratives of the Robinson family in Turkey and

England, little is actually known of Hannah's life in India. While in Bengal, Hannah became the mother of two girls (one of whom seems to have died in her infancy) and at least four boys. One would assume that a portion of Hannah's time was allocated to bringing up her children.

There are countless stories of the lives of English women in India who were married to influential men such as viceroys or governors. Accounts of the lives of female eccentrics, adventurers or missionaries in India are also easily accessible. However, there were women from a range of backgrounds who left Britain to follow their partners who had embarked on new careers in India. We know much less about the lives of these women. A number of middle-class women were able to find occupations as teachers and doctors. There were also the working-class wives of soldiers, although these were supposedly fewer in number. The social status of most British women in India was greatly dependent on the profession of their partners. These women, who often in practice had little or no domestic duties, were essentially 'incorporated wives'.[30] Prominent members of the Indian Civil Service with their wives formed an elite grouping. Lower-level civil servants and their spouses were 'on the outer edge of respectable society'.[31] As a tea planter, businessman and official, Hannah's husband occupied a place on the Indian social ladder at least one rank above the clerical workers, small shopkeepers and common soldiers.

It has been argued that it was 'imperative' for couples and the Raj 'that the imperial wife enjoy the outdoorsy, sports-oriented life led by the typical Indian official'. In particular, a skill in horse riding was deemed 'a necessity'.[32] Hannah may have had to accommodate herself to a cycle of dinners, balls, social rounds and sports activities which was expected of women of a certain social status. We should not doubt that she was up to this task. A decade later Hannah appeared to have little difficulty in establishing contacts and negotiating a path through the byzantine workings of the Ottoman court.

Life for many of these 'incorporated wives' could be lonely and quite dull, especially if they did not live in the centre of the larger hill stations. Raising children and looking after the home were not necessarily time-consuming tasks. The *memsahibs* were expected to have servants to carry out most of the domestic chores. In order to maintain a particular standing and respectability, ten servants were regarded as 'the barest minimum' to run the household. There were servants of many different types and categories. These included cooks, cook's helpers, sweepers, waiters, messengers, grass-cutters, gardeners, cowmen, tailors, watchmen and horse grooms. A *bheeshi* was employed to carry water for the bathrooms, while the washerman was known as the *dhabi*. Given the restrictions of the caste system at the time, it was not possible to find a servant willing to perform a range of household tasks.[33] Children were usually looked after by nannies or *ayahs*. The latter wore saris, while nannies usually wore European dress. These maids invariably developed very close ties with the children of the household and often spoiled them. Even relatively poor British families employed nannies or *ayahs*,[34] who fed and bathed infants, played with young children and put them to bed. They also often served as wet nurses.[35]

Such a leisurely existence would have been tedious for many English women. Living in or near the smaller settlements of Kurseong and Kalimpong, or especially on an isolated tea plantation, in contrast to the relative hustle and bustle of Darjeeling, must have made life more difficult for a *memsahib*. However, given her background and her experience in housekeeping, it is likely that Hannah attempted to retain as many hands-on responsibilities as possible in her own household. This could have been a challenge given the rising social status of her husband, although for all we know she may have been in her element in supervising and allocating tasks and duties to various servants.

In effect, Hannah may have assumed the role of house manager while keeping a close eye on the upbringing of her children. Because of the expenses involved in sending children back to England to attend boarding school, it seems likely that the older children, Maud and Spencer Bernard, were educated in the schools provided for European children in the hill stations. The contrast between Hannah's environs and those of other members of the Rodda family back in London's East End could not have been more striking.

We do know a little more about how the Robinsons lived in India from correspondence in the second half of 1885 when Spencer was confined in the Presidency Jail in Calcutta. In one of his letters appealing for aid, Spencer Robinson noted that his wife had no servants, no *ayah*, no cook and 'no bearer'. His wife was 'quite worn out with work' given that there were two children who could not wash themselves and one who did not dress herself.[36] Clearly, the Robinsons were accustomed to having domestic support in the household.

However, letters also revealed that Hannah was quite the businesswoman. In spite of her presumably limited education, and the distractions of raising a large family, Hannah seemed to have hands-on control of the 'Rajbaree' estate. Writing from her residence on the estate, which was intriguingly called 'Roddaville', Hannah stated that she was responsible for the servants' housing, managing the coolies and working with the factory. In fact, 'everything in short connected with the place' fell within her domain.[37] According to Spencer, she had spent 'considerable money' on the estate.[38] While her husband was in a state of panic in his prison cell, Hannah exuded in her letters a state of calm and steely resolve – and this was at a time when she was about to give birth.

Naming her home 'Roddaville' suggests Hannah had a close identification and pride with her family's past. Extended members of the Robinson family living in Turkey today are all aware of the Rodda surname. Hannah must have impressed upon her children the importance of her origins. She may have felt a sense of success and achievement in managing a residence which she could name after her family. After all, only a few years earlier she had been working as a domestic servant for Dr Pearl.

It is quite possible that Hannah also took up employment, perhaps on a part-time basis, while in India. In the period when she lived in the country, the annual Bengal and India directories refer to a Mrs Robinson working as a midwife/nurse in the district of Darjeeling. Could this have been Hannah? Indian midwives were 'used as a last resort' by the British/European community. A so-called 'imperial mentality' prevented many *memsahibs* from hiring local midwives, who were deemed to be incompetent.[39] British or European midwives were preferred, even though many of them had little or no formal training.[40] Hannah, then, may have been employed as a midwife, but there is no proof of this.

The death of her husband at a relatively young age must have led to a period of upheaval for Hannah. While suddenly becoming the sole parent of at least four young children in India, Hannah was again pregnant. George M. Robinson was listed as being born in Bengal in 1890. Sometime after the birth of George, Hannah embarked on what must have been a difficult journey back to England with her five young children.

According to the census of April 1891, Hannah Robinson was 'occupied in keeping house' at 6 Regency Square, Brighton. Having only recently returned to England, how was Hannah able to find such a post at what was a very prestigious address? She may have benefited from past contacts made by her late husband. Interestingly, after the death of Edward Stephen Lintott, his widow, Georgina, had started to run a lodging house at German Place in Kemptown in Brighton. I do not know if Hannah had contacts with the sister-in-law of her sister, Mary Ann, and if Georgina's choice of occupation had any influence on Hannah. In Victorian England, running a decent lodging house was one of the few respectable jobs open to widowed or unattached women of the lower or middle classes.[41]

There are also rumours that Hannah had secured the boarding house by tapping into money from her daughter's inheritance. According to the immediate relatives of Spencer Robinson still living in England, Gertrude was outraged when she later discovered how she had been deprived of money to which she was entitled. However, as will be seen, the terms and conditions for funds allocated to Gertrude in Dr Pearl's will were precisely stipulated, and it would have been difficult for Hannah to secure access to this money.

Regency Square, a residential quarter by the seafront in Brighton, was designed by the well-known developer Joshua Hanson. The square's terraced houses were generally regarded as some of the best examples of early nineteenth-century architecture. In what was clearly a superior boarding house, in April 1891 there were ten other occupants at 6 Regency Square in addition to Hannah and her immediate family. These included Lord and Lady Gilbert Kennedy. The Kennedys were an established family of Scottish aristocrats. Archibald Kennedy, 13th Earl of Cassilis, was the father of Lord Gilbert. Sir Archibald Kennedy, 1st Marquis of Ailsa, was Lord Gilbert's grandfather. At the time, Lord Gilbert served as the director general of the General Life and Fire Assurance Company. Also, residing at 6 Regency Square in April 1891 was the affluent shipbroker Charles Shaw Lovell. Lovell later became a major shareholder in the Bristol Steam Navigation Company, which operated shipping services between Bristol and ports in southern Ireland. There was quite a rapid turnover of occupants at the Brighton address, and other distinguished families and individuals were transient residents of 6 Regency Square throughout 1891.

The story of Hannah Robinson may well have concluded with her settling into a reasonably comfortable living in Brighton with her children. However, in a completely unforeseen chain of events, Hannah converted to Islam, married a self-proclaimed Afghan warlord and then emigrated to Constantinople.

Abdullah Quilliam: A Sheikh in Liverpool

The recent surge of interest in relations between Christianity and Islam and the role of Muslims in Western communities has led to an increased focus on the life of William Henry 'Abdullah' Quilliam. A convert to Islam in late Victorian England, the life of the Liverpool-born solicitor is the subject of much controversy.

Quilliam's supporters have praised his charitable work, arguing that in the society of today we can still learn and benefit from his efforts to introduce a form of soft Islam more attuned to the concerns of Victorian society. Currently, the organisation known simply as Quilliam (formerly The Quilliam Foundation) is spearheading a campaign to counter extremism and promote moderate Islam. Quilliam's detractors tend to focus on his personal weaknesses and shortcomings. He was known for his eccentric behaviour. Quilliam's pet marmoset, sporting a small, specially made fez, would go everywhere with him while perched on his shoulder. The lawyer also seemed to have a weakness for the fairer sex. His legal career lay in ruins after his incompetent, if not corrupt, handling of a divorce case. He became a greater figure of ridicule after his somewhat clumsy efforts to then adopt a new identity.

Attempts to spread the word of Islam did encounter opposition in Victorian society. Some people were alarmed at what they perceived was a threat to established norms and values. Many were not convinced by Quilliam's efforts to emphasise the similarities between Christianity and Islam.

It seems that Quilliam may have played some role in Hannah's conversion to Islam. He definitely developed a close interest in Hannah and her family and this connection later had an impact on Hannah's son Ahmet Robenson. However, Quilliam himself does not figure in any of the narratives of the Robinson family.

Born in Liverpool, William Henry Quilliam (1856–1932) came from a much-respected Wesleyan family of Manx origins. His father was a watchmaker and a Methodist preacher. Trained as a solicitor and based in Liverpool, where he presided over the local temperance movement, Quilliam converted to Islam and changed his name following a life-changing visit to Morocco. After initially forming a small Koran-reading group, Quilliam established the Liverpool Muslim Institute (LMI) and the British Muslim Association in September 1887. By 1889, he had opened arguably the first functioning mosque in Britain at Broughton Terrace in Liverpool. The first public Muslim funeral in Britain was held there in February 1891, and two months later it was the site of the first public Muslim marriage ceremony in Britain. The LMI played a role in the conversion of Christians to Islam, although the numbers involved were very small. By the end of 1891 there were about fifty converts.[42] In that year, there were reportedly fifty-two members of the LMI, of whom fourteen were 'ladies'.[43]

Referring to the mosque as the 'Islam church', some locals were not opposed to Quilliam's pioneering work. However, the work of the LMI did attract negative publicity. There were exaggerated concerns that Quilliam and his small community posed a grave threat to the Church and society in Liverpool, if not the country as a whole. Very shortly before Hannah's own marriage at the LMI, ostensibly provoked by the muezzin's call to prayer, a mob attacked the mosque. Some 400 'roughs' threw stones and fireworks and the muezzin was struck several times. Several of the missiles fell within inches of one of Quilliam's young sons.[44]

While a subject of some concern and curiosity in England, Quilliam and his small band of followers arguably attracted greater interest abroad. In October 1890, they successfully protested against the staging of a play titled *Mahomet* which was about to open at the Lyceum theatre in London. Newspaper reports of the planned performing of Hall Caine's production, in which the Prophet would play a central role, had triggered demonstrations among the Muslim community in the British Raj.[45]

Quilliam's efforts to counter the negative image of Afghans, who were often portrayed as fanatical Muslim warriors threatening the stability of British India, was appreciated by the amir of Afghanistan. Abdur Rahman Khan gave financial backing to the LMI and funded

the newly refurbished mosque which opened in Liverpool in 1895.[46]
The activities of Quilliam and his supporters also attracted the
attention of the Ottoman sultan. In April 1891, Quilliam and his
eldest son, Robert Ahmed, were invited to Constantinople and
received by Abdülhamid II himself. The young Robert Ahmed had
the distinction of being appointed lieutenant-colonel in the sultan's
elite *Ertuğrul* regiment (the Imperial Guard).[47] A close personal
relationship was struck up between Quilliam and the sultan. In return
for swearing his personal allegiance, in 1894 Quilliam was appointed
by Abdülhamid II to become his personal representative in Britain –
the Sheikh al-Islam of Britain.[48]

Only a handful of marriages were conducted at the LMI prior to
the wedding ceremony of Hannah and a 'Dr Gholab Shah'. The first
marriage between a convert and a Muslim took place at the mosque
in Liverpool in April 1891 between the originally Protestant Charlotte
Fitch and Mohamed Ahmad. The latter was a barrister working in
London. Prior to the marriage in Liverpool, a wedding ceremony was
performed in Camberwell in London.[49] This started what appeared
to be a common practice of having a legal, civil wedding in London
before holding a religious Muslim ceremony in Liverpool.

The legality of marriages carried out at the LMI was questioned by
the Home Office. Referring to a later marriage carried out in 1905 by
one of Quilliam's sons at the Liverpool mosque between a Muslim and
a seventeen-year-old girl, the Home Office declared that the couple
were not married in English law. According to the report, the so-called
marriage was 'a mere device for setting up a pretence of responsibility
for what is an immoral contract of union'. The Home Office added
that 'Mohammedan marriages' between persons who were both
believers should rather be solemnised at foreign consulates.[50]

What role, if any, did Quilliam perhaps play in Hannah Robinson's
decision to convert to Islam? One account in *The Crescent*, the
newspaper produced by the LMI, described how Hannah had become
acquainted with Quilliam's wife, also called Hannah, on a visit to
Liverpool, and then decided to renounce Christianity and enter
the Islamic faith together with her family.[51] I do not know if
Hannah Quilliam played any role in Hannah Robinson's conversion.
Interestingly, unlike Quilliam's mother, who followed her son into
the Islamic faith, the Liverpool sheikh's wife remained a Christian
throughout her life. Quilliam's spouse was the daughter of William

Johnstone, a businessman and an enthusiastic member of the Wesleyan Methodist Society.[52] Hannah Quilliam died in November 1909. In her will it was stated that she wanted her body 'to be buried in the manner used amongst Christians'.[53]

Perhaps Hannah Robinson was influenced by Fatima Cates (Elizabeth Cates), the first English woman to convert to Islam with Quilliam's encouragement. Adopting Islam in 1887 at the age of just nineteen, Fatima Cates became the first treasurer of the LMI. She was involved in helping Quilliam in his missionary activities. This included establishing working ties with leading Muslims in India. In autumn 1890, Fatima Cates sent a letter to the Hyderabad-based Muslim activist Moulvi Hassan Ali, seeking his support in the LMI's quest to expand the number of Muslim converts in Britain.[54] Is it possible, therefore, that Hannah Robinson could have been in prior communication with Fatima Cates before visiting Liverpool? Or was Quilliam himself more directly involved?

It is difficult to imagine Hannah, in the months after her husband's death, coming into contact with what was then a minuscule Muslim community in Kalimpong. More probably, Hannah started to contemplate the possibility of converting to Islam after coming into contact with the supposed former Afghan warlord 'Gholab Shah' – her future second husband. This may have prompted Hannah to visit Liverpool to meet Hannah Quilliam, and here she quite possibly encountered Fatima Cates and 'Abdullah' Quilliam.

Dr Gholab Shah, alias Eliahie Bosche: Charlatan and 'Blackguard'

One of the main claims to fame of Professor Arminius Vambery, a Hungarian Turcologist and expert on Central Asia, was that it was he who introduced Bram Stoker to the legend of Dracula. Stoker's creation, the vampire hunter Abraham Van Helsing, was evidently modelled on Vambery. The Turcologist, who was known to travel around Central Asia in the guise of a dervish, was also in the employ of the British government. For services rendered, King Edward VII later appointed him an Honorary Commander of the Royal Victorian Order – an order of knighthood created by Queen Victoria in 1896.

On 21 September 1892, Vambery despatched a confidential letter to Sir Philip Crowe, the permanent undersecretary in the Foreign Office.

Given his personal access to Sultan Abdülhamid II and the Ottoman court, Vambery sent regular reports to the British government on the state of Ottoman affairs. In his missive, Vambery noted excitedly that in Budapest a few days previously he had met an Afghan named Gholam Singh who claimed to be well-connected to the amir of Afghanistan, the Ottoman sultan and the sheriff of Mecca. Gholam Singh declared that he was travelling as a Russian emissary on a mission to convince the world of the superiority of Russian rule over British.[55] This was at a time when London was apprehensive about the possible Russian penetration of the mountainous Pamir region of Afghanistan. The governments of the day, led by Lord Salisbury and then by William Gladstone, were determined to ensure that Afghanistan remained a neutral buffer state between Tsarist Russia and the British Raj in India.

Six days later, the Foreign Office penned a reply to Vambery. The individual in question was not called Gholam Singh (nor Gholab Shah, another of his aliases) and he was not an Afghan. The self-proclaimed Russian emissary was actually named Elichi Bux or Eliahie Bosche, and he was an Indian oculist who had assumed the name of his former master. The letter then briefly referred to Bosche's 'past matrimonial misdeeds' and observed that 'he seems to be one of the greatest blackguards alive'. This 'scoundrel' was the same so-called Dr Gholab Shah whom Hannah married at the mosque in Liverpool in November 1891.[56] By September 1892, the Foreign Office was in possession of two letters posted from Constantinople by Hannah in which full details of the terrible ordeal Hannah and her family had faced at the hands of Bosche were painstakingly presented.

In the light of these events, it was perhaps not surprising that Hannah should choose not to recount this part of her life to her family members. No member of the Robinson family was aware of the existence of 'Dr Gholab Shah'. According to the story handed down by family members living in Turkey, Hannah had converted to Islam while in India and the Ottoman sultan, attracted by this story, had invited her and her children to the Ottoman Empire and had offered one of his leading military officers as Hannah's new husband.

There were a number of itinerant Indian oculists in late Victorian England who claimed to be eye experts and promised miracle cures. They advertised themselves in local newspapers together with glowing testimonials from supposed past patients. More gullible members of society, eager to find a cheap cure, were taken in by the bold claims of these charlatans. At the time, no formal qualifications were required to be recognised as an eye doctor. Indian oculists became less popular following a trial of four so-called eye doctors at the Old Bailey in London in October 1893.[57] Although the four were found not guilty of fraud, the negative publicity which surrounded the trial meant that the oculists would find it much more difficult in future to hoodwink clients.

In the case of the marriage of Hannah and the so-called Gholab Shah, there was no report in the media of an initial civil wedding before the holding of a Muslim ceremony. News of the impending marriage was covered by the local press in late October 1891.[58] The broader media coverage of the Liverpool wedding reported that Hannah and her family had converted to Islam a few months earlier. The marriage took place according to the rites of Islam at the mosque in Liverpool on 26 November 1891.[59] The ceremony was a private one, with only around thirty people in attendance. Dr Shah 'was attired in the picturesque Afghan cap, flowing turban and other characteristic garments'. Hannah – who had taken the name Fatima after her conversion – was 'dressed in a travelling costume of fawn-coloured cloth, with feather trimmings'. She was accompanied by her eldest daughter.[60] It is highly unlikely that Gertrude, by that time almost sixteen years of age, had also converted to Islam (there would be no references to this in accounts of Gertrude's later life after she had married a prominent German Jewish businessman). After the wedding, the couple left by the afternoon train to London en route to Constantinople.

The wedding certainly attracted national attention, which was not surprising given that such marriages were rare occurrences. However, not all press coverage was positive. One account argued that it would be a pity if this precedent was followed, adding that 'we do not desire that our free, Christian women should be transferred to Mahometan harems'.[61] Another critical news item noted how Hannah must have thought that the title 'Mrs Dr Gholab Shah' 'sounded better than Mrs Robinson' and so she had willingly assented to the title even though it meant a conversion to Islam.[62]

Newspaper reports stated that 'Dr Gholab Shah' of Kabul was the eldest son of the late Sheikh Mohammed. As a chief of one of the Afghan hill tribes, Dr Shah had ostensibly actively fought in the

Second Anglo-Afghan War (1878–80) against the British. He was supposedly one of the leaders of a company of *Ghazis* (fanatical warriors and devout followers of Islam). Nothing more was reported about him. The British had certainly suffered many casualties in the Second Anglo-Afghan War to the *Ghazis*. It may have seemed odd that Hannah, the one-time wife of quite a prominent British representative in India with close links to the government of the British Raj, should choose to marry a notorious former Afghan warlord. The marriage did not last long.

According to the British embassy in Constantinople, the story of Eliahie Bosche prior to his first encounter with Hannah was as follows.[63] In 1887, Bosche had arrived in Plymouth together with his master, Dr Gholab Shah, an Indian oculist. The pair were travelling the world offering their services. They quarrelled and separated, with Bosche setting up his own practice. While in Plymouth, Bosche met a Miss Lillicrap. Discovering that the young lady had property and was well connected, Bosche arranged to marry her. Immediately before the marriage, Bosche declared that he was a Muslim. Miss Lillicrap broke off the engagement, but Bosche continued to hassle and threaten her. Miss Lillicrap suffered a breakdown and was placed in a lunatic asylum in Exeter. This story does appear to be accurate. Records show that a Miss Amy Roberts Lillicrap of Tamerton, Devon, was admitted to an asylum at Plympton in July 1887. She was discharged in March 1888, but was later admitted to the Digby asylum in Exeter where she died in 1899. When her father, a yeoman, died, he left in his will a personal estate of over £6,800.

In April 1888, Bosche proceeded from Plymouth to Hull where he advertised himself as an 'eminent oculist' who had earned a first-class degree from Lahore College. Professing to be a Christian, he married a Miss Lait in September 1888 in a church ceremony. After the marriage, Bosche admitted that he was already married and Miss Lait promptly left him. Again, this story does tally with the facts. Edith Mary Lait was the daughter of a railway clerk from Hull. In the 1890s she was engaged as a singer, pianist and performer of recitals in concerts in the Bridlington area of Yorkshire.

The story continues. In December 1888, Bosche was working as an oculist in Newcastle. There, he met a domestic servant whom he married, travelled with to Quebec, and then abandoned. By 1890, Bosche was back in England making his living as an oculist in

Hartlepool before moving to London. He was now referring to himself as Gholab or Goolab Shah. By the time of the 1891 census, he was living in Mornington Crescent in London; later he resided at 35 South Street, Greenwich.

What became of the original Dr Gholab Shah? According to the British Embassy in Constantinople, he died in India in 1892. Prior to his arrival in Plymouth, he had worked and travelled in Australia and New Zealand, presumably with Bosche. There are reports that a 'Goolab Shah', who was barely able to speak English, was arrested in Australia for performing an operation without having the necessary qualifications.[64] When in England, the real Gholab Shah had also worked as an oculist in the north-east and in Cornwall for a period in 1889 and 1890.

Hannah, therefore, was one of a string of women who had fallen for the charms and wiles of Dr Gholab Shah, alias Eliahie Bosche. The maltreatment of Hannah and her children at the hands of Bosche in Constantinople, her desperation to seek a divorce, and her determination to remain in the Ottoman capital in spite of financial problems are recounted in some detail in correspondence held at the National Archives. Her first letter, posted in June 1892, was received by the Office of the Prime Minister, Lord Salisbury, and was then passed on to the Foreign Office. A number of memoranda were then exchanged between the British government and its representatives in Constantinople, together with another letter posted by Hannah to the office of the new prime minister, Gladstone, in September 1892.[65]

In her letters, Hannah described how she had first made Bosche's acquaintance while he was working as an oculist in Greenwich under the name Gholab Shah. This must have been after the April 1891 census. The engagement between the two therefore happened quite swiftly. Hannah was told how Gholab Shah had supposedly received the name 'Eliahie Bosche' – meaning 'blessed of God' – as a result of his successful campaign fighting against the British in the Second Anglo-Afghan War. Bosche recounted how, aged only eighteen, he had led 42,000 men into battle. He described how, after being imprisoned for a period by the British in India, he could not return to Afghanistan as his family posed a direct threat to the rule of the amir. Having lost all his possessions, he trained as an oculist in India before travelling to England. According to Bosche, he had been received by the queen at Windsor Castle and was well known to other members of the royal family. He convinced Hannah that Sultan Abdülhamid II would welcome them in Constantinople. Taking Bosche at his word, Hannah believed that her marriage to such an eminent figure could be 'greatly instrumental' in helping create close ties between the Afghan and British governments.

The marriage quickly broke down after the couple moved to Constantinople. Hannah learned that Bosche had four other wives and had driven one poor English woman to an asylum. She soon realised that her husband was a charlatan who had told her a string of lies. Trapped alone in a hotel room in a foreign country, and barely able to speak the local language, Hannah started to fear for her safety and that of her children. Referring to himself as Jack the Ripper, Bosche behaved abominably, insulting her, and acting 'like an absolute mad man'. In his regular violent rages, he threatened to 'dash' her children 'to pieces'.

Hannah sought to secure a divorce in the local courts. She secured the services of an English lawyer, Frederick David William Hatton, who was the family's solicitor 'for many years'. In the legal proceedings, they were able to use testimony from Edith Lait, Bosche's earlier wife. Ultimately, after further ordeals and delays, Hannah succeeded in obtaining a divorce.

However, in her letters Hannah also revealed that she had not lived a life of complete isolation. She had somehow established close contacts with key officials at the Ottoman court and had even communicated with Sultan Abdülhamid II himself! After Hannah wrote to the sultan about the plight of her family, arrangements were made at the palace for money to be paid monthly to help support Hannah, her five children, and her English maid. Bosche had apparently frittered away most of Hannah's money. Hannah had established contacts with Mustafa Zeki Pasha, the Field Marshal of the Imperial Arsenal of Ordnance and Artillery, and with 'Kurt' İsmail Pasha, a former army commander and governor of Diyarbakir. İsmail Pasha was nicknamed 'the Wolf' because of the tactics he had employed when fighting with rebel tribes. Both men were close confidants of the sultan. Hannah also knew personally the wife of the grand vizier (Ahmed Cevat Şakir Pasha).

Hannah urged the British government to lobby on her behalf so that she could obtain more funds from the sultan, because of the difficulties in securing access to the palace directly. To support her case,

Hannah argued that she came 'from a civilised European family' accustomed to 'civilised refinement' and so it was impossible for her to continue in her current situation. In addition, she requested the British authorities inform the sultan that she was willing to be of service to him, 'being practical, energetic and from England', and hoped that 'his Majesty will attach me to his family in this way'. One could certainly not fault Hannah for her determination to attempt to secure the best for herself and her family.

Contacts with Mustafa Zeki Pasha turned out to be especially fruitful. He was one of Sultan Abdülhamid II's most loyal generals, and his powers overlapped with those of the minister of war. He was also in charge of the empire's military schools. Mustafa Zeki Pasha had risen up the ranks serving as an *aide-de-camp* to the sultan before becoming tutor to the sultan's sons. Well versed in English, French and German, he played a prominent role in the modernisation of the Ottoman military.[66]

In her letters, Hannah noted that her daughter Maud (Adile) was currently living with Mustafa Zeki Pasha and his daughters. She was forced to accept the pasha's offer to take Maud in because the girl needed an education, proper food and clothing. The pasha's daughters in his household at the time would have been younger than the ten-year-old Maud. Maud must have stayed either at Mustafa Zeki Pasha's summer residence on Büyükada, the largest of the Princess Islands on the Sea of Marmara, or at the pasha's house in Nişantaşı, near the centre of Constantinople. The latter is now the site of the American Hospital in Istanbul. Mustafa Zeki Pasha did not relocate to his well-known, imposing, baroque-style mansion on the European shore of the Bosphorus until the waterfront dwelling was completed by the Italian architect Alexandre Vallaury in 1895.[67]

I contacted one of the great-grandsons of Mustafa Zeki Pasha, but neither he nor his brother recalled hearing of an English girl living temporarily in the household of the field marshal. Nor does Maud herself appear to have passed on to her children and grandchildren memories of her time in the pasha's residence. Interestingly, Sabiha, a daughter of Mustafa Zeki Pasha born in 1895, would later marry Ali Kemal, the great-grandfather of the one-time British Foreign Secretary Boris Johnson.

Through the recommendation of Mustafa Zeki Pasha, two of Hannah's sons were attending for free the famous military college at

Kuleli. Founded in 1845 on the Asian shores of the Bosphorus, Kuleli was the oldest and most prestigious military educational institution in the Ottoman Empire. However, Hannah expressed regret that her 'four-and-a-half-year-old son' had to attend school so young. Confusingly, this suggested that perhaps Eugene (by then renamed Abdurrahman) was born in 1887 and not in 1885. Hannah took solace in the fact that at school her young son was safe from any possible physical attack from Eliahie Bosche.

How did the British government and its officials in Constantinople react to Hannah's entreaties? Concerns were expressed with regard to Hannah, her children and the maid. It was noted that although Hannah lived as a Turkish woman and a Muslim, and did not want to leave Constantinople, she was still a British subject. The Foreign Office therefore stated that Hannah was 'very lucky' to be receiving anything from the sultan and that if the ambassador, Sir Francis Clare Ford, was to press for more support it could backfire.

The British authorities were especially worried about the future well-being of the children. When Hannah was living with Bosche, arrangements had been made for Maud to marry an Indian merchant who was both a Muslim and a British subject. This fell through after Maud was received by the pasha's family. Suggestions were made that enquiries could be carried out as to whether the Robinson children had relatives in England who could possibly take charge of them. Officials expressed alarm at the 'grave scandal' if the children of the late Mr Robinson converted to Islam – although earlier media reports had indicated that Hannah and her family (apart from Gertrude) had already converted to Islam. However, these officials added that if the embassy interfered and the children were removed from their Turkish homes, they would probably starve unless some Christian religious or charitable society intervened.

Hannah remained in Constantinople with her children. In spite of the concerns of the British government, Hannah's sons and daughter would be raised in public as Muslims. I do not know what happened to the maid. And what of Bosche? An Indian oculist called Gholab Shah was offering his services in Dublin in late 1894.[68] Bosche then disappears from the scene for the next twelve years.

On 13 July 1906, the British consul general in Marseilles, Mr Gurney, asked the India Office in London if he should issue a passport to a 'Goolab Shah'. This 'native of Afghanistan' was travelling from

London to Mecca, via Port Said. In its reply, the India Office noted that the foreign minister, Sir Edward Grey, had requested that attention should be given to correspondence in 1890 and 1891 concerning the status and history of the said Goolab Shah.[69]

This chain of communication revealed that Goolab Shah had previously applied for a passport in London without success. This begs the question whether 'Goolab Shah' had married Hannah in an attempt to secure a British passport in addition to seeking to gain access to her funds. In the India Office's reply to Consul General Gurney, the delicate diplomatic nature of the passport request was noted. A refusal 'may cause trouble' with the amir of Afghanistan, while the granting of a passport could cause difficulties with Constantinople. In these circumstances, it was recommended that No. 10 should be consulted directly, given that the Office of the Prime Minister had all the necessary correspondence. The occupant of No. 10 at the time was Sir Henry Campbell-Bannerman of the Liberal Party. It is not clear why the British government should have adopted such a circumspect approach given the information they had at their disposal on the past shenanigans of the Indian oculist.

Bosche had returned to England. The 1906 communication between Consul General Gurney and the India Office noted that 'Gholab Shah' was resident at 2 Chapel Street, Bloomsbury. The former oculist had apparently rebranded himself and had started up a new business as an Indian curry manufacturer. Specialising in the 'wholesale and export of chutney and Bomba duck', he had been awarded the gold medal for his produce in the Colonial and Indian Exhibition held at the Crystal Palace in 1905.[70]

'Goolab Shah' was present with his condiments and chutneys and 'in his robes of splendour' at the India Palace in the Franco-British Exhibition at the White City in 1908. The 'Afghan' was 'the intellectual among the natives of the show' with his knowledge of English, French, Spanish, Arabic, Hindustani, Punjabi and other Indian dialects, Tibetan, Persian and Afghan.[71] He then opened an Indian restaurant in Holborn sometime around 1909. This may have been the Salut-e-Hind, which was one of the first Indian restaurants in London to serve the local clientele rather than simply feeding South Asian emigres.

'Shah' also attracted media attention through other channels. According to him, the decline in the popularity of the Crystal Palace was due to an Egyptian curse after mummies looted from Egyptian temples were brought to be exhibited there.[72] The so-called Afghan was also sought after on account of his 'addiction to prophecy'. In what became a much-quoted prediction, he had noted that the English race and nation was destined to be 'glorious' after a seven-year period of troubles and sickness commencing in 1910. He prophesised that the time would come when France, Canada and the US would work together under the British flag. Because of its possession of Jacob's pillar as a coronation stone in Westminster Abbey, Britain was destined to be a great power.[73] This was a reference to the claim that the Stone of Scone used in coronations of monarchs of the United Kingdom was actually the stone consecrated to God by the biblical Jacob.

A 'Mr Gholab Shah', merchant, aged fifty-six, travelled third class from London to Colombo on a ship which embarked on 26 September 1914. England was listed as the last permanent residence of the merchant, and India was recorded as the intended future permanent residence of the passenger. It is quite possible that Hannah's erstwhile husband never returned.

Ahmed Bahri: The Sultan's Colonel

There is an extensive literature on the thoughts and observations of British women travellers in the late Ottoman Empire. In general, these were the works of upper-middle-class 'ladies'. Much attention was given to the daily routines of women in the sultan's harem. This fascination of Western women with the roles of their counterparts in the Ottoman Empire can be traced back to the early eighteenth century and the letters of Lady Mary Wortley Montagu, the wife of the then British ambassador in Constantinople. These later British women travellers paid particularly close attention to the traditions, rituals and ceremonies of Ottoman daily life. There is also another collection of writings which concentrated on the personal experiences of female Christian missionaries and pilgrims in the final years of Ottoman rule.[74]

This body of work was written by Western women who were essentially outside observers of Ottoman society. Even teachers were excluded from many aspects of local life and would have tended to focus their activities on the relatively small British, American or European communities living in the Ottoman Empire. However, those relatively few Western women who married Ottoman subjects had potentially much greater access to local culture and society.

After Hannah's messy divorce from Eliahie Bosche, details are lacking for the next few years of her life in the capital of the Ottoman Empire. In a March 1895 edition of *The Crescent* there was a brief item about how Mrs Fatima Robinson, residing in Constantinople, had lost 'her youngest son'.[75] This was most probably a reference to George M. Robinson (renamed Abdül Kadir), the last son of Spencer Robinson.

Given Hannah's past history with Sultan Abdülhamid II, it was quite possible that the Ottoman ruler did recommend that Hannah should marry one of his dashing young military officers, Ahmed Bahri. Indeed, Abdülhamid may have provided Hannah with a husband in an attempt to foreclose further requests for financial or other support. Relatives of the family currently living in Turkey have suggested that the couple were provided with a house on the street known as Akaretler, which was close to the sultan's palace at Dolmabahçe, near Beşiktaş in the Ottoman capital; the story goes that food from the palace was provided to the Bahri household on a daily basis.

The smart row of houses on Akaretler, extending up the hillside from the Bosphorus, was designed by the Armenian architect Sarkis Balyan and built in the 1870s on the instructions of Sultan Abdülaziz. Some of the houses were used to accommodate staff who were employed at the Dolmabahçe Palace, but most of the apartment buildings were occupied by prominent diplomats, bureaucrats and high-level government officials. Between 1896 and 1908, Fausto Zonaro, Abdülhamid's court painter, resided at No. 50, the most imposing of the street's buildings. Artists, intellectuals and statesmen flocked to Zonaro's home – including Winston Churchill when on a cruise of the Mediterranean in 1907 – and for a period the thoroughfare became the hub of high society and cultural life in Constantinople.

For a time, Hannah did indeed live on Akaretler. Like Zonaro, a 'Fatma Robenson Hanım' was fortunate to live in rent-free guesthouse accommodation on the street. Details of this have been registered in the official Ottoman Archives.[76] Many of the other properties were rented out at exorbitant rates. It seems that Hannah's earlier appeals to the sultan about her financial plight had been particularly effective and she was still benefitting from Abdülhamid's largesse even after her marriage. This highly convenient arrangement may have been terminated after the deposition of the sultan in April 1909. Certainly, with the fall from grace of his imperial sponsor, Zonaro was forced to vacate his residence as he could not afford to pay the 500-franc annual rent which was asked of him.

Hannah must have married Ahmed Bahri before the birth of their son, Fevzi, on 11 March 1895. Bahri was the son of Captain Mustafa Effendi, an officer with close ties to the sultan. Ahmed Bahri later distinguished himself in the Greco-Turkish (Ottoman) War which was fought largely in April and May 1897 in the Greek territory of Thessaly and Epirus. This conflict had erupted following an escalation of tensions between the Greek and Turkish communities on the then Ottoman-controlled island of Crete. Newspaper accounts report that the sultan had conferred upon Ahmed Bahri three decorations for his military services.[77] It is not clear what exact role Bahri had played in what is also known as the Thirty Days War of 1897, but it seems that around this time he had been promoted to the rank of *Kolağası* (senior captain) in the Ottoman Army.

The Bahri family were invited to be a part of the official welcoming committee when Abdullah Quilliam and his wife arrived in Constantinople by train in early May 1898. However, delays due to heavy traffic meant that the Bahris could only meet the Quilliams later in the day at the famous Pera Palace Hotel. According to reports, the reception committee at the train station was composed of a number of prominent dignitaries including Woods Pasha, vice admiral of the Ottoman Fleet; Ahmed Pasha, head of the Imperial Arsenal (this was actually incorrect as Mustafa Zeki Pasha, well known to Hannah, was then in control of the Imperial Arsenal); and Hakkı Bey, the principal legal councillor to the Sublime Porte (the Ottoman government).[78] Clearly, the Bahris were mixing with elevated company.

Hakkı Bey (aka İbrahim Hakkı Pasha, 1862–1918) had visited the mosque in Liverpool in October 1892 as Imperial Commissioner for the Ottoman Court.[79] He later held various ministerial positions and was appointed Ottoman ambassador to Germany and Italy. Between December 1909 and September 1911, he served as grand vizier. Unusual for the time, he was a freethinker who had a respect for constitutionalism and freedom of the press. Hakkı Bey once reportedly said that he was not at all concerned about being regularly caricatured by the media: 'My caricature is really good; I can't forbid such things.'[80]

Woods Pasha is also remembered in history as Sir Henry Felix Woods (1843–1929). He had previously worked at the British Embassy in Constantinople before joining the Imperial Ottoman Navy and rising to the rank of admiral. Woods Pasha also served as an *aide-de-camp* to Sultan Abdülhamid II. In effect, he operated as the sultan's public relations advisor, receiving visiting dignitaries from the English-speaking world. He was a keen advocate of close ties between the Ottoman Empire and Britain. Other Englishmen worked for the Ottoman government, but arguably none had risen to such a prominent position and had established such a close rapport with the sultan.[81] In his later memoirs, Woods Pasha recounted how he had found Quilliam to be 'an extraordinary person' whom he had believed to be 'perfectly sincere in his conversion to Islam'.[82]

When welcoming the Quilliams, Hannah and her daughter Adile (Maud) were veiled, while Hannah's sons Yakup (Spencer Bernard), Abdurrahman (Eugene B.) and Ahmet (Peel Harold) wore the uniform of the military school which they attended. It appears that the infant Fevzi was not part of the delegation. After the reception at the hotel, the Quilliams departed for the nearby Yildiz Palace, to be received by the sultan. Later in the month, the Bahri family were on hand to accompany the Quilliams to the ship which departed for Smyrna. As a parting gift, Ahmed Bahri's father, Captain Mustafa Effendi, presented Quilliam with a picture bearing quotations from the Koran written in Turkish characters.[83]

It is not known if Hannah and Ahmed Bahri were included in other delegations which received Quilliam on his later trips to Constantinople. The British Sheikh al-Islam visited the Ottoman Empire on several other occasions in the following years before his fall from grace in 1908 after being accused of forging evidence in a divorce case for one of his clients. Surprisingly, as will be seen, the repercussions of this case would have a direct impact on one of Hannah's sons – Ahmet Robenson. Quilliam himself disappeared from public view for a period after 1908 and in his absence the LMI was closed down.

The Bahris may well have been in London in the spring of 1900. On 2 May of that year, helped by Mr Hatton, the 'family solicitor', 'Fatima Bahri' received effects totalling over £587 'from the will of Spencer Robinson'. According to Spencer's last will and testament, drawn up twelve years earlier, all his estates and effects were to be left to Hannah and their children. This latest sum of money actually originally came from the estate of Isabella Robinson, Spencer Robinson's first wife. Isabella died intestate. Spencer then passed away without having taken upon himself letters of administration to secure access to his first wife's personal estate. Hannah and Ahmed Bahri secured the services of their solicitor to make the necessary legal arrangements to obtain effective control of what had been Isabella's personal estate. The distribution of money from Spencer's (and Isabella's) legacy would later be challenged by Hannah's daughter Gertrude.

It is difficult to find much more information about Ahmed Bahri. However, it seems that, together with Mehmed Raif (Davutpaşalı, 1863–1917), he was the surprising co-author of the work *Mir'at-ı İstanbul*. This was a book describing the Islamic monuments and places of historic interest in Constantinople. The first printing of the book in 1896 only listed Mehmed Rauf as author, but the second printing two years later included Ahmed Bahri. A *Kolağası* like Ahmed Bahri, Mehmed Rauf had fought in the Greco-Turkish War and was probably a close associate of Bahri. Mehmed Rauf also penned a number of other works on the history, architecture and archaeology of Constantinople, as well as undertaking studies on Turkish, Persian and Arabic literary epigrams.[84] Unlike his colleague, Ahmed Bahri does not appear to have had major literary or scholarly pretensions; *Mir'at-ı İstanbul* appears to have been his only work.

Little else is known of Ahmed Bahri. The family have in their possession an undated photograph of the silver-bearded Ahmed Bahri in full military uniform standing together with Hannah. His wife, with hair and chin covered, has her arm locked into her husband's. They look relaxed and contented.

Ahmed Bahri died around 1920. In personal correspondence to his half-sister Gertrude from early 1924, Ahmet Robenson noted that 'the Colonel' had died four years ago.[85] The cause of death was not given. In the years since the Greco-Turkish War, Ahmed Bahri had evidently been promoted to hold a senior military post.

Certainly, Hannah had benefitted from close ties with Sultan Abdülhamid II and prominent members of the Ottoman Court. The provision of a third husband by the sultan would have enabled Hannah to remain in Constantinople with her children without the fear of any reprisals from Eliahie Bosche. These imperial connections would have had much less significance after the overthrow of Sultan Abdülhamid II in 1909, and after the demise of the Ottoman Empire following the First World War.

The Later Years

By the early 1920s, Hannah had apparently fully settled into leading a life in what was to become the Republic of Turkey. After the death of her third husband, Hannah remained a widow. Most of her days appeared to be dedicated to family matters. While seemingly receding into the background, Hannah remained a pivotal figure within her family as a mother, grandmother and indeed great-grandmother. It is not known if she attempted to keep contact with her relatives in England. Given their circumstances, it may not have been easy for her to maintain ties. She may have consciously chosen to distance herself from England given her past experiences there, particularly when her social life and adventures in India and then in the Ottoman Empire are taken into account. This could help also to explain the lack of awareness among Turks about Hannah's humble origins back in London's East End.

Some insight into the latter years of Hannah's life may be gleaned from interviews with relatives based in Turkey and from the little personal correspondence that remains. By late 1926, Hannah had relocated to live in the Cennet district of the port city of Izmir (Smyrna) on the Aegean coast. A letter from Ahmet Robenson to his half-sister describes in some detail the property in which Hannah lived. The house consisted of six 'fair-sized' rooms together with a small room for a servant, a bathroom, box room, pantry, kitchen, laundry and stable. Attached to the house was a garden, not large in size but nevertheless containing 'a small vineyard, six fine pine trees, two almond trees, one walnut tree and a few rose and other trees'. Wire screens were fixed to the windows of the property to deal with the problem of mosquitos. Water was provided by an American windmill, and electricity was provided from the nearby American college (presumably, today's private Izmir American College).[86]

By the summer of 1943, Hannah had moved again and was residing at 5 Yeni Yol, in the Buca district of Izmir.[87] Buca, originally a largely Greek-populated village, and neighbouring Burnova became districts populated by the British community in Izmir in the decades before and after the First World War. Prior to the founding of the Republic of Turkey, enterprising merchants and industrialists were attracted by the expanding trade at the Ottoman entrepot and were eager to benefit from the fiscal and legal privileges offered by the Ottoman authorities – the so-called 'Capitulations'.

Buca and Burnova were famous for their splendid country houses and well-kept gardens, which were patrolled by Turkish guards to keep out local ruffians. For example, the impressive Forbes Mansion in Buca was the home of David Forbes of MacAndrews and Forbes, the famous liquorice manufacturers. The villa built in Buca by the prominent British businessman Tommy Rees, founder of the Egypt & Levant Steamship Company, was arguably even more grand than the Forbes Mansion, with its fifteen bedrooms, ballroom, billiard room and smoking room. The establishment of the British Chamber of Commerce in Smyrna in 1888 encouraged more entrepreneurs from Britain to set up businesses in the area. The British community spent their leisure time partying and mixing at balls, attending social clubs, or engaging in sports such as tennis and football. A Smyrna football club was founded by British expatriates as early as 1894, many years before professional Turkish football teams were permitted in the Ottoman Empire. The All Saints Anglican Church in Buca provided for more spiritual nourishment.[88]

Hannah's living quarters in Buca would certainly not have been as grandiose as the villas of the English merchants, and the ageing and increasingly frail English woman from Bethnal Green would presumably have avoided most of the social activities on offer. However, with a thriving British community at her doorstep, Hannah had the opportunity to maintain some ties with her English heritage, and perhaps this is why she opted to settle in Buca in her later years.

Reportedly, Hannah ran a tight ship at home. She was particularly punctilious with regard to the making of beds. Ahmet Robenson affectionately referred to her as 'Mother' and seemed to spend considerable time with her in her first years in Izmir. The relationship between Hannah and her only surviving son from her first marriage appears to have been especially close, with two other sons from her marriage to Spencer Robinson having perished in the First World War. In the fashion of Ottomans of an elevated status, she always addressed the young girls in the family as *Hanım* ('lady'). She could also be extremely authoritarian. Her youngest son, Fevzi, even when he was an adult, stood to attention like a soldier upon meeting his mother. In her last years, Hannah apparently had a bitter altercation with Fevzi over a court case involving allegations of theft. According to one of her letters she had previously helped Fevzi by paying for court expenses, but she was not prepared to do so again.[89]

One of Hannah's idiosyncrasies in her later years was her decision to have a number of visiting cards printed for herself. This was a highly unusual practice at the time for widowed ladies living in Turkey. For some unknown reason the name she chose to print on the cards was 'Fatima R. B. Kövi – the widow of the deceased Colonel Ahmed Bahri'. No member of the extended Robinson family in Turkey is able to explain why Hannah decided to use the name Kövi rather than Bahri. The 'R' may have referred to either Robinson or Rodda, given her close identification with her maiden name, and the 'B' to Bahri.

In her later years, Hannah suffered from various ailments. Writing to his half-sister in April 1928, Ahmet Robenson noted that she was 'doing well' but had 'suffered much' and had not left her room the previous winter because of attacks of rheumatism. They had travelled to Bursa in 1926 to benefit from the natural hot baths there. She enjoyed tending to the garden, sowing and watering in the summer mornings and evenings. In the winter, however, she was confined to her room and spent her time reading and doing 'very beautiful needlework'. If possible, mother and son went to bathe in the nearby sea, but this was becoming increasingly difficult given Hannah's condition; during the last summer they had only five or six short 'outings'.[90]

The death of one 'Fatma Robenson-Bahri' was announced briefly in a Turkish newspaper in May 1948.[91] In spite of problems with her health, she had lived to the grand age of ninety-three. According to Ahmet Robenson, his mother was buried in Sultantepe ('Sultan Hill'), a conservative district of Üsküdar on the Asian side of Istanbul.

*

Unlike the lives of other Robinsons mentioned in this book, Hannah's uniquely spanned the second half of the nineteenth century and the first half of the twentieth century. She was witness to a revolution – the Young Turk Revolution of 1908, which would eventually result in the overthrow of Sultan Abdülhamid II a year later. The forced abdication of the sultan, with whom Hannah had cultivated close ties, did not appear to have a marked impact on her well-being in Constantinople. Two of her sons would be casualties of the First World War, but Hannah was a survivor. She had already emerged unscathed from what was obviously an unhappy and disastrous marriage to Eliahie Bosche. Hannah was highly adaptable, resourceful and resilient. The deaths of Yakup and Abdurrahman notwithstanding, it seems that Hannah was left almost untouched by the turbulent and violent events of the *fin de siècle*, which culminated in the final dismemberment of the Ottoman Empire.

In sharp contrast, Hannah's daughter Gertrude Eisenmann, who lived in Wilhelmine and Weimar Germany, would be a tragic victim of the new Europe that emerged in the first decades of the twentieth century.

4

Gertrude Rodda/Eisenmann:
A Racing Amazon

Aide-toi et le ciel t'aidera
(Help yourself and Heaven will help you)
Jean de la Fontaine, *The Carter in the Mire*

Introduction
Surprisingly, none of the Robinson family members living in Turkey were aware of Hannah's daughter Gertrude and her sporting achievements. This is all the more difficult to grasp given the contacts between Gertrude and her mother and her half-brother Ahmet. Gertrude also maintained communications with Emily Robinson, the wife of Spencer Robinson's son Minick, but I do not know if she preserved links with other London-based relatives of her mother. There was an awareness among relatives in Turkey that a branch of the family lived in Germany, and rumours circulated that one of their German relatives was a 'countess' who lived in a grand house situated on a large country estate there. Although I knew that Gertrude married a certain Max Eisenmann, I did not connect Hannah's daughter with the famous sportswoman called Gertrude Eisenmann until I came across an article from 1905 in the magazine *The Motor Way*. This opened up a new and unexpected avenue for research which eventually led to correspondence with Gertrude's granddaughter Gertrud.

The name Gertrude Eisenmann is well known in select German motorbike and car racing circles. Gertrude fleetingly enjoyed celebrity status in her adopted homeland in the years leading up to the First World War, and she remains a cult figure today. Renowned for her

133

general sporting prowess, accounts of Gertrude's success and, indeed, her personal life, present a likeable, plucky and adventurous young woman. One Dutch newspaper of the time, describing how in her motoring exploits she would attempt to tackle mechanical problems herself rather than seek help from others, employed the above phrase of la Fontaine, the seventeenth-century French poet and fabulist, to refer to Gertrude.[1]

Although not, strictly speaking, a Robinson herself, Gertrude's personal story adds another dimension to the family history of the Robinsons. In this case, a confident and independent-minded young woman ventured from England to seek new opportunities abroad. Guaranteed financial security provided her with a springboard to receive an education in Germany, pursue her own calling and lead a separate life in a country where none of her relatives lived. Unfortunately, as in the case of other members of her family, Gertrude's life also had its share of difficulties as well as achievements. Her life ended on a particularly tragic note, and following her death her German Jewish husband suffered persecution under the Nazis.

Many questions remain unanswered concerning Gertrude, and there are frustratingly long gaps in the narrative of a life cut short. I was able to gather some written information from Gertrude's granddaughter living in Germany. Other details have been collected from newspaper reports, Gertrude's own observations, and the little personal correspondence that is available. They reveal a spirited and self-made woman who was endowed with a definite sense of humour.

The Formative Years

Did Gertrude spend time in India after the death of Dr Geoffrey Pearl, her presumed father? One article implied that she may have spent part of her youth in Bengal. Referring to Gertrude's initial claim to fame for her successes in cycling, it was noted that 'the sporting blood of her Anglo-Indian ancestry soon evinced itself in her once she was free of her teacher's shackles'.[2]

What is clear from the 1881 census is that in her early childhood Gertrude was attended to by Mary Pearl Watkins, the grandniece of Dr Pearl. After the death of Dr Pearl in 1884, it is possible that Gertrude was brought up at Purdis Farm in Nacton near Ipswich. This was the residence of Pearl's niece, also called Mary, who had married the wealthy Suffolk farmer, estate agent and valuer Joseph Watkins. Mary Pearl Watkins most probably also lived with her father at Purdis Farm in the late 1880s. In the period between 1887 and 1889, Mary was enrolled as an art student at the Ipswich School of Science and Art.[3] Mary married at the relatively late age of thirty in September 1891.

As a prominent member of the local Woodbridge Board of Governors, Joseph Watkins devoted much of his time to providing welfare for impoverished and illegitimate children. He was one of the three friends, executors and trustees mentioned in Dr Geoffrey Pearl's will. Given the close ties of Joseph Watkins and his daughter with the Pearl household, it is quite feasible that Gertrude spent a period of her childhood and early teenage years with the Watkins family in Suffolk before Gertrude's mother returned to England from India.

Gertrude was certainly with Hannah in Brighton at the time of the census in 1891, and she attended her mother's wedding in Liverpool in November of that year. In one of his letters to Gertrude, Ahmet Robenson recalled how in Brighton it was he who walked into the sea 'like a naughty boy – with his boots and stockings on' while she was fishing.[4]

However, what was also clear from Ahmet Robenson's correspondence with his half-sister, dated January 1924, was that the two had until recently been out of touch for a considerable period of time. He had to inform her that it was he and not Minick Robinson who had recently contacted her and that Minick, Spencer Robinson's son from his first marriage, had died the previous year. Ahmet noted how, in her reply to his earlier message, Gertrude had said that she was 'longing to know' all about the family. Ahmet had the painful task of revealing to her that his two brothers had died in the war. On a much more pleasant note, he also disclosed how his sister Maud had married and had children and was living in Constantinople. Ahmet asked about Gertrude's husband and child, adding that he thought her daughter was 'now quite a grown-up young lady'.[5] This indicated that he and Gertrude had been in communication at some point before this latest exchange.

According to the last will and testament of Dr Geoffrey Pearl, substantial funds were bequeathed to Gertrude, the 'reputed daughter of Hannah Robinson'. The trustees were instructed to use £5,000, of a total personal estate of approximately £38,000, to invest in securities, shares and bonds for 'the maintenance, education and benefit' of Gertrude. On reaching the age of twenty-one, or when she married before that age, the trustees were to pay to Gertrude any accumulations together with £500 from the original £5,000. The remaining £4,500 would continue to be invested, and any income from this sum would be passed to Gertrude 'for her separate use'. Upon her death, the £4,500 was to be divided equally between her children when they reached the age of twenty-one. Finally, it was noted that these provisions for Gertrude 'shall be in addition to any other provisions I may have already made for her'. These 'other provisions' were not specified.

This generosity shown by Dr Pearl strongly suggests that Gertrude was indeed his daughter. Gertrude could benefit from a financial safety net and follow her interests, pursuing a life which none of her mother's immediate relatives in Bow or Bethnal Green could have imagined.

It appears that Gertrude did not spend much if any time with her mother in Constantinople. Certainly, Gertrude was not in the Ottoman capital when her mother was subjected to sustained abuse by Eliahie Bosche. What I do know, from information gathered from a magazine article, is that in her youth Gertrude was sent to Germany to learn German. This education would have been quite expensive. In the 1890s, there were a number of establishments in Germany which 'offered instruction in the German language for daughters of gentlemen'. It is not known why Gertrude received an education in German. Gertrude decided to make Hamburg her home 'on gaining her majority'. Long before her marriage, she was famous in German cycling circles using Rodda, not Robinson, as her surname. While making Germany her adopted home, it was noted that 'she is English so far as her birth, extraction and an almost overwhelming love of sport can make her'.[6]

Gertrude and Max Eisenmann

At the start of the twentieth century, a boom in trade and a dramatic surge in population growth had resulted in Hamburg becoming the world's third-largest port after London and New York. The shipping magnate Albert Ballin headed the Hamburg–America Line, which then boasted that it was the biggest transatlantic shipping company. Vast quantities of goods were loaded onto vessels docked at the port. There was also a substantial movement of people at the time as individuals fleeing from persecution or in search of adventure came from across Germany and continental Europe in order to continue on their journey to the American continent. As 'Germany's Gateway to the World', Hamburg had become a major cosmopolitan centre. In this environment, new industries and businesses were established and quickly prospered.

Gertrude Rodda married Max Eisenmann – like Ballin, a successful German Jewish businessman – at a registry office in Fulham on 26 July 1901. Fourteen years older than Gertrude, Max was born in Heidelberg in December 1861. His father, Julius, was also a well-to-do entrepreneur. Julius died at the age of fifty-five in 1885. Max's mother, Adelheide, lived long enough to witness her son's marriage to Gertrude, eventually passing away at the age of seventy-two in 1911. Both father and mother were buried at the Bergfriedhof in Hamburg.

In 1890, Max had married Alice Bella Simonson, the daughter of another German Jewish businessman, Herrmann Simonson, who had stakes in the shoe industry. The couple had two children before they divorced. Olga was born in October 1891 and Fritz Julius in June 1893. Alice died in Hamburg in September 1932.

As a young man, Max also made a name for himself as a sporting personality. He participated in gymnastics and wrestling tournaments in Germany and abroad. Much of his youth was spent in London and in Paris. He was a prominent member of the well-known Hamburg-based rowing club Allemannia, which was founded in 1866.[7] Max also developed an interest in road and motor sports and took part in various competitions. A keen racing cyclist himself, in 1895 he established a company in Hamburg to sell bicycles. Max Eisenmann & Company imported bicycles from the US and from Humber & Co. Ltd of Beeston, Wolverhampton and Coventry. Humber bicycles were particularly well known at the time for their quality. By 1897, Max Eisenmann & Company was the first firm to import automobiles from the UK to Germany.[8] As well as becoming a car dealer, the company also sold motorbikes. By 1900, Max Eisenmann & Company was advertising itself as the first business to open a garage in Hamburg.[9]

It is not known when, where and how Gertrude and Max first met. They could have been introduced to one another in Hamburg or they may have encountered each other in England given Max's business interests there. What is clear is that Gertrude had already made a name for herself in Germany as a cyclist before her marriage to Max. Mistakenly reported as being an American lady rider, a cyclist of 'the weaker sex', the press noted that a Miss Gertrude Rodda, as an amateur, had in 1900 applied for and been granted a licence from the French Society of Athletic Sports. This was evidently the first of its kind to be issued.[10] Gertrude and Max obviously shared common interests.

At the time of their marriage, Max and Gertrude gave as their places of residence the addresses of two different boarding houses on Beaumont Crescent in Kensington. In the case of Gertrude, the columns of the marriage certificate referring to 'father's name and surname' and 'rank or profession' of the father were both left blank. The two witnesses to the marriage were Frederick Hatton, the 'family solicitor' of the Robinsons, and Ida Mary Lintott, the previously mentioned wife of William Bernard Lintott.

Gertrude and Ida Lintott may have been on close terms for a long period. It is possible that Ida regularly made the trip to Hamburg to visit Gertrude. Certainly, in October 1899, the forty-nine-year-old Ida Lintott, married and living in London, had departed from Hamburg to London on board the *Olivia*. I wish I could have discovered more about the relationship between Ida and Gertrude, bearing in mind the ties between William Bernard Lintott and Mary Ann Rodda, the sister of Gertrude's mother. Unfortunately, there are no details available about Ida's life following her tour of America in the mid-1880s with the cast of Miss Mary Anderson's company. My attempts to learn more by contacting relatives of William Bernard Lintott were unsuccessful.

Did Gertrude's mother and other members of her family, based at the time in Constantinople and London, attend the wedding in 1901? Indeed, did any brothers or sisters of Spencer Robinson participate in the ceremony? It is perhaps unlikely that Hannah and her family would have made the long journey from Constantinople to Fulham. What is clear, though, is that only months after her marriage, Gertrude was made a shareholder in Max Eisenmann & Company.[11]

Motoring Amazons in a Men's World

The 'New Woman' of *fin de siècle* Europe was regarded by many men, and indeed women, as a threat to women's hallowed role as mothers. The term was purportedly coined by the Irish feminist writer

Sarah Grand, in an article published in 1894. Grand referred to women 'awaking from their long apathy' and declared that 'the day of our acquiescence is over'.[12] Posing a challenge to the conventional Victorian view of motherhood and womanhood, the New Woman was looked upon as someone who was dangerous and a threat to the status quo. The term 'new', though, was vague and could not be defined with any precision. To some, however, these early feminists conjured up images of sexual decadence, if not deviance.[13] They were not perceived as proper women, whatever that may have meant. Those pioneering women who took up cycling, motorcycling and automobile driving were often, in effect, looked upon as examples of New Women who had dared to set themselves loose from the family household. Women may have experienced a sense of liberation in riding a bicycle or steering a motor car, but some commentators felt that these were irresponsible young ladies who posed a menace to a world that was dominated by men and had until recently been accepted as such.

Bertha Benz, the wife of the pioneering automobile designer Carl Benz, has gone down in history as arguably the first woman to drive a motor car. One evening in August 1888, without her husband's knowledge, Frau Benz, together with her two teenage sons, embarked on the 106-kilometre drive from Mannheim to Pforzheim in the Patent Motor Car built by Carl Benz. The ostensible reason for the trip was a visit to Bertha's mother. In reality, Frau Benz was determined to prove to her overcautious husband that his patented vehicle could actually travel such a long distance. With no service stations available to provide petrol, Bertha was forced to top up on supplies of 'ligroin' – as petrol was then known – from chemists along the route. Without the power and thrust to negotiate steep ascents, mother and sons had to dismount and push the vehicle uphill at times. Totally exhausted, the three would have failed to reach their destination had it not been for the exertions of two willing young farmhands who helped push the Patent Motor Car over the final climb.[14]

In spite of the celebrated adventure of Frau Benz, at the turn of the century, motorbikes and automobiles were undoubtedly regarded as the prized playthings of a male-dominated world. An article in *The Times* in 1907 claimed that it was 'difficult to reconcile the practice of motor-driving with the feminine lot and temperament'.[15] In the 'male-generated discourse' at the time about whether it was fit and proper for ladies to ride bikes and cars, there was much discussion about women's lack of physical strength, emotional maturity and technical know-how. There was also extensive debate over what negative impact there might be on women's health, and in particular on their reproduction capabilities. Scepticism, if not outright hostility, was directed at the 'motoring amazons' who dared to attempt to break into this men's world. Such women were seen as 'socially suspect'.[16] Motorcycles were looked upon as 'particularly inappropriate vehicles' for women.[17] As for automobiles, would the ladies be strong enough to crank a car handle? Would their vanity prevent them from wearing suitable clothing and getting their hands dirty?[18]

Campaigns were initiated to attempt to encourage ladies to drive electric rather than gasoline cars on the grounds that they were cleaner, quieter, more comfortable and easier to handle.[19] The automobile manufacturer Henry Ford purchased an electric car for his wife Clara. However, many women refused to operate electric cars, which were more expensive, limited in range and speed, and regarded as much less exhilarating to drive.[20]

Following the exploits of Bertha Benz, there were a few famous and adventurous women pioneers who took to the road, such as Camille du Gast in France and Dorothy Levitt in Britain. These women needed monetary backing or independent means given that car ownership at the time was very expensive and only for the privileged few. Levitt, for example, was born to a wealthy Jewish family, and led a 'bachelor girl' lifestyle, waited on by two servants in her pad in London's West End.[21] Initially, female motorists were a small, elite group. The inaugural meeting of the Ladies' Automobile Club in London in April 1903 mustered only seventeen participants. By 1909, however, membership had increased to around 400.[22] In Germany in 1903, only one woman was a member of the German Automobile Drivers' Association (the DMV – *Deutsche Motorradfahrer-Vereinigung*). Founded in that year, the DMV then had a membership of almost 1,000. By 1910, only 2.5 per cent of the 7,100 members of the Imperial Automobile Club (the KAC – *Kaiserlicher AutomobilClub*) were women.[23]

In Germany in the first decade of the twentieth century, there were three 'motoring Amazons' who attracted particular attention – Lilli Sternberg, Emilie von Opel and Gertrude Eisenmann. All were financially supported and encouraged to drive by their husbands, who were German car manufacturers or dealers. Lilli Sternberg was the wife of Dr Alfred Sternberg, who established the Protos car manufacturing company in Berlin in the late 1890s. Lilli, perhaps ironically driving an Opel, was the first woman to drive single-handedly along the whole route of the Prince Heinrich Trial in 1910 – named after the kaiser's brother, who was an avid motoring enthusiast. Emile von Opel, the wife of the famous car manufacturer Heinrich von Opel, also competed in time trials and car rallies.

Gertrude herself had sufficient resources to participate in competitive cycling before meeting her husband. However, the financial outlay required to maintain an automobile and take part in speed trials and car rallies across Europe was another matter. In practice, at the turn of the twentieth century, very few women would have had the means and access to drive automobiles and compete in international competitions without the backing of rich partners who were often themselves key players in the motor industry.

Given their elite backgrounds and privileged circumstances, most early women motorists were not directly involved in political movements pushing for women's suffrage, access to education, reforms to divorce laws, free access to contraception and abortion, etc. Many motoring women were not politically confrontational. Rather, they enjoyed driving as a social pastime.[24] However, exclusion from competing in specific competitions or from membership of particular automobile clubs solely on account of their gender may have prompted certain women motorists to pursue agendas which had more political overtones. The Suffragette movement itself would have been keen to win the public support of the early female drivers.

Intentionally or not, the exploits of early women motorcyclists and motorists did play an important role in the 'history of feminist activism'. Challenging the commonly held assumption at the time that a woman's place was in the home, the activities of the early female motorists attracted much media attention. Driving at the time was a highly public spectacle, with the motorist sitting high up behind the steering wheel in an open vehicle. A number of these New Women, including Gertrude, did publish newspaper accounts or full-length stories of their motoring experiences. The most widely publicised of these accounts was Levitt's *The Woman and the Car: A Chatty Little Handbook for all Women Who Motor or Want to Motor*. In effect, this was a manual advising female motorists how to dress, carry out car repairs without the need of assistance, and comport themselves in a manner which at the same time preserved their femininity. In their writings, the early female motorists showed what it might mean to be a modern woman, challenging views about women. In such a context, they were thrust into the wider debates over femininity at the start of the twentieth century and they were engaged, in effect, in a form of political action, even if they were not fully aware of this.[25] Suffragettes, themselves, also attempted to recruit female motorists to promote their publicity campaigns. Decked automobiles were exploited as public platforms upon which leading suffragettes made impassioned speeches.

Gertrude 'rapidly gained fame' in northern Germany, first as a cyclist who rode 'for speed and comfort, in bloomers'. She reportedly toured nearly the whole of Europe 'on her wheel'.[26] But, it was through motorcycles that Gertrude attracted more international attention, making use of her links with the firm *Naeh-und Strick Union* (NSU), nominally the Sewing and Knitting Union.

Established in the 1870s, NSU originally produced knitting equipment. However, by 1885 the company, based in Neckarsalm in Baden-Württemberg, had started to manufacture safety bicycles. Turning its focus to selling bicycles, the firm halted its production of knitting equipment. In 1901, NSU produced the first motorised version of their bicycle. After further rebranding of the business, two years later the company developed the first 'true' motorcycle with a 2.5 horsepower (hp) engine. In her racing exploits, Gertrude provided NSU with much favourable publicity. She became the first motorcyclist riding an NSU bike to win the 660-kilometre Eisenach–Berlin–Eisenach road race. While triumphing in the race she set a new record for a 2 hp motorcycle with an average speed of 42 kilometres per hour. Talking almost as if she was giving a sales promotion for NSU, Gertrude explained that the NSU bike, with its engine and frame, had 'everything you can reasonably ask for'.[27]

Gertrude Eisenmann became known in Germany as *Die Meisterin des Motorrads* ('The Champion of the Motorbike'). Her first actual competition was a relay race in Stuttgart. Without any training, she won a silver medal in the last relay. Gertrude later explained, 'I became a motorcyclist for the fun of the thing.'[28] She took part in a number of motorbike races. As the only lady competitor in the Munich race of the Herkommer Konkurrenz, held in the German Automobile Week in

August 1905, she finished a highly commendable fourth.[29] And, in the Hamburg–Hedersleben road race, held in the same year and for 4 hp motorcycles, it was reported that she would have won the event 'had not unscrupulous rivalry severed the tires of her tricycle'.[30] At the time, Gertrude was apparently surprised by the amount of public attention she was receiving. Declaring that the praise she was receiving was not justified, she added that just as 'nobody wonders why a duck swims', there should be no fuss over women riding motorbikes.[31]

Gertrude was equally known for her presence behind the wheel, often in the make of cars sold by her husband. The English press portrayed her as a serious threat to their local heroine, Dorothy Levitt. The two clashed in June 1908 in the gruelling nine-day Prince Heinrich Trial, which extended over 1,260 miles across Germany. Of the 130 starters in one of the best-known long-distance rallies, there were only three women including Levitt and Eisenmann. According to a newspaper report, Gertrude's 'Prince Henry car' looked like 'a rakish racer'.[32] Max Eisenmann also competed in car trials against his wife. In August 1906, on the second day of the competition for small automobiles held at Bielefeld, Max came first driving a Belgian-made Minervette, with his wife placing third after finishing four minutes later in another Minervette.[33]

Clearly, Gertrude had a real enthusiasm for motor racing. In 1904, Germany was chosen to host the then annual Gordon Bennett Cup. This very prestigious international race was named after James Gordon Bennett, the owner of the *New York Herald*, who provided the trophy which was given to the winner of the rally. A suitable course needed to be prepared for the proposed eliminating trials for the rally. It was Gertrude who scoured northern Germany and plotted what she believed to be an appropriate route for the trials. She then drove Baron Rudolf von Brandenstein, the general secretary of the German Automobile Club (AvD – *Automobilclub von Deutschland*), around the circuit. Ultimately, the course would not be used as the trials did not take place due to the scarcity of entries.[34]

Baron von Brandenstein had close ties with Kaiser Wilhelm II. The kaiser had taken up a personal interest in motoring; he was apparently the one who selected the course for the 1904 Gordon Bennett Cup race, which ran around a castle in the Taunus region near Frankfurt. After extending his patronage, in 1905 the AvD was renamed the

KAC. In the same year, working together with the kaiser's brother, Prince Heinrich, the baron was appointed secretary of the German Volunteer Automobile Company, an automobile corps organised along military lines and modelled on the British motorised corps.

Gertrude appeared to know Baron von Brandenstein quite well. In March 1904, the two were photographed in their individual cars on the Lüneberger Strecke before the departure from Salzhausen to Garlstorf, two towns in the district of Harburg in Lower Saxony. In his Berlin-made Protos Rennwagen, the baron was watched by a group of children. Behind the baron in her 14 hp Cudell car was Gertrude, possibly consulting a map with a male official. Given her connections and rising fame, it is quite possible that Gertrude may have been introduced to the kaiser.

Enhancing her celebrity status, in the years before the First World War Gertrude competed in other races and participated in other sideshows such as matching her motoring abilities against the speed of early biplanes.

From Hamburg to Frankfurt, and Back Again

In the early 1900s, a literature developed in Germany on the theme of driving for leisure while also appreciating nature and culture. This was when cars were not very reliable and the chauffeur often had to contend with the forces of nature. The German poet and Impressionist writer Otto Julius Bierbaum was one of the leading proponents of this 'road-trip literature'. He became famous for his motto: 'Drive, don't race.'[35] Railways were condemned for crowding passengers into closed and cramped compartments. Slaves to the constraints of the railway timetable, these passengers had effectively become hostages on trains which trundled between fixed points on the map. In contrast, motor-touring liberated the driver and his or her passengers from such shackles. As with the horse-drawn vehicles of yesteryear, the occupants of the motor car were exposed to the elements and free to travel along any road, thereby experiencing more directly the pleasures of rural and urban life.

Gertrude's published thoughts and observations about a road trip she made in Germany was essentially an early contribution to this literature on the romance of the motor car and the interaction between machine and nature.[36] Generally regarded as the first guidebook for motorists in Germany, Bierbaum's famous work *Eine empfindsame*

Reise im Automobil von Berlin nach Sorrent und zurück an den Rhein
(*A Sentimental Journey by Car from Berlin to Sorrento and back to the Rhine*) was published in 1903, the year Gertrude undertook her tour of parts of Germany. Gertrude was not simply a speed merchant; she wrote about themes and events which Bierbaum would have understood. In particular, her expression 'Like the people and their customs' would have resonated with the Impressionist author.

Much can also be learned about Gertrude's character from her own personal recollection of the 2,000-kilometre tour she undertook by car in 1903. Five years earlier she had actually cycled along most of the route. Accompanying Gertrude on the trip from Hamburg to Frankfurt and back was her trusted pet English terrier, Dickey, who as a mascot travelled with her on many car journeys.

The 'motor watchdog' was an essential accoutrement for many early lady (and in some cases gentleman) automobile drivers. As well as providing entertaining company, they also served as guard dogs, protecting items, including motor car rugs, from being stolen when the chauffeuse briefly stepped out of the car to visit the shops or call on a friend. Only certain breeds of dog were suitable. They had to be reasonably sturdy but not too large. Long-haired dogs were not appropriate given the amount of dust they would have accumulated in an open vehicle. Bulldogs were apparently a popular choice, but they were susceptible to the cold. Poodles were also favoured. Some car owners were accompanied by other pets on their travels. These included a cat, a parrot and a pig. Perhaps most unusual of all was the American lady who shared her car with her pet penguin.[37]

'Master Dickey', to give him his full name, was 'one of the most famous motor-dogs in Germany'. Evidently, he had the 'sweetest possible temper on all occasions' except when a stranger approached the car of his mistress when he was on guard duty. As Frau Eisenmann was prone to drive her car 'unconcernedly through days of downpour, hail and snow', Dickey had to be dressed for the part, as a 'weather proof and chill-resisting motorist'.[38] Goggles, hoods and neat-fitting dust-coats were essential items of the motor dog's regalia. Boots were another feature.

The sixty-eight-year-old Frau Schrader was the second passenger on Gertrude's road trip. The wife of one of Max Eisenmann's associates, she had never left Hamburg. The three made the journey in the French-produced 10 hp Dion-Bouton car. The Dion-Bouton was affectionately named 'Töff Töff' ('Choo Choo') by Gertrude. A full account of the journey is described by Gertrude herself in a six-page piece for an Austrian newspaper.[39] The story is recounted in a humorous and colourful manner as Gertrude transported Frau Schrader and terrier stage by stage from town to town across Germany. She had resolved to go ahead with the trip to attend the races in Frankfurt after brushing aside her husband's concerns that neither he nor a mechanic would be available to accompany her on the journey. Max was worried enough to remove the headlamps from the car so that Gertrude would not dare to risk driving by night. Gertrude had the skills and know-how to identify what was wrong with the vehicle when problems arose, and she occasionally repaired the car herself. This did not prevent a number of interested male on-lookers from offering the chauffeuse their support. Pedestrians she passed asked if they could join her on her journey. Completing the first leg of her trip with a stopover in Hannover, she was watched by a large crowd as she parked her vehicle in the garage of Herr Wagener. The owner of the garage enthused that he could not have wished for better publicity.

Along the journey, Gertrude and her companion had to negotiate steep mountain climbs and steer along roads blocked by horse carriages or wandering farm animals. On one occasion, Dickey sprang out of the car to bark at an especially obstreperous goat. Another time, the terrier attacked and killed a goose and hen; Gertrude felt obliged to compensate the farmers for their loss.

By chance, the ladies picked up a gentleman hunter at Kassel who revelled in the novelty of being driven by a lady motorist. Arrangements were swiftly made for his overcoat and shotgun to be despatched separately by train so that he could proceed with his lady companions to Rothenburg. In another encounter, Gertrude recounted how a group of officials crossing a bridge on horseback refused to give way to her. She suspected that this was because there was a woman behind the driver's wheel. When they eventually arrived at Frankfurt, an officious attendant insisted that Gertrude should vacate the car to allow the driver to take the vehicle to the nearby parking place. The attendant was taken aback when Gertrude countered by saying that she was the driver and how could he not see that this was the case.

On the return journey, in another bruising encounter, seeking to park her car in front of a hotel, Gertrude clashed with a coachman who stubbornly refused to move his carriage. While recounting the incident, which could only be resolved with the intervention of staff of the hotel, Gertrude referred to the coachman as a 'dickhead'.

Returning to the outskirts of Hamburg, Frau Schrader became highly emotional at her imminent homecoming. In contrast, Gertrude noted that she could happily have repeated the drive right away. Max said of his wife that she 'can never have enough'. He added that perhaps she would only be content after she had toured the world by car. Gertrude, however, chose to disagree.

The English press enthused about Gertrude's story, which they noted was written 'in sparkling and fascinating style'.[40] They also reported how Gertrude had brought her lady passenger home safe and sound and that the journey was completed in 'a highly respectable time', adding that 'few ladies could beat this record'.[41] The media evidently continued to be obsessed with speed, although the road trip was certainly not intended to be a time trial.

What is also evident from Gertrude's account is that she was a determined and bold young woman, able to calmly handle any obstacle thrown in front of her. Full of a zest for life and keen to assert herself in what was an obviously male-dominated world, Gertrude also appeared to take confidence from her social standing. She did have a temper. Other sources have noted that 'a certain Mrs Gertrude Eisenmann' was known 'for shooing away awkward coachmen by firing her revolver'.[42] Apparently, Gertrude did not need to resort to the use of a revolver on her round trip from Hamburg to Frankfurt. However, she may well have possessed such a weapon. Certainly, her contemporary Dorothy Levitt was known for always carrying a pistol for self-defence.

Gertrude retired from competitive racing before the First World War. She gave birth to a girl, named Georgina. In her later years, Gertrude was mentioned in the local media from time to time. She also gained some further recognition as a highly accomplished horsewoman, being covered in newspaper reports of some equestrian events.

There are a few letters available in which one can catch at least a glimpse of the nature of Gertrude's interaction with other members of her family in Turkey and in England. In a letter addressed to 'Gerty' in April 1928, Ahmet Robenson wrote how he had received her last letter 'with very great pleasure' and that 'mother also liked it'. He went on to say that she had not written him often and that their mother had received fewer than a dozen over the years, and none for some time. Her half-brother extended an invitation for her to visit them in Smyrna (Izmir) whenever she could, 'especially after so many years'. Ahmet signed the letter off 'Your loving brother "Toto"' – obviously a term of affection, the origins of which are unclear.[43]

Sometime in 1931, Gertrude had visited England and had met with Emily, the widow of Minick Robinson (the son of Spencer and Isabella), who was living in Southsea. Their encounter was described in a letter Emily wrote to Maud, the daughter of Spencer and Hannah Robinson. 'She is very nice, and we had quite a nice time together,' noted Emily, but problems over money were raised by Gertrude. In her letter, Emily wrote that Gertrude believed that 'quite a lot of money' had been left to her mother. Gertrude wanted this to be shared between the family and that 'she hoped to get the money owing to her'. Emily speculated that Gertrude may have read about the money in one of the English newspapers and asked Maud if she had heard about it.[44]

Spencer's last will and testament had noted that all estates and effects were to be left to his wife for the benefit of her and their children. Perhaps most, if not all, of this money was actually consumed by Hannah in her dalliance with the Brighton lodging house, her doomed marriage with Bosche, and in her later life in the Ottoman Empire and Turkey. Certainly, Hannah and her third husband had appeared eager to wrest control of assets left by Spencer's first wife, Isabella. However, Gertrude herself was a major beneficiary of the Geoffrey Pearl estate. Married to a rich businessman, Gertrude was probably in much less need of family money than her half-brother, Ahmet. Whatever the case, doubts and concerns raised over the use of Spencer's legacy caused friction within the family and Gertrude appeared to be at the centre stoking these tensions.

Gertrude Eisenmann tragically died on 15 January 1933 in Hamburg. The circumstances behind her death are unclear. Only one day before her death she had participated in an equestrian event which had attracted media attention.[45] According to her granddaughter, Gertrude was upset at Nazi threats to seize control of her husband's factory and had taken her own life. However, this seems difficult to reconcile with developments in Germany, and in Hamburg in particular, at that time. The death certificate merely noted that she had died free from any outside interference. Her death remains a mystery.

Max Eisenmann & Company

What happened to Max Eisenmann and his company following Gertrude's untimely death? The firm, which had originated as an importer and seller of bicycles, had developed in the first decades of the twentieth century to become a major car dealer. Briefly, between 1905 and 1907, the company had produced its own automobiles. Two makes of Immermobil produced on French lines were manufactured in Hamburg. In 1921, the business's main facility at Wandsbeker Stieg in Hamburg became the first installation and repair shop for the Bosch Company. Extensive customer service could be provided to automobile owners. Maintenance and repairs were offered together with the sale and installation of Bosch car service products. This filled a gap in the market at a time when there were few car dealerships and filling stations. This pioneering after-sales service had the full support of Robert Bosch, the founder of the Bosch Company.[46] Max Eisenmann's business would certainly have benefitted from the prestige of providing the first Bosch car service in the world. Six years later, a Bremen branch of Eisenmann & Company's Bosch car service was opened.[47] Fritz Julius, Max's son from his first marriage, had stakes in Eisenmann & Company and in the late 1920s he worked as a commercial agent for the enterprise.

Max Eisenmann himself became a towering figure in the Hamburg Automobile Club. One of the founder members of the club in 1905, he was the only living founder member at the celebration of the club's twenty-fifth jubilee in 1930.[48] He also served for many years as a regional head for the General German Automobile Club. In short, Max Eisenmann was a very well-known figure in German motoring circles. He was also one of a number of prosperous German Jewish entrepreneurs in Hamburg who were destined to fall victim to Nazi rule.

Jews living in Hamburg had enjoyed the benefits of a largely tolerant local regime in what had become a major trading hub. With its window to the outside world, by the mid-nineteenth century Jews had formed a thriving and active business community in the port city. As prosperous merchants they formed a part of the higher social echelons, although they were not completely politically, culturally and socially integrated with the wider local society. Nevertheless, Hamburg was an attractive location for German Jews and by the start of the First World War the community in the port city numbered around 19,000.[49]

Hitler came to power, initially as head of a coalition government, on 30 January 1933. However, the Nazis had been steadily accumulating support well before Hitler was appointed chancellor, and anti-Semitism had also been on the rise for some time as Germany experienced a period of prolonged economic recession. Jewish graves and synagogues in Hamburg were desecrated as early as 1931. On 17 July 1932, the Nazis organised a 'monster demonstration' in Altona, a town neighbouring Hamburg and a traditional stronghold of Marxists. In the clashes which ensued on 'bloody Sunday', eighteen were killed and over sixty injured as snipers targeted people from rooftops. According to one commentator, 'this changed the political landscape in Hamburg'. Although still relatively few in number, Nazi thugs were emboldened and took to the streets to engage in acts of violence.[50] By the time Gertrude perhaps committed suicide, the Nazis clearly posed a serious threat to the fledgling German democracy of the Weimar Republic, although the closure of Jewish businesses in Hamburg was still some years off.

The position of Jews in Germany started to deteriorate rapidly after Hitler consolidated his position in power following national and local elections held in March 1933. A Nazi-organised boycott of Jewish businesses on 1 April 1933 had little obvious impact in Hamburg as the campaign attracted little support from the townsfolk.[51] For a period, Jewish companies were still able to function under the Nazi regime. However, the situation dramatically worsened with *Kristallnacht* on 9–10 November 1938, when Jewish stores and businesses were targeted in brutal, coordinated attacks throughout Germany, including in Hamburg. The showroom of Citroen cars in Hamburg was vandalised – the company had once been under Jewish ownership.[52] Following this orchestrated spate of violence, Jews in Germany were excluded from economic life. Jewish owners were stripped of their property rights. They were forbidden to operate retail and mail-order businesses and workshops after 1 January 1939. The compulsory Aryanisation, or liquidation of Jewish enterprises in Germany, was carried out rapidly in late 1938 and early 1939. Many Jews in Hamburg were forced to emigrate.[53]

Robert Bosch, the head of Bosch Company, refused to dismiss on 'racial grounds' any employees working in his various sales establishments. The influential entrepreneur had good working relations with Hjalmar Schacht, the Nazi minister for economic affairs since July 1934, but Schacht was removed from office in the autumn of 1938. Bosch was determined to protect the rights of his workers.[54] However, even the Jewish companies affiliated with Bosch could not escape the events of 9–10 November 1938. Max Eisenmann & Company was one of the Jewish firms Aryanised in the 1938–39 period. It was taken over by Alfred Kruse, a factory manager with operations in Stuttgart. Earlier, in 1937, under pressure from the Nazi authorities, Max Eisenmann had been forced to sell the Bremen branch of Hamburg Bosch Services to the businessman Franz Seeling for the sum of 45,000 Reichsmarks.[55]

What exactly happened to Max Eisenmann in the wake of these developments is not fully clear. There are reports that he, together with another employee of the Bosch Group, had emigrated.[56] If this was indeed the case, Max later returned to Germany. According to his death certificate, he died of a perforated ulcer in Hamburg on 27 May 1940. His granddaughter has noted that the family had earlier written a letter to the authorities complaining that the money he was allowed to receive was not enough to cover for the costs of his medicine.

Interestingly, on the death certificate it is stated that while Max was originally Jewish, he had later converted to evangelical Lutheranism. This begs the question, why would Max have decided to change his religion? In general, conversion to Christianity did not protect Jews from persecution by the Nazis. Jews were targeted on grounds of race. Referring to race, the Nuremburg Laws of November 1935 had forbidden future marriage between Germans and Jews, and Jews could no longer be citizens of the Reich.

This chronology of events indicates that at the time of Gertrude's death the Nazis were not about to seize control of Max Eisenmann & Company. However, given the climate of the time, by early 1933 her husband (and Gertrude herself perhaps, as the wife of a prominent Jew?) may have been subjected to threats and abuse from Nazi officials.

*

Even though Gertrude and her husband may have been the casualties of political developments, I do not know if Gertrude herself consciously dabbled in political affairs like her half-brother, Ahmet Robenson. In her writings and in her quoted pithy remarks, it is possible to observe a woman who was aware of her gender and who was determined to be regarded as an equal to her contemporary male peers. However, I have no evidence that this was transferred to a willingness to embrace, for example, the Suffragette cause. Given the financial means at her disposal and the backing of a prosperous husband, Gertrude did come from a privileged background – unlike many other members of her family living in London. However, she did not come across as one of those wealthy women who took to driving merely as some form of hobby or pastime. The impression I have is that Gertrude was a competitive soul endowed with a particular spirit, independence and sheer go-gettedness.

To all intents and purposes, Gertrude was an outlier in the Robinson family. An illegitimate child who was brought up by others, Gertrude does not seem to have enjoyed close relations with her mother, who had effectively abandoned her when she was an infant. Mother and daughter appeared to spend very little time together. This did not prevent Gertrude from establishing separate ties with Ahmet Robenson, and, perhaps surprisingly, she also went out of her way to meet with relatives of Minick Robinson, Spencer Robinson's son with his first wife, Isabella. I do not know if Gertrude also attempted to initiate contact with other members of the Rodda family. Her links with Ida Lintott suggest that a channel existed through which Gertrude could have grown closer with her mother if she had so wished.

Afterword

Becoming a teacher in a *gymnasium*, in 1934 Gertrude's only daughter, Georgina, married Fritz Parschalk and went to live in Mannheim. Fritz worked for a Swiss group of electrical engineering companies known as Brown, Boverie and Cie. Founded in Switzerland in 1891, the group had opened offices in Mannheim in 1900. The German branch became a key part of the group and was responsible for much of its sales. It produced technical equipment such as motors, generators, steam and gas turbines, transformers and electrical parts for locomotives. It seems that Fritz played an important role as a leading electrical engineer in the Mannheim branch, and some of his work was patented.[57]

The couple had two children: a boy named Alfred and a girl named Gertrud. Their son, born in 1935, visited Southsea in 1953 and was warmly received by the family of Spencer Palmer Robinson, son of Minick and grandson of Spencer Robinson. The family connection between relatives in Germany and Turkey may have been weakened after Gertrude's death. However, as late as the mid-1960s, Ahmet Robenson, the son of Hannah and brother of Maud, who by that time had relocated to the US, had informed Maud's granddaughter Gülperi that they had relatives in Germany and she should visit them. The suggestion was not taken up.

5

The Robenson Brothers:
In Peace and at War

The mystical bond of brotherhood makes all men brothers.
Thomas Carlyle, *Critical and Miscellaneous Essays*

Introduction

Abdurrahman (Eugene B.) and Ahmet (Peel Harold), two of the remaining three sons of Spencer and Hannah Robinson, became famous in the Ottoman Empire for their pioneering activities in sports and Scouting. Much less is known about the eldest brother, Yakup (Spencer John Bernard). There is very little information about Fevzi, the son of Hannah/Fatima and Ahmed Bahri, and the early life of Hannah's daughter Maud (Adile) largely remains a closed box.

Life for the young Robenson children would not have been easy. They were uprooted from India after their father's death to return to England, and were soon on the move again to Constantinople with a new stepfather. Perhaps none of the children were permanently scarred by the memories of living for a brief period with Eliahie Bosche. Ahmet, certainly, would have been too young to remember the traumatic first months of his mother's residence in Constantinople. It is not clear how much contact was maintained with their half-sister Gertrude and with their other relatives back in England in these first years.

Most of the available information on the brothers concentrates on Ahmet Robenson. Details of the young Ahmet, and, indeed, depictions of his later life, have led me to conclude that he could be regarded as both a liberal internationalist and a frustrated patriot. Living in an Ottoman society which was struggling to come to terms with its identity at a time of bubbling social change, Ahmet

Robenson appeared to believe sincerely that it was in the interests of his adopted homeland to cooperate with the wider international community and embrace some of the new social and political outlets that this engagement with the outside world offered. In particular, in the pre-war period, this found expression in Ahmet's avid desire to introduce various sports and Scouting to Ottoman society. These attempts were at different times frustrated and co-opted by the authorities of the day.

Late Ottoman society was uncertain to what degree it should accommodate or keep itself aloof from new ideologies, fashions and tastes, which often originated from Europe at the end of the nineteenth century. Islamic and Islamist, Turkish and Pan-Turkic views, as well as Western and reformist ideas, were present and vying for influence in the Ottoman Empire. In such changing times, those who were perceived as outsiders or foreigners might be respected or suspected and questions raised over their identity and their loyalty.

The last years of the Ottoman Empire were a time of tumult and change. Rival powers sought to secure territorial, political and financial advantage from the increasingly indebted and beleaguered 'Sick Man of Europe'. Within the empire, nationalist groups, especially in the Balkans, aimed to gain autonomy if not independence. Other internal political forces sought to curtail the powers of the authoritarian Sultan Abdülhamid II and introduce genuine constitutional reforms while simultaneously attempting to preserve the unity of the empire.

Reforms had been introduced in 1839 in an effort to modernise the Ottoman Empire and ensure its survival (the so-called *Tanzimat*). These measures covered important sectors such as the military, the bureaucracy, the judiciary and education. With the Constitutional Revolution of 1876, Sultan Abdülhamid II had been pressured to agree to the drafting of a first constitution and the formation of an inaugural parliament, but these advances were abruptly curtailed with the Russo-Ottoman War of 1877–78. The Young Turk Revolution of July 1908, principally instigated by junior officers in the Macedonia-based Ottoman Third Army and supported by various political groups including the Committee of Union and Progress (CUP), resulted in Abdülhamid II being forced to recall parliament. There then followed a period of turbulence and great uncertainty. An attempted counter-revolution led by a motley group of Islamists and liberals was crushed in April 1909. Abdülhamid was deposed and replaced by his brother, Mehmet. After the imposition of martial law, a string of unsuccessful governments, parliamentary elections and wars in north Africa and then in the Balkans, the CUP seized power in a coup on 23 January 1913. With the sultan in effect a mere figurehead, control lay in the hands of the Central Committee of the CUP.

Throughout this period, relations between the Ottoman Empire and Britain fluctuated. Given Abdülhamid's close ties with Germany, Britain initially appeared to benefit from the Young Turk Revolution. The Anglophile Kamil Pasha was appointed grand vizier in August 1908, and the new constitutional regime that was established looked to Britain for support and guidance.[1] Relations deteriorated, however, when the British Embassy in Constantinople was suspected of backing the failed counter-revolution after Kamil Pasha had been forced to resign. It was rumoured that Britain had close ties with the liberal opposition leader, Prince Sabahattin.[2] Nevertheless, on the eve of the First World War, Britain still enjoyed firm links with the ruling authorities in the Ottoman Empire. Eager to secure oil concessions in Mesopotamia, British officials had influence over the customs and finance branches of administration and also over the ministries of justice and the interior, while a British admiral served as chief naval adviser and was in effective command of the Ottoman fleet.[3]

The priority of the CUP was to ensure that the Ottoman Empire remained secure and intact. To further these goals, leaders of the CUP toyed with stressing variants of Islamic, Ottoman or Turkic identities. The concept of 'Ottomanism', in which ethnic and religious communities could unite under the umbrella of a common Ottoman citizenry, was jettisoned after defeat in the Balkan Wars in 1912–13.[4] Eager to limit the role of the empire's Christians, who had traditionally dominated trade and industry, the CUP increasingly stressed the importance of associating the state with the Muslim majority. And, quite quickly, this concept of the Muslim majority became closely tied to the idea of a Turkish identity.[5] This stress on Turkish nationalism was promoted by a diverse range of thinkers. For example, Yusuf Akçura, a political activist born in Russia to a Tatar family, emphasised the importance of a common Turkish ethnicity. On the other hand, Ziya Gökalp, a member of the Central Committee of the CUP after 1912, underlined the significance of a shared Turkish culture. Gökalp stressed the importance of language, religion and education as well as morality and aesthetics. The Turkish Hearths (*Türk Ocakları*) were founded in 1911 to propagate Turkish and pan-Turkic nationalism through schooling and by mobilising popular opinion.

In this time of uncertainty and upheaval, life may not have been comfortable for the Robenson brothers. Attempted moves by the authorities towards allowing more open political debate, and officials being more receptive to outside influences, would have provided the brothers with opportunities. However, the CUP's growing emphasis on supporting the Muslim majority and the Turkish elements within the Ottoman polity may have posed difficulties for children with an English background, whose parents could have been regarded as potential spies. Moreover, after a period of relatively close ties between London and Constantinople, the outbreak of war between the Ottoman Empire and Britain in 1914 must have placed further strains on the Robenson/Bahri family.

Sporting Achievements with Galatasaray

The date was Sunday 25 November 1906, and the time was two in the afternoon. Galatasaray kicked off their inaugural official football match in the Istanbul Sunday League. Having belatedly registered to play in the league, Galatasaray were given special permission to participate in the tournament. Galatasaray were the first team to play in the league with an eleven which included no British expatriates and no representatives of the Levantine community – i.e. Europeans, primarily engaged in trade, who had settled in the Ottoman Empire. The opponents were British sailors from HMS *Imogene*. Founded in 1904 by the crew members of the small special service vessel which was attached to Britain's Mediterranean Squadron and which served as the ambassadorial yacht, HMS *Imogene* football club had been the champions of the Istanbul Sunday League in the league's opening 1904/05 season. The venue for the eagerly anticipated match between Galatasaray and HMS *Imogene* was the Priest's Field – now the site of the stadium of the Fenerbahçe football club. The match referee was James La Fontaine, the Levantine businessman who had helped establish the Istanbul Sunday League and who had personally ordered from Britain the shield which was presented each year to the champions of the league.

The Galatasaray players were all young students. Some of them had lacked the funds to purchase appropriate boots and socks for the game. A day before the match, sums of money were hastily collected and the necessary gear was procured from G. A. Baker Ltd, a reputable retail store in downtown Pera in the Ottoman capital. The players were kitted out with a strip of deep blue and yellow, ironically very much like the colours worn by the current Fenerbahçe eleven. Galatasaray had yet to lay claim to their famous red and yellow outfit.

Earlier in the year, the Galatasaray students had played two friendly matches against the local Kadiköy team. Composed mainly of Greeks born in Constantinople, the experienced Kadiköy outfit had thrashed the students, winning 11-0 and 7-0. But before the start of the 1906/07 campaign, the Galatasaray squad had been reinforced with the recruitment of several new players, including Ahmet and Abdurrahman Robenson.[6]

Immediately before the start of the match against HMS *Imogene*, the Galatasaray players encountered another serious problem: there did not appear to be a nearby facility in which the team could change. Stripping off in the Priest's Field itself was clearly out of the question. Fortunately, a local Muslim Albanian, Zeynel Ağa, came to the players' rescue. The Albanian ran a small pudding shop quite close to the Priest's Field. In return for making use of a shed in the back yard of his shop, the Galatasaray team agreed to buy a number of Zeynel Ağa's puddings. The makeshift locker room was full of the mixed aromas of puddings and the smells of a nearby chicken coop.

Ahmet Robenson was Galatasaray's goalkeeper. A tall, impassive figure, famous for his huge hands, Ahmet was undeniably the best goalkeeper in Constantinople at the time. His older brother, Abdurrahman, had become the team's established left-back. A very educated and cultured footballer who was always smiling, Abdurrahman was also known for his boundless energy. Unfortunately, though, he had had to withdraw from the match at short notice as he was suffering from one of his periodic severe headaches.

In a hard-fought encounter, the match ended with honours even, with the score at 1-1. The Galatasaray team had rallied to equalise after HMS *Imogene* had opened the scoring. This was a very creditable result for the Turkish debutants.[7]

*

Contemporaries of the Robenson brothers have provided us with glimpses of their personalities. According to Ruşen Eşref Ünaydın, a writer and journalist who also served as ambassador to the UK, Yakup was the tallest of the three and acted like a tough guy. In contrast, Abdurrahman was very reserved, while Ahmet was the most friendly, warm and active of the brothers. All three were depicted as Muslims who had been thoroughly Turkified. Ünaydın had heard that there was talk of another younger brother (Fevzi), but he had never met him.[8] In contrast to Ünaydın, one of Ahmet Robenson's students at the Vefa School in Constantinople noted that he and his peers could not figure out if their teacher was English or Turkish.[9] Another journalist and popular sports commentator, Burhan Felek, noted that Yakup was an uncomplicated chap who wanted to be everyone's friend.[10]

First enrolled in the Kuleli Military High School upon the recommendation of Field Marshal Mustafa Zeki Pasha, the three brothers were later transferred to Galatasaray High School in Constantinople upon the wishes of their mother, who was keen to ensure that her sons would lead lives as civilians.[11] According to family members, while at Galatasaray, one or more of the brothers may also have spent a period of study at the Sorbonne in Paris. Since 1868, Galatasaray High School had followed the French *Lycée* model and most of the teaching was in French. The French education system had been held in high esteem by the Ottomans ever since Sultan Abdülaziz visited France in 1867.

Following graduation, Ahmet became a physical education instructor at Galatasaray High School and his brother Abdurrahman took up the same position at Istanbul Boys' High School. Ahmet also taught physical education for a time at the Vefa School, which was also in the Ottoman capital. Both brothers were products of the system of sports teaching introduced by Ali Faik, one of the first Muslim gymnastics instructors in the Ottoman Empire. Faik had received his training at the Central Gymnastics Institute in Berlin in the mid-1870s, before commencing teaching at Galatasaray High School in 1879. According to Faik, gymnastics was important both for the body and soul and helped to produce a complete, well-rounded individual.[12]

Ahmet Robenson was influenced by Faik's teachings and philosophy. In an article published in July 1913, Ahmet discussed the importance of playing games in the education of primary school children. He believed that games led to children being raised as clear-thinking, strong-minded and able-bodied individuals. According to Ahmet, participation in games encouraged thinking and innovation, taught children how to protect themselves and learn to compete, and laid the foundations for rule-making and administrative behaviour in their later adult lives.[13]

This emphasis on individual- and society-centred education was to some extent influenced by Western views on pedagogy. Childhood education was to be geared towards producing healthy adults equipped with the necessary problem-solving skills. The value of this for the nation was obvious. Ahmet's views would later be developed by educationalists in the Republic of Turkey.

Ahmet and Abdurrahman were both proficient sportsmen, and the two played key roles in introducing new sports to the Ottoman Empire and helping to popularise them. They were also regular contributors to sports magazines, journals and newspapers.

The Ottoman authorities had objected to Muslims playing football. The sport was seen as distracting the youth from pursuing their education. Officials also frowned upon the wearing of inappropriate dress, with the wearing of shorts seen as tantamount to nakedness. Football was viewed as an expression of an alien, Western culture. More significantly, it was seen as blasphemous by the religious rulers. The kicking of a ball too closely resembled the actions of the killers of the Prophet Mohammed's grandson in AD 680 when they kicked around the severed head of Hussein after the Battle of Karbala.[14]

In this environment, it was not safe for Muslims to play football. The first football matches in the Ottoman Empire were played by teams composed of Englishmen, Greeks, Jews and other minorities. The first Turk known to play football was Fuad Hüsnü Bey, a student at the Naval Academy. In 1899, he formed a team composed of Muslims called the Black Stockings. The team had deliberately chosen an English name in an attempt to prevent the authorities from banning them from playing. However, news of the Black Stockings was soon reported to the authorities and the team was forced to disband.[15] A few years later, before their admission to the Istanbul Sunday League, Galatasaray players were apparently arrested for playing football, but Ahmet Robenson was quickly released because of his English background.[16]

Restrictions on Muslims were gradually lifted and the playing of football was openly encouraged after the CUP gained power. Galatasaray Football Club, now known as the Galatasaray Sports Club, was established in October 1905. The three Robenson brothers became members. Ahmet Robenson was ninth on the list of founder

1. A window in St Helen's Church, Saxby, Lincolnshire. It was made around 1870 in memory of John Wheelwright Robinson. (Courtesy of J. Guffrogg & J. Hannan)

Above left: 2. William Henry 'Abdullah' Quilliam, founder of the Liverpool Muslim Institute. Quilliam knew Hannah Robinson well.

Above: 3. Mustafa Zeki Pasha, field marshal and loyal servant of Sultan Abdülhamid II. He provided refuge for Hannah Robinson's young daughter Maud (Adile).

Left: 4. Sultan Abdülhamid II in his youth. He provided important financial support for Hannah Robinson and her family.

Above: 5. Fort Graham, Gnatong.

Below: 6. Darjeeling. (Courtesy of S. Shankar)

Above: 7. Ahmed Bahri and the sons of Hannah Robinson (Fatima Bahri).

Left: 8. Maud (Adile) Robinson.

Right: 9. Gertrude Eisenmann.

Below: 10. Galatasaray's 1908/09 football team. Ahmet Robenson is standing in the white top.

11. Ahmet Robenson, dated around 1911.

12. Members of the camel corps pictured sometime before the Battle of Katiya. Yakup Robenson is standing on the left in battle dress. (Courtesy of the Library of Congress)

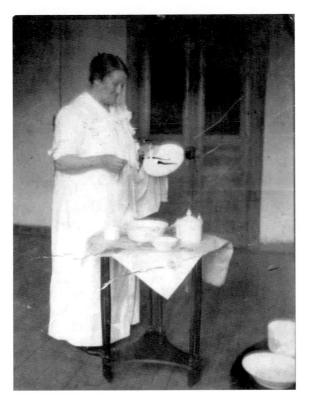

13. Hannah Robinson (Fatima Bahri).

14. Ahmet Robenson and members of family at the Lyndhurst estate, Tarrytown, New York.

15. Bernard Robinson.

16. Ahmet Ceylan.

members published after the club was legally registered as an association in 1913. Ahmet soon became a legend, playing for the team in its early years through to the First World War. As goalkeeper, Ahmet starred for the team that won the Istanbul Sunday League for three consecutive seasons between 1908 and 1911. His brother, Abdurrahman, featured as an outfield player in the championship-winning team of 1908/09, in which season only three other teams competed. Over the next two seasons the league expanded in size, and Galatasaray won all of the fourteen games played in those years. In those games, Galatasaray scored fifty-one goals and, with Ahmet Robenson as goalkeeper, conceded only four.

Ahmet Robenson also played an instrumental role in introducing basketball to the Ottoman Empire. Basketball remains a very popular sport in today's Turkey, and the name 'Ahmet Robenson' is almost synonymous with the game. Ahmet helped translate the rules of basketball into Ottoman Turkish. He organised one of the first basketball matches played in the Ottoman Empire in 1911 at Galatasaray High School. The story goes that he came across an American magazine on basketball and decided to try playing the game with his students. The magazine article was short on details of the rules of the sport, but Ahmet Robenson attempted to improvise and organised a game. Two makeshift paper baskets were placed on opposing walls of the gymnasium and twenty pupils were rounded up. The game had to be abandoned with the score at 8-3 as most of the players had injured themselves. There were bleeding noses, swollen eyes and battered faces. The sport was then largely forgotten in the Ottoman Empire and was only played occasionally at American-run educational institutions such as Robert College in the capital and the American College in Smyrna. However, Ahmet Robenson helped revive interest in the sport after the First World War.[17]

Field hockey and hockey played on a rink with roller skates were also popularised in the late Ottoman Empire by Ahmet Robenson. Hockey was first played in Istanbul by English expatriates in 1910. Ahmet Robenson participated in the first roller-skating hockey match in Constantinople, in which Galatasaray played against a team named the Scorpions.[18] The Scorpions were formed from American crew and troop personnel from the USS *Scorpion*, the US ambassador's steam yacht, which was stationed in Constantinople. The Scorpions were hard-running, tough opponents, but the Turkish roller skaters were more than able to hold their own. The match was held at the Skating Palace in Beyoğlu in Constantinople – later the site of the famous Emek cinema. The Skating Palace had been opened in 1908 and soon became a social venue frequented by Ottoman youth and those from the Levantine community. The rink was surrounded by bars where spectators sat on wicker chairs padded with palm leaves. When the rink was used by the general public, a jazz band often played on a balcony to help set a rhythm for the roller skaters. Roller-skating hockey became fashionable for a period and a roller-skating hockey league was briefly established between 1923 and 1925.[19]

The first tennis court was built at Galatasaray in 1909, and Ahmet Robenson was involved once more. In 1913, members from Galatasaray sports club (including Ahmet Robenson) and the rival Fenerbahçe club toured Anatolia to introduce various sports. The delegation visited towns such as Izmit, Eskisehir, Konya, Isparta and Smyrna. Hockey exhibition matches were played.[20] By 1914, Ahmet had been appointed captain of Galatasaray's rowing team and had been elected to the executive board of the Galatasaray High School. He and Abdurrahman were also members of Galatasaray's eight-man tug-of-war team, which won national championships in 1913 and 1914.[21]

Another claim to fame for Ahmet Robenson was that he was arguably the first football journalist in the Ottoman Empire. While still playing competitive football, he penned commentaries on the football leagues for the local magazine *Terbiye ve Oyun*.[22]

The role of Ahmet Robenson in pioneering a range of sports in the Ottoman Empire is recognised in present-day Turkey. His background and possible contacts outside the empire helped him to become, in effect, a sports ambassador. In contrast to the period under the rule of Sultan Abdülhamid II, the CUP, especially after defeat in the Balkan Wars, was keen to stress the importance of football and other sports in helping to shape a healthy and robust Ottoman youth. The government's focus on physical well-being would be particularly evident in the Scouting movement, which Ahmet and Abdurrahman Robenson also helped introduce to the Ottoman Empire.

In the Footsteps of Baden-Powell
Is it possible to be at once a patriot and a liberal internationalist? The terms 'patriot' and 'patriotism' have been used by some in a

derogatory sense and have become increasingly equated with hard-line nationalism. The terms appear to be directly juxtaposed with the notion of 'liberal internationalism', with the latter's focus on interdependence, greater cooperation, and the importance of interactions between peoples. While being a 'matter of sentiment', patriotism may also refer to the 'privileges' and 'responsibilities' of citizenship. In this context, patriots are the first to experience and suffer shame if their country is perceived to be responsible for any serious wrongdoing.[23] Attachment, in this instance, is not necessarily to a particular nation or ethnic group, but a homeland or territory. These emotional bonds may also be connected to certain institutions and organisations associated with this homeland or territory, such as a particular school or sports team.

'Internationalism' is linked with the notion that we are, and should be, part of a broader community than that pertaining to one nation or state. The term 'liberal internationalism' has strong normative connotations in that it seeks to promote understanding, peace, prosperity and freedom between states, nations and peoples.[24] It is possible, then, to be both a patriot and a believer in liberal internationalism. Working together with the international community and being receptive to new and developing cultural and social ideas and movements could bolster one's homeland and enable it to perform a more effective role on the global stage.

Arguably, given his personality, background and upbringing, Ahmet Robenson was ideally positioned to feel at home both in the wider world and in the Ottoman Empire. With one foot in each, he was able 'to straddle the global and local'.[25] However, authorities at the local level could misinterpret the efforts of a liberal internationalist and view his words and deeds with suspicion. Officials could also seek to co-opt, if not blatantly hijack, his work in order to pursue their more limited nationalist goals and ambitions. This seems to have been the case with regard to Ahmet Robenson, the CUP and the Scouting movement.

The world's first experimental Scout camp was organised on Brownsea Island off Poole in Dorset in the first week of August 1907. Around twenty boys from different backgrounds were selected. A number came from the public schools Eton and Harrow, and others were chosen from nearby towns. Training included topics such as woodcraft, observation, discipline, health and endurance, chivalry, saving lives and patriotism. A rigorous daily programme included wake-up at 6.00 a.m. and prayers before breakfast, with lights out at 9.30 p.m. after prayers. The boys did not wear uniforms, but the four patrols which were set up were distinguished by shoulder knots of different coloured wool.[26]

General Robert Baden-Powell, proclaimed a 'hero' in Britain because of his role in the defence of Mafeking in the recent Boer War, organised the Brownsea Island camp. The sons of some of his friends had been invited to the experimental Scout camp. In 1908, Baden Powell's well-known book *Scouting for Boys* was first published; the Brownsea Island camp was a way to promote it. Drawing on his interest in military Scouting and on his personal experiences in the Boer War and service in India, Baden-Powell had come to believe in the importance of character-building, citizenship, patriotism, sports and health for the youth in the British Empire. Scouting apparently sought to help nurture respectable future citizens, although its critics also believed that the movement could be exploited for more sinister militaristic purposes. Baden-Powell's papers reveal that he sought to stress the peaceful nature of Scouting. However, it appears that this new passion came about —after he was frustrated in his attempts to reform the training of British cavalrymen to prioritise the building of individual character over drill-based work. It is also important to note that Baden-Powell had been an admirer of the Volunteer Force, Britain's part-time citizen army, and was eager for boys to practice marksmanship like the Volunteers.[27]

The importance of Christianity in the origins and development of the Scout movement in England has also been disputed. Certainly, church groups were attracted to the principles that Baden-Powell sought to instil in the youth, and prayers were a part of the daily routine of Scout camps, as seen on Brownsea Island. Baden-Powell himself, though, was not known to be particularly religious.

Scouting very rapidly attracted huge interest in Britain. In 1909, King Edward VII agreed to introduce the King's Scout Award. The following year, the Boy Scouts Association, along with a Girl Guide group, was established. By 1910, there were more than 130,000 Scout members in Britain and its colonies, and a further 150,000 in other countries. However, it was only after the war in 1919 and 1920 that Scouts and Guides in Britain initiated serious efforts to coordinate Scout activities globally.[28]

Ahmet and Abdurrahman Robenson helped set up some of the first Scout groups in the Ottoman Empire at Galatasaray High School and Istanbul Boys' High School in 1911.[29] They also established the first Scout camps. Ahmet played an influential role in encouraging the formation of the first Girl Guide group at the Haydarpasha İttihad School in Constantinople.[30] Apparently, the idea of introducing the Scouting movement was first hatched by Ahmet and other members of the Galatasaray Sports Club in June 1911 on an excursion to the then wooded area of Beykoz along the Asian banks of the Bosphorus. At Galatasaray High School, to plan his Scouting activities and hold meetings, Ahmet was allocated a special small room on the second floor, overlooking the large courtyard and next to the chemistry/ physics laboratory. Seriously dedicated to his work, he spent most of his nights in the week at school preparing Scouting lessons.[31]

Much-liked as a teacher, Ahmet Robenson was known to often lead his students on long hikes in the countryside. This was actually a custom at the time that was followed by other teachers and their pupils, and was seen as an important part of staff-student bonding. On one occasion, in April 1912, fifteen students from the Vefa School with their packed lunches accompanied Ahmet on a long trek to Kağıthane. Now an unattractive industrial suburb of Istanbul open to urban regeneration, before the First World War families were accustomed to picnic at Kağıthane and take pleasure boat rides along the clear waters of the Cendere stream which wound through the lush tulip fields. In the words of one of his students at the time, Ahmet Robenson was 'the man who made us love nature'.[32]

The Scouting movement was initially regarded with suspicion by Ottoman society. Questions were raised over the use of an English handbook. The uniforms worn by the first Scouts – short trousers and white tennis caps – also attracted negative feedback. Rumours spread that the movement was a vehicle used by the English through which Muslim children could be converted to Christianity.[33]

These objections were no longer raised when the ruling CUP leadership realised the value of the Scouting movement for building a healthy and disciplined Ottoman youth. The defeats and losses in the Balkan Wars of 1912 and 1913 had dramatically revealed the ill health of the Ottoman armed forces. Apparently, 90 per cent of men called up for military service were not fit for duty.[34] The CUP was forced to take action. The Turkish Strength Association was set up in June 1913 with the aim of creating a healthy and obedient Ottoman/Turkish youth. Most of the association's leading members were military officers who had served in the Balkan Wars. The association coordinated its work with the recently established Turkish Hearths.[35] The Turkish Strength Association also linked its activities with the Scouting movement. Scouting clubs for those aged between ten and seventeen were encouraged; the intention was for Scouts to move on to Turkish Strength clubs once they had reached the age of seventeen. In these clubs, the stress was on rowing and shooting practice under the supervision of officers of the Ottoman Army. Arms and ammunition were provided by the War Ministry.[36]

Further moves to centralise and institutionalise the shaping of a healthy youth fit for military service led to the formation of the Ottoman Strength League in May 1914. Unlike its predecessor, the Turkish Strength Association, which had been a private club, the Ottoman Strength League was a public body open to all, and schools were compelled to set up branches. It seemed that the goal was to prepare a 'nation-in-arms' along the lines advocated by Marshal Colmar Freiherr von der Goltz.[37] This high-ranking German officer had been an advisor to the Ottoman Army since 1908. The Ottoman Strength League absorbed Scout units which had been grouped together in the Ottoman Scout Committee in April 1914. The CUP leadership had invited Harold Parfitt, a British citizen who had headed the Belgian Scouting Organisation since 1909, to coordinate the Ottoman Scout Committee.[38]

In April 1916, in the middle of the First World War, the Ottoman Strength League was replaced by the Ottoman Youth League. The German officer Colonel Heinrich Leonard Emmanuel von Hoff was appointed its general inspector. All Ottoman male youth – including unschooled peasant boys – were forced to become members of the new body and Scouting organisations lost what little autonomy they still had.[39] In this changing environment, one of the CUP's leaders, Enver Pasha, was accorded the title of Chief Scout. What had commenced as a small number of voluntary Scouting groups set up by the Robenson brothers had rapidly been transformed into a mandatory and centralised production-line system set up to prepare a strong and obedient Ottoman/Turkish youth.

How did the Robensons react to this turn of events? They had initially responded to official calls for encouraging the spread of

Scouting groups throughout Anatolia by helping to form a branch in Bursa,[40] but would the brothers have welcomed the co-opting of the Scouting movement by the CUP leadership to serve what were nationalist and militarist goals? Parfitt was a guest at the first Scout camp set up by Ahmet Robenson for the Istanbul Boys' High School in Kilyos by the Black Sea in the summer of 1914,[41] which was unsurprising given Parfitt's prominent position in the Scouting movement in the Ottoman Empire. In a letter dated 26 July 1914, Ahmet Robenson invited students to apply to attend the ten-day summer camp. Only the nine top students from the school would be accepted. 'Good manners' and a 'pleasant character' were deemed essential prerequisites.[42]

More significantly, perhaps, in December 1915 Ahmet Robenson was photographed in his Scout's uniform together with members of the General Inspectorate of the Ottoman Strength League. Included in the photograph amid austere, fez-wearing officials was the then relatively unknown Colonel Mustafa Kemal, later founder of the Republic of Turkey, who had recently returned from the battlefields of Gallipoli, and Ahmed İzzet Pasha, who was destined to take command of the Ottoman Second Army in the Caucasus in the spring of 1916.[43] One should bear in mind that this was a time of war. The Scout units in Britain, for example, were also contributing to the war effort through activities such as guarding railway lines and monitoring the coastline, while the Army Cadets had greatly expanded in size and had formed branches in grammar schools. Baden-Powell had himself lobbied unsuccessfully for the deployment of Scout units to the battle front. Ahmet Robenson's support for the Ottoman cause through his past work with the Scouting units should therefore come as no surprise, even though he may have felt some unease over a conflict which pitted the Ottoman Empire, a member of the German-led Triple Alliance, against the Triple Entente backed by Britain.

As a side note, one cannot help being struck by the similarities between the energy and enthusiasm of the Robenson brothers in their sporting and Scouting activities in the Ottoman Empire and the tireless efforts of their father to help establish the volunteer militia in Spilsby half a century earlier. Baden-Powell's interest in the Volunteer Force should here be recalled.

In their social and cultural work, then, it seems that the Robenson brothers were making use of their experience, background and presumably contacts to help provide certain services and in so doing enable elements of Ottoman society to tap into wider cultural currents and trends. This may have initially raised suspicions among more conservative groups in the Ottoman Empire. The brothers would also have had to contend with the rising swell of nationalist feeling which was cultivated by the CUP leadership after the debacle of the Balkan Wars, when large stretches of Ottoman territory in eastern Europe were irretrievably lost. In such circumstances, in the months before the outbreak of the First World War, it must have been increasingly difficult to project oneself as a liberal internationalist and a patriot at the same time.

The Young Ahmet Robenson

Ahmet Robenson was not just an able sportsman and a professional organiser of social activities for the Ottoman youth. Like his brothers, he was also an accomplished linguist, fluent in English, French and Ottoman. Ahmet made full use of his language skills to secure other employment. In his youth, for example, he also worked as a guide and interpreter.

In the summer of 1909, the famous American journalist Herman Bernstein employed Ahmet as his guide and translator when visiting Constantinople to interview the Sheikh al-Islam, who was based there. The sheikh was the sultan's chief religious scholar. Bernstein interviewed many of the leading personalities of his time, including Leo Tolstoy, Albert Einstein, Leon Trotsky, Bernard Shaw and Auguste Rodin. Later in his career he would serve as US ambassador to Albania. Bernstein also received much acclaim for preparing a book which proved that the notorious *Protocols of the Learned Elders of Zion*, used by Hitler to justify the Holocaust, was based on forged texts.

In a lengthy article published in *The New York Times*, Bernstein referred to his companion 'Ahmed Robinson Bey', a former classmate of the son of the Sheikh-al-Islam. Bernstein's guide and interpreter was clearly familiar with the etiquette required of him on such formal occasions. Upon meeting Sahib Molla Effendi, Ahmet kissed the sheikh's hand and then performed a low bow when the sheikh indicated that they should be seated. In their conversation the sheikh, known for his liberal views at the time, declared that he was not sure if women would ever be emancipated in the Ottoman Empire. After the interview was over, Bernstein and Robenson were shown around the various departments within the Islamate. This included the room in which, a few months earlier, the *fatwa* that led to the deposing of Sultan Abdülhamid II had been issued.[44] Interestingly, the fact that Ahmet Robenson's family had been so closely connected with the recently deposed sultan did not appear to have had any negative repercussions for the young Ahmet. It appeared that he was able to circulate freely among the very people who had conspired in the overthrow of the sultan.

*

More significantly with regard to the personal life of the young Ahmet Robenson, I have found material which indicates that he was engaged at one time to a Mrs Martha May Thompson. The Foreign Office has records of a Mrs M. M. Thompson, of 165 Salisbury Road, Liverpool, inquiring about the whereabouts of a 'missing friend' in Constantinople. Dated 6 November 1917, and addressed to the Foreign Office, Mrs Thompson was 'extremely anxious' to learn about the whereabouts of her fiancé, Ahmed Robinson Bey, and to find out if he was well. She went on to explain that her fiancé was about twenty-seven-years-old and born in Brighton, and that his mother had married 'Major Fahri Bey' in the Turkish army. His mother was known at the British Embassy in Constantinople as 'Mrs Robinson'. All the family were known at the 'Yildiz Kiosk' (Yildiz Palace) to the officials and to some members of the royal suite.

At the outbreak of war, according to Mrs Thompson, 'Ahmed' was working as a pay clerk at the Post Centrale in Pera in the centre of Constantinople. He lived in the township of Marakem (today's Bakırköy) on the outskirts of the Ottoman capital. Mrs Thompson stressed that she would be quite satisfied not to communicate with him provided she knew that he was well. In her letter, though, she directs a number of questions to her fiancé: Where and how are you? Where is your mother and youngest brother? Is there any hope of you coming to England after the war? In the Foreign Office document, the reply to this enquiry was left blank.[45]

This communication raises a number of intriguing issues. I have no conclusive proof that Mrs Thompson was indeed Ahmet's fiancée, but she was obviously so concerned about his well-being that she sent a letter of enquiry to the Foreign Office even though Britain at the time was at war with the Ottoman Empire. The letter provides further evidence of the surprisingly close ties between the Robinsons/ Robensons and high-level Ottoman officialdom. Most illuminating, perhaps, was the reference to Ahmet working as a humble pay clerk in a post office. Had his career somehow dramatically plummeted, perhaps in reaction to the CUP assuming control of the Scouting programme? Had a well-known sports personality abruptly become a pen pusher in a nondescript clerical post?

Alternatively, Ahmet may have briefly worked with the Ottoman Post Office before becoming a sports instructor. There is evidence that he was employed as a civil servant at the telegraph centre in Pera. He was used as an intermediary, communicating between the Ottoman Post Office and the Union Factory in Birmingham which produced bicycles. The Ottoman Post Office had decided to purchase bicycles for its postal workers.[46] In September 1909, the security office of the local police made inquiries to the Ottoman Post Office about the effectiveness of using bicycles.[47] Quite possibly, then, Ahmet may have initially been contracted to work for the Ottoman Post Office upon graduating from Galatasaray High School.

But who exactly was Mrs Martha May Thompson? Here the story becomes even more interesting. She was the same Mrs Thompson who was responsible for the end of the legal career of Abdullah Quilliam, the founder of the mosque in Liverpool. The notorious divorce case of 1908 involving Mrs Thompson led to the closing of the LMI. Reluctant to return to England in the face of the ignominious collapse of the Thompson divorce case and the negative publicity that ensued, Quilliam had lingered in the Ottoman Empire for about eighteen months and had not returned to England until late 1909. The relationship evidently formed between Ahmet Robenson and Mrs Thompson seems to suggest that Quilliam had maintained contact with the Robinson/Bahri family in Constantinople over the years.

On 17 June 1907, Mrs Thompson had made a petition for divorce on the grounds that her husband, Enoch Griffiths Thompson, had committed adultery and had deserted her.[48] In her petition. Mrs Thompson outlined in detail a history of cruelty and violence dating back to the first weeks of her marriage. According to her testimony, Enoch Griffiths had first committed adultery in February 1900, a month before he then deserted her. The case was taken up by Quilliam, and on 16 January 1908 the decree nisi was awarded. Allegedly, on 31 May 1907, Mr Thompson had visited a brothel in

Glasgow and had sex with a prostitute named Susie Burns. A Mr George Evans was a witness to the act. However, the case was overturned and the decree nisi rescinded later in 1908 when it was suggested that Quilliam had not brought certain facts before the court. Investigations revealed that Evans had previously been employed by Quilliam as a clerk. Evans had evidently sought to befriend Mr Thompson and plied him with drink before leading him to the brothel. A Glasgow barman said that Evans had told him that Mrs Thompson had wanted to get rid of her husband because she was getting a man who would drive her about in his car.[49] The King's Proctor accused Mrs Thompson and her solicitor of attempting to frame Enoch Griffiths in order to secure the divorce. Quilliam was ordered to pay substantial costs and was later struck off the Rolls.

At the time when the King's Proctor had decided to look into the case of Mrs Thompson, Quilliam was in Constantinople following a summons from the sultan. Quilliam seems to have returned to England after the death of his wife Hannah in November 1909. Remarrying, and then later living with another woman, by 1912 Quilliam had adopted a new identity and had started to refer to himself as Henri de Leon. His ties with the Ottoman Empire had suffered a serious blow with the forced abdication of Abdülhamid. It is not clear what Quilliam was doing in the Ottoman Empire in the eighteen months prior to his return to England. His activities in the period between 1910 and 1913 were also unclear, although he may have returned to the Ottoman Empire from time to time. From 1913, Quilliam/Henri de Leon abandoned overseas travel and remained in England.[50]

There were rumours that Mrs Thompson and Quilliam had intimate relations. Quilliam had acquired a reputation as a womaniser and this would have been fuelled by society's perceptions of Islam at the time, with the lurid tales about the harem. Some sources have noted that Mrs Thompson had accompanied Quilliam to Constantinople in 1908.[51] Press reports in November 1908 stated that Martha May was believed to be 'in Turkey'.[52] It is possible, therefore, that the two may have been involved in some sort of relationship. For what other reason would an impoverished tobacconist from Liverpool make the arduous and costly journey to Constantinople?

Martha May Thompson was born Martha May Peters in January 1880 in Edge Hill, Liverpool, one of seven siblings. Her father was a musician and her aunt an unabashed preacher of the Bible. She married

Enoch Griffiths Thompson in January 1899 and in the following year the couple had a daughter, also called Martha May. Mrs Thompson lived and worked in Liverpool. At one time, she kept a tobacco stall at a railway station in the port city.[53] In the 1911 census, she was registered as living at 68 September Road, Liverpool, along with her two sisters and her eighty-two-year-old widowed aunt. Martha May was still listed as 'married'. Her occupation was listed as tobacconist's assistant. It is not known when Martha May returned to Liverpool from Istanbul. Perhaps she may have visited and stayed in Istanbul on other occasions, although clearly, she would not have been able to finance the travel herself.

Enoch Griffiths Thompson was born in Birkenhead near Liverpool in 1877. The son of a shipwright, Enoch Griffiths worked as a joiner's apprentice and carpenter before being employed as a ship's steward at the time of the divorce case. In line with a part of Martha May's testimony, at the time of the baptism of his daughter in April 1900 Enoch Griffiths had left Britain and was living in Yonkers, New York, with the family of his brother, William. He may have stayed in New York for some time as his name does not appear in the 1901 UK census. In 1911, Enoch Griffiths was living separate from his wife in Bootle, near Liverpool, with his father, who had been recently made a widower. The following year, Enoch Griffiths became father to a son, Victor. Eliza Harriet Phillips was the mother. It seems that Eliza did marry Enoch Griffiths some time before his death in 1920. Death records refer to an Eliza Harriet Thompson. This indicated, then, that a divorce may have been finally agreed which would also have enabled Martha May to remarry.

Little is known of the later years in Martha May's life. In 1939, the records somewhat confusingly refer to the 'widowed' Martha May Thompson living at 44 Garden Lane, Liverpool. Other occupants of the household were her daughter, a single unemployed domestic servant and one of her sisters, Emma, and Emma's husband, Robert Burne. Martha May eventually died in Liverpool in 1952.

I do not know exactly how and when Martha May met Ahmet Robenson. Perhaps Quilliam introduced the two when Martha May was in Constantinople in 1908. The tobacconist's assistant from Liverpool, who had most probably never travelled abroad, would presumably have welcomed contacts with a family in Constantinople which had close ties with England. It is difficult to envisage how a relationship between Martha May and Ahmet could have been sustained over a long period. Perhaps, Ahmet visited Liverpool on occasion. The relationship may have actually ended prior to the outbreak of war. Martha May did not appear to be aware of Ahmet Robenson's career as a sports instructor and Scoutmaster. Surprisingly, the Robenson family in Turkey were not aware of the connection with Martha May. Were the two ever actually officially engaged? We do not know. What is clear, however, is that Mrs Thompson had some knowledge of the Robenson/Bahri family. If the two had been engaged, the relationship had definitely ended by 1919 when Ahmet Robenson met his wife-to-be.

The relationship between Quilliam and the Robinsons/Robensons seems to have been a surprisingly long-lasting one. Hannah and her family get only a passing mention in the literature on the life of Abdullah Quilliam, and in the various writings on Quilliam no mention is made of the Robinson family's connection with the lawyer-cum-sheikh via Mrs Thompson. This seems to be another example of how the Robinsons' presence in the lives of key characters in history has been totally overlooked.

A Family at War

In war, a belief in liberal internationalism is invariably trumped by impassioned appeals to defend the homeland. The Robenson brothers heeded these calls to come to the defence of the Ottoman Empire, even though this meant that they would come into direct conflict with the nation of their parents (or mother, as in the case of Fevzi). Family members based in Turkey who were interviewed stressed how throughout the war the Robenson brothers felt an especial need to demonstrate their loyalty to the Ottoman cause. The brothers were quick to place themselves at the spearhead of any planned attack regardless of the risks involved. This may explain the possible death of Yakup Robenson leading a cavalry charge in the sands of the Sinai Desert.

However, stories referring to the exploits of the Robenson brothers in the First World War need to be handled with care. For example, there are references to a 'Feyzi Robenson' (i.e. Fevzi Bahri) serving as a military pilot. One account notes that 'Feyzi', also apparently a football player for Galatasaray, was injured in the war.[54] Another source erroneously alleged that when serving as a pilot he was killed on the Iraqi front by the British.[55] In contrast to his older brothers, very little is actually known about Fevzi – who was, of course, not a Robenson – although he certainly did not perish in the First World War. The exact nature of the death of Yakup Robenson is also the subject of some controversy.

There are many accounts relating to the Galatasaray High School alumni who gave their lives. In particular, there are narratives about famous Galatasaray footballers who fell on the battlefield. The firm bond between soldiers linked with Galatasaray was clearly important. With regard to the Robensons, there are Turkish accounts which are full of praise for the brothers and their choice to fight for the Ottoman Empire against their original homeland. However, some of these tales, presumably chiefly for propaganda purposes, have been embellished. One account, for example, explains in some detail how the Robenson brothers explained to their father (apparently still alive, converted to Islam, and renamed Abdullah) and mother (supposedly originally called Sarah) their decision to go to war on the side of the Ottomans. This was ostensibly after Abdurrahman had had an extensive talk with Hasnun Galip, a member of Galatasaray's football and hockey teams, about his desire to enlist in the Ottoman military. The story goes that Hasnun Galip had without success attempted to dissuade Abdurrahman from serving because of his English origins. Hasnun Galip was then called up and soon died on the Gallipoli front. This prompted Abdurrahman to decide to enlist together with his brother Yakup.[56] Hasnun Galip was indeed a casualty of the Gallipoli campaign, falling in battle on 21 June 1915.[57] However, Abdurrahman had actually enlisted with the Ottoman forces at the outset of the war.

At the start of hostilities, Ahmet and Abdurrahman Robenson received their initial military training while stationed at the Harbiye camp in the centre of Constantinople. Abdurrahman was well known among his company colleagues at the camp. A creature of habit, every night when lights were out and the toilets had been emptied, Abdurrahman would go to a wash basin in the lavatories and soak himself in ice-cold water. Each evening in the dormitory the men chatted among themselves. The loudest and happiest voice always boomed out from the far corner of the room where Abdurrahman sat.[58] These evenings of camaraderie came to an end with the posting of troops to the battle zones.

The Ottoman Empire had entered into conflict with Tsarist Russia in early November 1914 after attacking Russian shipping in the Black

Sea and shelling the Crimean port of Sevastopol. The CUP leadership was keen to reoccupy the Muslim provinces of Kars, Ardahan and Batum, which the Russians had annexed following the Russo-Ottoman War of 1877–78. Enver Pasha also harboured ambitions to connect the Ottoman Empire with other Turkic peoples in the Caucasus and Central Asia. The Russians were seeking to fulfil the longstanding dream of seizing Constantinople – the so-called Tsarigrad – for the Orthodox world.

The poorly equipped Ottoman Third Army suffered a major defeat at the hands of the Russians at the Battle of Sarıkamış (December 1914–January 1915). In scenes reminiscent of Napoleon's famous retreat from Moscow more than a century before, the Third Army withdrew in the face of hostile weather. There were no railroads in the region to facilitate movement. The Ottoman forces lacked proper clothing and food to cope with the harsh winter climate. Their Russian counterparts were too exhausted, though, to mount a pursuit and then storm the Ottoman garrison at Erzurum. The fortress only fell into Russian hands in February 1916.

In a moving letter addressed to his friend and fellow Galatasaray club member Ali Sami (later known as Ali Sami Yen), posted from Sivas (in today's central Anatolia) on 21 January 1915, Abdurrahman requested that in the event of his death a day of memorial should be held to commemorate the deaths of himself and other fallen comrades.[59] His wish would be fulfilled. Galatasaray remembers its war dead each year on 25 June.

In a later letter sent from Erzurum, dated 13 February 1915, Abdurrahman described to Ali Sami how he had undertaken a thirty-six-day journey across Anatolia to reach Erzurum. This indicated that Abdurrahman had not participated in the debacle at Sarıkamış. The letter also noted that his brother, Ahmet, would remain in Erzurum. Eager to hear of news, Abdurrahman urged his friend to send mail to him care of the Erzurum post office. According to an oft-quoted account, Abdurrahman spoke of how he wore the Galatasaray club emblem close to his chest and that if he died the emblem would be buried with him. The letter ended with the flourish, 'Long Live Galatasaray!'[60]

Abdurrahman later became a casualty of war. Many of the troops on the Russian Front died of typhoid as a result of contaminated food, water and clothing. Abdurrahman, though, evidently perished from the extreme weather. A victim of the bitter cold, his feet suffered from frostbite and then from gangrene. Abdurrahman's feet had to be amputated, but this did not save him. One of his comrades noted how Abdurrahman's death had a devastating impact on morale.[61] According to one source, quoting an article published in the sports journal *Spor Alem*, Abdurrahman passed away in the Bayburt hospital near Erzurum on 11 January 1916.[62] Other accounts note that Abdurrahman died on 11 April 1915.[63] In a scribbled note held by the family, Hannah/Fatima gives the impression that her son passed away in 1915.

In contrast to his brother, Yakup Robenson was probably killed in action by the British. Signing a secret treaty of alliance with Germany on 2 August 1914, the CUP leadership had fatally committed themselves to enter into war against the Triple Entente, which included Britain and France as well as Russia. The British decision to requisition two warships they had been building for the Ottomans, and which the Ottomans had paid for in full, had forced the CUP's hand. This was in spite of the close ties between the Ottoman and British navies. Yakup had reportedly fought against the British at Gallipoli some time in 1915. It seems that he fell at the Battle of Katiya, fought in the Sinai Desert in Egypt against the British on 23 April 1916.

Yakup had become a second lieutenant in one of the Ottoman Army's camel companies. Perhaps it was while he was in Jerusalem en route to Sinai that Yakup addressed a letter to his former Galatasaray classmate, Ali Sami. Yakup noted how his brother, Ahmet, had informed him of Abdurrahman's death. Resigning himself to fate, Yakup added that it would be up to God if he too would die or would live to become a hero.[64]

The first concerted effort by the Ottoman Fourth Army in February 1915 to seize control of the Suez Canal from the British had swiftly ended in failure. The heavily defended canal was an essential conduit through which Britain transferred substantial numbers of troops from India to the Egyptian theatre. The Ottoman objective in the spring of 1916 was the more limited one of grabbing control of territory on the eastern bank of the Suez Canal, which would be within artillery range of shipping using the waterway. In this context, the Katiya settlement and oasis, about 30 miles to the east of the canal, was an area of strategic importance. By March 1916, the British had commenced work on extending a railway and water pipeline from the town of Kantara on the Suez Canal towards Katiya.

According to one account, there was a certain degree of complacency among the British forces in the desert at that time. Settled in their oases, they assumed a 'picnic-like frame of mind', bringing with them their dressing tables and golf clubs.[65] Seeking to surprise the British units, an Ottoman force of approximately 3,500 was in the area, led by the German General Friedrich Freiherr Kress von Kressenstein. The Ottomans were determined to prevent the British from completing their engineering work. This Ottoman detachment included a unit of Ottoman regular camel troops, and the Hedjaz Camel Regiment, which largely consisted of Arab irregulars.[66] It is not clear to which force Yakup was attached.

Yakup Robenson was photographed, together with other officers of a camel corps, in the desert some time before the engagement at Katiya. In an almost surreal yet vivid image, Yakup is standing in battledress while second lieutenant Ali Halet (another Galatasaray schoolmate) is seated together with the apparent commander of the corps, Captain Sürreya Bey. The officers are refreshing themselves. There is a table laden with a teapot and cups. All appear to be in good spirits and full of confidence.[67] We do have a little information about Ali Halet. Apparently a courageous and diligent officer, according to one anecdote Halet loved his camels so much that he would willingly brush their teeth every morning.[68]

There is some disagreement over whether Yakup Robenson and his colleagues were killed in action on 23 April 1916 (Easter Sunday). One source that is used by several other commentators alleges that Yakup died in the Sinai Desert on 16 December 1916.[69] However, little of note happened on that date. The Ottomans were in retreat and were evacuating the town of El-Arish after their defeat at Romani in August 1916. British forces only entered El-Arish on 21 December.

It is quite likely, therefore, that Yakup Robenson and his colleagues were killed early in the morning of 23 April 1916 in one of two skirmishes. The camel units were split into two columns to attack enemy forces gathered at Oghratina and Dueidar.

The assault against the settlement of Oghratina marked in effect the first phase of the Battle of Katiya. Oghratina lay 5 miles to the east of Katiya. At Oghratina, two squadrons of Worcester Yeomanry – also known as the Queen's Own Worcestershire Hussars – were protecting a party of fifty Royal Engineers who were working on boring water wells. However, the Worcester Yeomanry had not had time to dig a proper trench to provide more security for the camp. British troops in the area had been dispersed quite widely and they had little intelligence with regard to the whereabouts of von Kressenstein's force. At 4.30 a.m., under the cover of mist, an approaching Arab camel company had been fired upon by the Worcester Yeomanry. General von Kressenstein immediately ordered a full-scale assault. However, the first attack was repulsed as the Ottoman force found it difficult to ascend the hill because of the soft sand. The Ottomans suffered 'numerous' casualties, even though the defenders only possessed one mounted machine gun. After two hours of intense fighting, what was left of the two squadrons of Worcester Yeomanry was forced to surrender. They had suffered the losses of eleven officers and 135 other troops.[70] Energised by their victory, the Ottoman force swiftly moved on to attack Katiya itself, which was guarded by Gloucestershire Hussars and another squadron of Worcester Yeomanry. Eventually, the Ottomans gained control of the oasis by mid-afternoon following further fierce fighting.

This series of encounters turned out to be a notable albeit relatively minor victory for the Ottomans. According to one contemporary report from the British side, the 'affair' at Katiya was a 'lamentable occurrence' with the total loss of three and a half squadrons of yeomanry.[71] At the time, Cemal Pasha, then the governor of Syria as well as one of the key leaders of the CUP, noted how the victory at Katiya 'raised the confidence of the troops to a remarkable degree'.[72] In practice, though, work on the railroad and water pipeline was only temporarily disrupted. Australians and New Zealanders later pushed the Ottomans back in a larger encounter in the Sinai Desert at the Battle of Romani in August 1916.

Another Ottoman attack against British and Indian units at a garrison post at Dueidar, about 10 miles south-west of Katiya, had been repelled on 23 April 1916. According to an official news correspondent attached to the British-led Egyptian Expeditionary Force, Dueidar was 'a pretty oasis on the old caravan route across the desert to Syria'.[73] A second company of camel riders had been despatched to Dueidar as part of a column led by Major Carl Muhlmann. This unit may have chiefly consisted of Arab irregulars that had been placed under Muhlmann's command and which would have been staffed by Ottoman officers. The German-led Ottoman/Arab unit of around 500 suffered eventual defeat at the hands of a battalion of the Royal Scots Fusiliers and a small number of Indian troops forming part of the Bikaner Camel Corps.[74] The Ottoman attack had been hindered by a thick, swirling mist, barbed wire and a strategically placed machine gun.[75] In the clash, there are reports of how Ali Halet was killed.[76] In total, approximately seventy-five Ottoman troops perished in the fiercely contested engagement and were buried on-site by the British.

Yakup Robenson may have fallen in the heated initial melee before the seizure of Oghratina. Although the Ottoman force had greatly outnumbered the British defenders and was much better armed, the nature of the terrain seems to have put the leading camel company at a serious disadvantage. Perhaps, in a tragic twist of irony, Yakup was killed in a clash with fighting units which bore close resemblance to the volunteer rifle corps that his father had helped set help several decades earlier. Traditionally, the yeomanry was a volunteer mounted militia whose ranks were filled by farmers and lower rural gentry. With the Territorial and Reserve Forces Act of 1907, yeomanry units such as the Worcestershires were to become the cavalry arm of the new Territorial Army, whose primary purpose was to defend the homeland. With the outbreak of war, such units volunteered to serve overseas.

If Yakup was, instead, a victim of the bloody skirmish at Dueidar, he would have been killed by a defending force which included regular British and Indian forces in its ranks. The Bikaner Camel Corps was a legendary Indian fighting unit, from the northern Indian state of Bikaner, under the command of the Maharaja Ganga Singh. The combat effectiveness of the Bikaner Camel Corps at Dueidar was praised at the time. According to a war correspondent present at the skirmish, half a dozen men of the corps had laid down in the open to bolster the Scots' line and had 'behaved with consummate coolness'.[77]

There are other disputed accounts, however, which claim that Yakup did not die in action but was instead sentenced to execution by the Ottoman authorities in December 1916 after being charged with treason. The Ottoman archives noted that Yakup was found guilty of passing intelligence to the British. According to other sources, he was accused of handing over sensitive information to the Americans about the Ottoman Empire's treatment of its Armenian subjects.[78] These stories should be handled with extreme caution. The Ottoman records, for example, also noted that Yakup Robenson was the son of a certain 'Abdullah Gevilyan'. Some Turkish historians believe that this Gevilyan was none other than Abdullah Quilliam! In contrast, websites linked to the Galatasaray Sports Club consistently refer to Yakup as a martyr. Members of the Robenson family living in Turkey today believe that the Robenson brothers at the time of the First World War were very much aware of the need to prove their loyalty to the Ottoman Empire. Rumours and tales of espionage were rife in the late Ottoman Empire. In the immediate aftermath of the war, Ahmet Robenson himself would be suspected of working as a British agent.

Ahmet Robenson survived the war. He was also based on the Russian Front for at least a part of the campaign. In a letter dated 14 March 1916, Ahmet sent to his former classmate Ali Sami a signed photograph of himself in army attire. He referred to himself as a member of the Third Army, a sledge instructor, and a member of the Galatasaray Sports Club.[79]

*

The loss of her two sons in the First World War must have grievously pained Hannah. I do not know Hannah's views on the war itself. Ahmet must also have suffered with the deaths of two of his brothers. With her two eldest sons the casualties of war, much closer ties may then have developed between Hannah and Ahmet.

Although there are frustrating gaps in the narrative of Ahmet's life, much more is known about him than his brothers, particularly in the period before the outbreak of war. For example, I do not know how Yakup occupied himself following his graduation from Galatasaray High School. There is very little information on Fevzi. Nevertheless, it is still possible to gain an impression of each of the three sons of Spencer and Hannah. Yakup comes across as a more gregarious and impetuous character. Abdurrahman appears occasionally more taciturn and reserved, although he could also be outspoken. Ahmet strikes one as being a warm, likeable person. In contrast to Yakup and Abdurrahman, one is also able to compare the young Ahmet with his persona in his middle and later years.

Ahmet and Abdurrahman Robenson, in particular, left their mark on a rapidly changing Ottoman society in the first years of the twentieth century. These were exciting but also dangerous times as Constantinople witnessed revolution, attempted counter-revolution, and a coup with the backdrop of wars in north Africa (in today's Libya) and in the Balkans. In this maelstrom of conflict and political unrest, new, foreign modes of thinking and behaviour were unleashed. The Robenson brothers, at the time, were able to surf successfully upon waves of innovation and action which crashed against and breached the Ottoman defences.

Regardless of their background, each of the three brothers appeared to have been accepted by many of their peers as fellow Turks and Muslims. Membership of the Galatasaray Sports Club seems to have helped solidify bonds between the Robenson brothers and their contemporaries. A passionate identity with Galatasaray gave the Robensons a definite affiliation as well as a cause to fight for.

Notwithstanding his services to sports and Scouting in the Ottoman Empire, it will be seen that in the months following the war's end Ahmet Robenson's English origins put him under a cloud of suspicion. Reports of the possible treasonous behaviour of his brother Yakup would not have helped. Lingering doubts over Ahmet's loyalties may have eventually forced him to abandon Turkey in the late 1920s. In the face of repeated public dressing-downs and insidious mutterings of conspiracy, the patience of frustrated self-styled patriots is not necessarily boundless.

6

Ahmet Robenson: A Man of Many Names

I had done all that I could, and no Man is well pleased
to have his all neglected, be it ever so little.
James Boswell, *The Life of Samuel Johnson*

Introduction

Paradoxically, although quite a lot is known about Ahmet Robenson, there are certain key events in his life which remain unclear. This has led to unsubstantiated rumours that he may at one time have served as a spy for the British. He was certainly actively engaged in Turkish politics in the 1920s, but, surprisingly and controversially, by the end of the decade Ahmet had decided to emigrate to the US.

After serving in the Ottoman Army in the First World War, Ahmet Robenson was employed as an interpreter and, in effect, intermediary between the occupying British forces in the Caucasus and what would come to call itself the South-West Caucasus Democratic Republic. Following the collapse of the Ottoman Empire and the establishment of the Republic of Turkey, Ahmet was briefly president of the Galatasaray Sports Club. However, it was his active part in negotiations between the Turkish authorities and American officials seeking to develop closer cultural ties between the US and the fledgling republic that resulted in Ahmet playing an influential role in the politics of the time. After a reversal in his fortunes, Ahmet, together with his wife, emigrated to New York, where he took up a job as an oriental rug merchant. In his later years, he helped maintain the well-known Lyndhurst estate in Tarrytown, New York. His eventual death in 1965 went seemingly unnoticed in the local American media. While not remembered for his involvement in politics, Ahmet Robenson remains a sporting legend in Turkey, especially for his exploits in basketball and football.

Clearly, Ahmet Robenson had a chequered career. There are specific episodes in his life which may never be fully explained. In particular, his decision to leave his ailing mother in Izmir and abandon Turkey for New York is difficult to comprehend. Strikingly, perhaps, Ahmet did not attempt to begin a new life in England, the land of his forefathers. This was in spite of the fact that he had relatives in England, such as the family of his deceased half-brother Minick Robinson in Southsea.

There are other unanswered questions about both Ahmet and his wife that may be partly connected with issues over identity and politics. What is in a name? While living in the US, Ahmet Robenson used a number of different names in census records and other official registers. He first referred to himself as 'Ahmet Robinson', then 'Ahmed Robinson', before later calling himself 'Ahmet Abdullah Robinson'. Much more puzzlingly, in his final years he assumed the name of his late eldest brother, 'Spencer John Bernard Robinson', rather than adopting his original birth name, Peel Harold. The death certificate of 'Spencer Robinson' recorded the exact birth date of Ahmet Robenson's eldest brother – 23 February 1884.

Ahmet's wife Nina, or Emily Nina as she was known by her husband, also employed a range of names when living in New York. Originally called Nina Yankovski (Yankowsky), she assumed the Muslim name Fatma after marrying Ahmet. However, according to official American records, 'Nina Yankowsky Robinson' was also known as 'Fatima Nina Robinson', or 'Nina Stevens'. Why Nina should have chosen to use the surname Stevens is not at all clear. The political intrigue about Nina's early life may help to explain, at least in part, her simultaneous use of different names. Regrettably, there are few details of Nina's life in New York.

Turbulent Times: The Occupation of Istanbul

Following the defeat of the Ottoman Empire in the First World War, Constantinople – soon to be generally known as Istanbul – was occupied by several of the victorious powers. *De facto* Allied occupation of the city in November 1918 was made official in March 1920 in the face of mounting opposition from local nationalist supporters. Remnants of the defeated CUP had set up nationalist resistance organisations in outlying parts of Anatolia. One of these bodies, the Islamic or Muslim National Council in Kars, later formed the short-lived South-West Caucasus Democratic Republic. In the ensuing upheavals, the Ottoman Empire was dissolved, the Sultanate and the Caliphate abolished, and a nationalist resistance movement eventually led by Mustafa Kemal 'Atatürk' established the Republic of Turkey in late October 1923 after winning a war of national independence. The long and painful demise of Ottoman rule was finally complete. Revolution and war had forced the Turks to hastily adapt to the brutal realities of the early twentieth century.

Contrary to initial British reassurances that there would be no Allied military presence in Istanbul, an Allied occupation began on 13 November 1918, supposedly the result of security concerns. British, French and Italian forces fanned out to control various parts of the capital.[1] The local police were compelled to take orders from the occupying forces. Controlling Pera, the business centre and diplomatic quarter of the city, the British turned out to be the most enthusiastic backers of the occupation regime. With their very survival at stake, Sultan Mehmet VI and his ministers attempted to engage with the occupying forces. Although the CUP had disbanded itself on 5 November 1918, a nationalist resistance organised around former CUP members and opposed to the sultan's attempts to work with the foreign occupiers was quickly established in Istanbul and throughout Anatolia. This resistance movement attracted further support after Greek forces landed in Smyrna – soon to be known as Izmir – in May 1919 in a brazen attempt to grab Ottoman territory.

The Allied forces declared the official occupation of Istanbul on 20 March 1920. The increasingly popular nationalist resistance movement had been gaining strength in Anatolia, aided by much war material being smuggled out of the capital. The occupying forces had arrested suspected nationalist supporters in Istanbul. At the same time, those political groupings attempting to work with the occupying authorities were becoming increasingly discredited. The Ottoman parliament dissolved itself on 18 March 1920, two days after a couple of its members were unceremoniously dragged out of the building where the parliament was convened; the two deputies were arrested by the British. Many of the parliamentarians of the dissolved legislature escaped to Anatolia, and days later a new opposition government was officially announced in Ankara.

The British had believed that by declaring the *de jure* occupation of Istanbul it would be easier to arrest nationalist supporters and clamp down on resistance. However, in the months that followed, the nationalist opposition waged a successful military campaign against the invading Greek army, culminating in the recapture of Izmir in September 1922. The sultan and his government had lost further support after the signing of the humiliating Treaty of Sevres in August 1920, according to the terms of which the Ottoman Empire would have become a rump state concentrated around Istanbul and parts of Anatolia. Much of eastern Anatolia would have become part of an independent Armenia. The treaty was never implemented due to rapidly changing circumstances on the ground. Confronted by the successful nationalist forces led by Mustafa Kemal, the Allies evacuated Istanbul on 2 October 1923. The sultan had been removed from the city by the British the previous November after supporters of the nationalist movement had started to take control of the local gendarmerie and police. Turkish troops marched into Istanbul on 6 October 1923, and the Republic of Turkey was declared on 29 October.

When Istanbul was under Allied occupation, some of the local inhabitants were vehemently opposed to the 'Godless' nationalist rebels and supported the British, who were perceived as supporters of the sultan. On 20 May 1919, the Friends of England Society was founded in Istanbul and led by Sait Molla, the editor of a local newspaper, *Türkçe İstanbul*. Branches of the society were rapidly opened in Ankara, Edirne and Bursa. In an attempt to attract wider support, each day Molla's organisation distributed large quantities of meat to Turks living in poorer districts.[2] Molla was in correspondence with Dr Robert Frew, a popular Scottish Presbyterian minister at the Evangelical Union Church, who had been preaching in Pera since 1902. Frew was apparently a key 'recruiting agent' for the society. Many Turks later regarded him as a British spy. Atatürk himself, in a famous speech he delivered in 1927, referred to Frew as a 'British adventurer'. A notable commentator on Turkish affairs believed that Frew was more likely a freelance go-between, seeking to secure support for the society.[3] The British government's decision at the time to support the Greek landing at Izmir likely resulted in the society attracting much less local backing.

In early 1919, there had also been talk of permanently transferring control of Istanbul from the Ottoman Empire to either an international body or to British or American mandate rule. The Friends of England Society lobbied for the establishment of a British mandate. Throughout 1919, British and French diplomats held a series of delicate negotiations on the issue in which the possibility of according Sultan Mehmet VI a special Vatican-type status in Istanbul was seriously entertained. The opposition of the War Office and the India Office in London, who were concerned that Muslims in India could rise up if Istanbul was taken from the Ottoman Empire, finally led to these plans being aborted in January 1920. Instead, the British became more enthusiastic supporters of the sultan.[4]

In these troubled times, life may not have been comfortable for the Robenson/Bahri family given both their British connections and their established close ties with the Sultanate. But, there also appear to have been nationalist sympathies within the family. According to one family narrative, Ahmet Robenson's sister Maud was confronted with a particularly traumatic experience. The story goes that Maud's stepbrother Fevzi informed the British occupying forces in Istanbul that Maud's husband at the time, Mehmet Emin Sabri İnal, with whom Maud had four children, was involved in operations to smuggle weapons out of the capital to nationalist forces in Anatolia. Emin was arrested by the British and was about to be hanged. His life was saved when Maud personally intervened and persuaded the British authorities to release him from the dungeon where he was being held. The family account adds that Emin was shot in the leg during the War of Independence, but further details as to how, when and where this incident took place are not known.

Under the Allied occupation of Istanbul, some families were indeed divided, pledging their continued allegiance to the sultan and his advisers or transferring their support to the nationalist resistance movement. The Robenson/Bahri family may well have become entangled in the divisive and bitter politics of the time. What is definitely known, though, is that in late 1918 and throughout at least the first half of 1919, Ahmet Robenson was not in Istanbul. In this period, Ahmet was playing an instrumental role in the politics of what would become the Kars-based South-West Caucasus Democratic Republic.

A Spy in Kars?
The city of Kars sits on a plateau in what is now north-eastern Turkey close to the border with Armenia. Once the capital of a medieval

Armenian kingdom, over the centuries the city was occupied in turn by the invading Seljuks, Mongols, Georgians, Persians and Russians. It is famous for its austere-looking castle or citadel, dating back to at least the thirteenth century, which is perched high on a cliff overlooking the city. Kars recently attracted more international attention after it was used by the Nobel Laureate Orhan Pamuk as the backdrop for his novel *Kar* ('Snow'). In this novel, Pamuk referred to the city's well-known 'Baltic Houses'. These were the low-level dwellings and cottages built when Kars was a Russian garrison town. They can be recognised by their distinct window frames and neoclassical elements.

Through most of the nineteenth century, Ottoman and Tsarist Russian armies fought to gain control of the disputed territory of Kars and its surrounding region. Following defeat by the Russians in the war of 1877–78, the Ottomans were forced to surrender the areas around Kars, Ardahan and Batum (territories near the current Turkish–Armenian and Turkish–Georgian borders). The major Ottoman defeat at Sarıkamış in the First World War was a result of a failed attempt to reconquer the city. The Ottomans briefly re-established control of Kars, Ardahan and Batum after Russia withdrew from the war in the wake of the Bolshevik Revolution in 1917. Once the defeated Ottoman authorities signed an armistice with the British at the end of October 1918, the latter were keen for Ottoman troops to be withdrawn from the Caucasus region. Units of the Ottoman Ninth Army under the command of Yakup Şevki Pasha delayed their departure, and when these forces eventually started to withdraw, caches of arms were left to the Turks living in the area, who were determined not to come under the rule of local Armenians or Georgians.

The defeated CUP had encouraged the formation of Societies for the Defence of the National Rights in outlying parts of Anatolia including the Caucasus. The primary aim of these societies was to defend the interests of Turks and Muslims. Within this framework, the Kars Islamic Council was established in early November 1918. To reduce the emphasis on its Muslim credentials, the following month it was renamed the Kars National Council. After organising parliamentary elections, the council named itself the Provisional Government of the South-West Caucasus on 18 January 1919. Two months later, it dropped the term 'provisional' and declared the establishment of the South-West Caucasus Democratic Republic. This was arguably the first democratic Turkish-majority government.

The new political entity, led by Cihangiroğlu İbrahim Bey, the former commander of a regiment in the Ottoman Army and a native of the region, claimed control over a large swathe of territory including areas in which there were considerable Armenian and Georgian populations. This presented the government in London with a dilemma. British forces were still deployed in the region. The government of David Lloyd George was under pressure to respect the rights of Armenians and Georgians. Playing for time, the British first decided not to oppose the Provisional Government and waited to hear how the Paris Peace Conference would rule on the fate of the Caucasus. However, this policy was soon reversed after clashes between the Turks/Muslims, Armenians and Georgians intensified and the British came to believe that the government based in Kars was essentially a puppet of the Ottoman regime.[5]

Ahmet Robenson certainly took an active and direct part in the politics of the short-lived Kars Islamic Council and its successor bodies, but his exact role has been a subject of some debate. He has been accused of serving as a spy, either for the British or for the Ottoman authorities. Other sources referred to him as a brigand or somebody who sympathised with the local Turkish population.

What is definitely known is that Ahmet Robenson served in the war as a conscript officer in the Ottoman Third and Ninth Armies. After the cessation of hostilities, he was employed as an English/Turkish interpreter for the Kars Islamic Council. According to one source, he was paid 100 Turkish liras for this post.[6] As an official interpreter, Ahmet was personally involved in the high-level negotiations between the British occupying forces in the Caucasus and officials from the Kars Islamic Council and its successor organisations. He was thus in attendance when General William Henry Beach, head of intelligence to the British Military Mission in the Caucasus, held a series of meetings with Fahrettin Pirioğlu, a key representative of the Kars Islamic Council and later foreign minister of the South-West Caucasus Democratic Republic. These talks took place on a train in Kars between 13–16 January 1919.[7] Ahmet also served as an interpreter when the British military governor, Brigadier-General Verney Asser, visited Kars on 1 March.[8] He was present when General William Montgomery Thomson, the commander of British Forces in the Caucasus, arrived in Kars in late March.[9] Most significantly, perhaps, on 12 April Ahmet held talks with the new military governor, Lieutenant-Colonel

George Allen Preston, in Kars, immediately before British units stormed the building where the government of the South-West Caucasus Democratic Republic was meeting.[10] Following the seizure of the building, the ministers were arrested and later deported to Malta. Kars and its surrounding territory then briefly became part of the recently established Republic of Armenia until Turkish forces liberated Kars from the Armenians in late October 1920.

Three months after British forces had forcibly intervened in Kars, Ahmet Robenson reappeared in the neighbouring district of Oltu. After the fall of the South-West Caucasus Democratic Republic, the government of the Oltu Council had declared itself independent. This administration, also composed of local Turks and Muslims, was later occupied by Armenian forces for a short period before Turkish nationalist troops recaptured the area. On 30 July 1919, Ahmet had acted as an interpreter between the local authorities in Oltu and a British delegation arriving from Kars led by Captain H. R. Prosser.[11] The purpose of Prosser's visit was to assess whether Oltu should, in effect, remain autonomous or come under the jurisdiction of the Republic of Armenia.

One of the reasons some Turkish sources have suspected that Ahmet Robenson was working as a spy for British intelligence was that he did not leave the Caucasus immediately after the dismantling of the Kars-based South-West Caucasus Democratic Republic. Suspicions were further aroused by an exchange of correspondence between Ahmet and other members of his family living in the Ottoman Empire about the prospects of Istanbul being partitioned and declared an international city. This correspondence attracted the attention of Kazım Karabekir, the recently appointed commander of Turkish nationalist forces in the Caucasus. According to Karabekir, such messages over the future of Istanbul could prove damaging to morale. The commander was led to ponder whether Ahmet Robenson and his family had been British spies all along, in spite of their established presence in the Ottoman Empire and their professed belief in Islam. In a coded telegraph despatched on 24 August 1919, Karabekir requested that the military authorities initiate an investigation into Ahmet and his family.[12] Interestingly, though, there appeared to have been no mention of Yakup's possible questionable wartime activities.

These were very serious and potentially gravely damaging allegations. However, there do not appear to be further official reports questioning the allegiance of Ahmet Robenson and his immediate family as a result of his activities in the Caucasus. In the following years, Ahmet was able to move freely in prominent social circles in the new Republic of Turkey. Nevertheless, one of Atatürk's closest commanders at the time had raised grave doubts over the loyalty of Ahmet Robenson. This cloud of suspicion over Ahmet may never have fully lifted, and could have contributed to his eventual decision to emigrate to the US.

According to another source, however, Ahmet Robenson had helped save the Kars-based government's head of gendarmerie from arrest by the British. After the British had arrested members of the government of the South-West Caucasus Democratic Republic, they despatched a unit to the nearby house of Mehmet Sungur Yenigazi. The head of the local gendarmerie lied to the British that he was actually Ahmet Yenigazi, the brother of Mehmet. The British did not have a clear impression of what the gendarmerie commander looked like, but their suspicions had been raised. Yenigazi was held under house arrest for twelve days. Ahmet Robenson was then summoned to act as an interpreter, and he apparently prevented Mehmet from being detained and deported by corroborating the story that the man in custody was in fact Ahmet Yenegazi.[13] In the opinion of Armenian commentators, Mehmet Sungur Yenigazi was a notorious figure who had been responsible for the large-scale massacres of Armenians and others in the area in the First World War.[14]

An article produced in a British journal in 1925 is full of mistakes with regard to the role of Ahmet Robenson in the Caucasus. He is mistakenly referred to as the President of the Republic of the South-West Caucasus. Depicted as 'nothing more than an adventurer', he apparently was still 'rather a fine figure, always well-turned out in contrast to his scallywag followers and always suave and self-possessed no matter how embarrassing the situation'. The article went on to explain that he had lived in Kars before the Russian Revolution and that he was the son of an Englishman and a mother of 'Tartar origin'. After the British overthrew the 'Tartar Republic', the presidentship was offered to Ahmed Robinson, who 'accepted it with alacrity'.[15]

A much more reliable account is available in the British Foreign Office records in the National Archives. A classified intelligence report confirmed that Ahmet Robenson was the official interpreter of the Kars-based government. A Muslim who was half-English and half-Turkish (incorrect), he was reputed to have been an agent of Şevki Pasha, the commander of the Ottoman Ninth Army. This claim was not substantiated. Most interestingly, though, Ahmet was noted to be 'on intimate terms' with a Miss Yankovski, the minister for post and telegraphs of the Kars-based government.[16] This detail appeared to give the intelligence report more credence as Ahmet Robenson married a Nina Yankovski in the same year. It is important to note that this intelligence report did not refer to Ahmet Robenson as a British agent.

The background and role of Nina Yankovski was also open to debate. The British intelligence report noted, in implied derogatory terms, that she was a 'suffragette'. At the time, the label was often used in a patronising sense to refer to troublemaking women who had little respect for the rule of law. However, Nina Yankovski was not listed as one of the ministers arrested by the British on 12 April 1919 and deported to Malta. Instead, Mehmetoğlu Muhlis Bey, the acting or assistant minister in charge of telegram, telephone and postal services, was detained. Other accounts do not refer to a Miss Yankovski as minister. A woman minister is often referred to, named 'Arlof' or 'Elena Orlova'. Apparently a teacher and an anti-Bolshevik Russian, she had held the post as general director of telegraph, telephone and postal services and had served as education minister for what was then the Kars Islamic Council in November 1918. 'Arlof', or 'Elena Orlova', was elected to be one of seventy-one members of the parliament of the South-West Caucasus Democratic Republic.[17] The role of a woman in the Kars-based government, and one of apparently Russian ethnic identity, was singled out to demonstrate the liberal and progressive nature of an administration which was thus not exclusively male, Muslim and Turkish.

This begs the question whether Nina Yankovski, who was born in Grodno, a Polish town controlled by Russia since 1795, and 'Arlof' or 'Elena Orlova' were one and the same person. This was quite possible given that Nina in her later life was prone to use various names in official records. Writing later to his half-sister Gertrude, Ahmet Robenson noted, with a sense of pride, that his wife was fluent in English, German, French, Polish, Russian, Ukrainian and Turkish.[18] According to family accounts, Nina had worked on her sewing machine to produce the perforated edges of stamps of the 'Van Republic' (i.e. the Kars Republic). Given his contacts with the British, is it possible that Ahmet Robenson protected his future wife, Nina, by ensuring that she would not be present at the government building in Kars on 12 April?

These were times when a Presbyterian minister long based in Istanbul could be looked upon by the Turks as a spy for the British. However, it seems highly unlikely that Ahmet Robenson operated as an agent of the British government while serving as an interpreter for the Kars Islamic Council and its successor bodies. Through his post in Kars, he certainly did liaise with key British officials and this could have triggered suspicion among Ottoman officialdom. He may well have used these ties to his advantage by preventing the detention of Nina Yankovski. On the other hand, there is also no firm evidence to corroborate the British intelligence report that Ahmet Robenson might have been in the employ of Ottoman or, indeed, Turkish nationalist intelligence. Turkish commentators have not suggested this, and the suspicions at the time that Ahmet Robenson may have been working for the British government appear to indicate that he was not working for the Turkish nationalist opposition. What is clear, though, is that some time shortly after the events of April 1919 Ahmet married Nina (who would adopt the name Fatma). By 1921, Ahmet had returned to occupied Istanbul and had started to work for the American-financed Young Men's Christian Association (YMCA).

Still the Sportsman

Present at the formation of a republic in the Caucasus that was effectively strangled at birth, Ahmet Robenson also played a public role in the formative years of the Republic of Turkey. His role was that of interpreter, broker and active participant in works and programmes backed by American officials and philanthropists in the 1920s in Istanbul, Ankara and Izmir.

Through their missionary and cultural work, and by developing commercial ties, the Americans had established a firm presence in the Ottoman Empire. The benefactor Christopher Robert and the missionary Cyrus Hamlin had founded Robert College, overlooking the Bosphorus, in 1863. The college had the mission 'of creating New England gentlemen out of Orientals'.[19] It was the oldest American institution of higher education formed outside the US, and the college would acquire an international reputation as a distinguished centre of learning. An American College for Girls was also founded in

Constantinople in 1871. Such missionary activity aroused suspicion among the Muslim population of the Ottoman Empire, but it also led to the Americans acquiring a good reputation for their educational work and technical enterprise.[20]

This positive image of the Americans carried over to the Republic of Turkey. On the one hand, the US was regarded with suspicion because of its sympathy for the Armenian cause. In this context, President Woodrow Wilson had seriously toyed with the idea of creating an American mandate in the Ottoman Empire which would have included territory traditionally populated by Armenians. However, Wilson notwithstanding, in contrast to the British, the Americans were less burdened with the historical baggage of seeking to carve up Istanbul and the Ottoman Empire. American officials on the ground were also quicker than their British counterparts to appreciate the support that the nationalist resistance movement enjoyed in Anatolia. Diplomatic ties between the US and the Ottoman Empire were severed in 1917 with the American entry to the First World War, and were not established with the Republic of Turkey until 1927, but this did not prevent the Americans from cultivating close economic and cultural ties with the new republic. The US was called upon by the Turks to give advice in a range of fields including education, cotton culture, mineral prospecting, public health, communications and economic development in general.[21]

The YMCA, and also the Young Women's Christian Association (YWCA), played an important role in supporting the missionary and collegiate activities of the US in the Ottoman Empire and in the first years of the Republic of Turkey. As well as physical and recreational work, the YMCA and YWCA also offered classes in subjects such as language skills, typing and bookkeeping. They also sponsored various social projects and organised summer camps.[22]

According to the English-language weekly newsletter published by the American Bible House in Istanbul, a 'Mr P. H. Robinson' was one of the assistant directors for the YMCA summer gathering at Camp Perry in June and July 1921. Up to 100 young men had assembled at the camp at Kilyos, immediately north of Istanbul on the shores of the Black Sea.[23] This was the same area where, seven years before, Ahmet Robenson had established one of the Ottoman Empire's first Scout camps.

In the early 1920s, Ahmet Robenson was the director of physical education at the YMCA's Beyoğlu branch in Istanbul. Located at 40 Rue Cabristan, immediately next door to the American Consulate, the branch was equipped with a modern gymnasium.[24] Here Ahmet Robenson worked closely with the American Chester M. Tobin, who would later be selected as the trainer of the 1924 Turkish Olympic team. Tobin wrote a guidebook on volleyball which Ahmet translated into Turkish. In a letter to his half-sister Gertrude written in January 1924, Ahmet gave as his address 40 Rue Cabristan, Pera, which indicated that he was still working for the YMCA at that time.

Dr Deaver, the manager of the YMCA in Istanbul in the period between 1919 and 1925, and a sports teacher himself, organised a basketball match which has come to feature prominently in the annals of Turkish sporting history. Certainly, any historical overview of the origins and development of basketball in Turkey refers to this match, which was arguably the first international basketball game contested in 'Turkey'. In contrast to ten years ago, Ahmet Robenson was now in full command of the rules of the sport. Played in the grounds of the Dar-ül Muallimin-I Aliye Mektup (the later Cağaloğlu Professional School) in Istanbul in April 1921, the match saw Ahmet Robenson captain the Turkish team against American opponents from the YMCA. The latter won a close encounter 18–14. The first basketball league was established in Turkey six years later. Ahmet was one of the first coaches in Turkey to earn a licence to referee basketball games, having passed the test prepared by the American Basketball Federation.[25]

＊

In the summer of 2013, Gezi Park became famous as a focal point for youth-led protests against what was perceived to be an increasingly authoritarian government in Turkey. The tree-lined site in the centre of Istanbul had previously housed barracks for the Ottoman Army before, in the inter-war period, becoming the venue for the Taksim Stadium – an 8,000-capacity sports complex which hosted football matches, athletics tournaments, and boxing and wrestling competitions. Before the opening of the stadium in 1922, the area had become increasingly rundown. A detachment of Senegalese troops, part of the French occupying forces, was stationed in what was left of the barracks. A rudimentary horse-racing track run by exiled

White Russians had been laid in the area immediately adjacent to the barracks. The land, which was owned at the time by the French bankers Perier, was being managed by a certain Bork (Joseph Borg), a thick-set Greek of Maltese extraction.

Ahmet Robenson was heavily involved in the plans to construct the first sports stadium in the Ottoman Empire at Taksim.[26] He worked together on this project with the sports journalist Burhan Felek and with Çelebizade Said Tevfik (also known as Sait Çelebi), the proprietor of the magazine *Spor Alem*. In this endeavour, Ahmet was able to make use of his friendship with Bork. He could also call drum up local interest by exploiting his close ties with the various sporting clubs. Said Tevfik was mainly responsible for raising the considerable funds needed to rent the land from Bork to build the sports stadium. The YMCA office in Beyoğlu was used as a meeting place to hammer out plans to finance and construct the stadium. It was agreed that representatives from the occupying forces, together with sportsmen from America, Russia and the local Jewish, Armenian and Greek communities, should be invited to participate along with Turkish athletes in a grand opening of the stadium.

Plans were well advanced to open the stadium in June 1922 with a spectacular sports competition when, suddenly, the heads of the Turkish sports clubs announced that they had decided to boycott the ceremony. It seems that they were unhappy that meetings to organise the event had been held in the office of an American-based organisation and they were less than enthusiastic about the open invitation for athletes from other nations to compete. They were also possibly jealous of Said Tevfik and the immense effort he had put in to enable the construction of the new stadium.

After a sleepless night, Said Tevfik called upon Ahmet Robenson early the next morning to break the bad news. He barged into Ahmet's lodgings in Glavani Passage, a narrow alleyway running through the heart of Beyoğlu in the old Latin quarter. At one end of the passage was the fashionable Grand Hotel de Londres, built by the Glavani family in the late nineteenth century. Ahmet's accommodation was literally a stone's throw from the YMCA mission in Beyoğlu. Said Tevfik broke in while Ahmet was in the middle of having his breakfast. Taken aback by the latest turn of events, Ahmet abandoned drinking his tea and the two held a crisis meeting to decide how to proceed. Undeterred, they opted to go ahead with the project.

In spite of the local boycott, Taksim Stadium was officially opened in June 1922 with a series of athletic competitions. Football matches were soon played at the new facility between players hand-picked from several Turkish football teams and on the other side from the British and French occupying forces. However, struggling financially, Said Tevfik had been forced to return the management of the site to Bork. The Maltese Greek responded by provocatively displaying a huge Greek flag at the entrance to the stadium. Turkish athletics teams only competed in the stadium after the end of the occupation regime. With the declaration of the Republic of Turkey, Bork fled the country and a Turkish businessman, Menazirzade Abdülaziz Bey, took over the running of the stadium.

For Ahmet Robenson, this was but a foretaste of events to come over the next decade. In the various projects with which he became involved, he would have to repeatedly confront the blinkered views of short-sighted, hard-line Turkish nationalist groups. The mounting frustration at having to deal with such narrow-minded individuals would gradually take its toll on Ahmet Robenson.

By 1925, Ahmet Robenson had given up active participation in sports and, instead, had become involved in high-level sports administration. He was appointed Galatasaray Sports Club's president on 17 July 1925 by a three-person committee headed by the club's founder, Ali Sami. Ahmet Robenson and Ali Sami had been close associates for many years. This was evidently a time of upheaval in the club, with polarised committee meetings and several resignations. Ali Sami had been forced to relinquish his post as the club's president to take up another senior administrative position.

Ahmet Robenson's reign would be brief. According to a newspaper report, fifty signatures were collected to call for an extraordinary meeting of the Galatasaray Sports Club, and it was held on 4 September 1925. Members apparently complained that although Ahmet Robenson had been an accomplished sportsman, he was not an able administrator. A new president was thus voted in. No further details were given.[27] This leaves open the question whether Ahmet Robenson was fairly treated by his colleagues. His tenure as club president lasted less than three months. However, Ahmet Robenson had other commitments. He was heavily involved acting as an intermediary and broker in the Turkish-American Clubs Project, the so-called Anatolian Project.

The Turkish-American Clubs Project

The American Asa K. Jennings, a prominent representative of the YMCA in the region, was the main driving force behind the Turkish-American Clubs Project, working closely with Ahmet Robenson. A Methodist pastor by training, Jennings had played a major role in organising the evacuation by ship of tens of thousands of Greeks from Izmir in September 1922 in the face of advancing Turkish troops and a vengeful and hostile Turkish mob as Turkey's war of independence drew to a close. Originally sent to Turkey on what was meant to be a temporary posting, Jennings spent the next several years cultivating close ties with key Turkish politicians. This work culminated in the formation of the American Friends of Turkey in June 1930.

The Turkish-American Clubs Project envisaged cooperation between the YMCA and the Turkish authorities to promote physical education and other social and cultural programmes in Turkey. Within this framework, the Cincinnati-based Arthur Nash, who ran a garment-manufacturing company and was also a believer in the Universalist faith, was prepared to give substantial financial support for the construction of a building in Ankara (the new capital) to be used by the Turkish-American Clubs. Given Turkish sensitivities about working with an organisation which had the word 'Christian' in its title, the Americans agreed to play down the role of the YMCA. Nevertheless, the planned building in Ankara was originally intended to be, in practice, another branch of the YMCA. One of the main aims of the Turkish-American Clubs Project was to boost friendship between the two states. As a Universalist, believing in the 'Brotherhood of Man', and contending that all belonged to the family of God no matter their religion, Nash was eager to allocate a considerable sum of money to kickstart the project.[28]

Obviously well connected with the YMCA in Turkey, Ahmet Robenson acted as an official translator in talks between Jennings and leading Turkish officials. In fact, in this role he also took an active part in attempting to persuade politicians in Ankara to agree with Jennings' views. Ahmet had evidently struck up a close relationship with the pastor. The respect was mutual. Jennings was noted as saying that Ahmet Robenson 'stands well among the Turks'.[29]

Important talks took place in Ankara on 6 August 1925 between Jennings and the then Turkish education minister, Hamdullah Suphi Tanrıöver. Ahmet Robenson was present as an interpreter for

Jennings. The negotiations were in danger of breaking down after the minister proposed that the money Nash was willing to offer should be used for a more general programme rather than setting up the Turkish-American Clubs Project as had been initially envisaged. Tanrıöver, who was a long-time president of the Turkish Hearths, also suggested that the Americans should work directly with the nationalist association.

The education minister had played a key part in reactivating the nationalist Turkish Hearths in 1924. The movement aimed to develop in the new republic a society based on 'Turkishness' in combination with social scientific principles from Europe. In the years 1925 and 1926, the number of branches of the Turkish Hearths expanded from 135 to 217. The Turkish prime minister at the time, İsmet İnönü, was himself a member of the body.[30]

Intervening in the discussion, Ahmet Robenson stated that, as the president of the most important sports club in Turkey, he would welcome international friendship between the Turks and the Americans. He added that cooperation between the two peoples would help raise the standards of sports clubs and other groups in Turkey.[31] Here, Ahmet could have been also indirectly appealing to the minister's connections with Galatasaray. Tanrıöver, a poet as well as a politician, had also studied at Galatasaray High School and had graduated a few years earlier than Ahmet. The minister must also have been very familiar with Ahmet's previous work for the Scouting movement, which nationalist groups had co-opted immediately before the First World War. It seems that the intervention by Ahmet Robenson helped stave off the collapse of the Turkish-American Clubs Project, if only temporarily.

In November 1925, in Ankara, Ahmet Robenson acted as an official interpreter in discussions between Jennings, D. A. Davies (the administrative secretary for the YMCA in Europe), and Refik Saydam, a leading figure in the governing Republican People's Party (CHP – *Cumhuriyet Halk Partisi*). The Turkish-American Clubs Project was again the focus of the talks.[32] Ahmet served in the same capacity when further negotiations were held between Jennings and Tanrıöver on 10 May 1926 at the Tokatlıyan Hotel in Istanbul. However, on this occasion, Robenson was unable to save the day. No longer minister of education, but still president of the Turkish Hearths, Tanrıöver insisted that for political reasons funds should come directly from Nash, rather than be transferred via the YMCA, to construct the planned building in Ankara. This led to Ahmet Robenson directly clashing with Tanrıöver while coming to the defence of Jennings. The 'interpreter' interjected to argue basically that Tanrıöver had gone back on what had been agreed in earlier meetings.[33] By this time, the Kemalists, the supporters of Atatürk, believed that the Turkish Hearths were in danger of spinning out of control and were threatening to turn into an alternative nationalist movement. The opposition of the Turkish Hearths to the introduction of the Latin alphabet by the Kemalists to replace the Arabic script eventually contributed to the demise of the nationalist federation in 1931.[34]

Following the meeting in the Tokatlıyan Hotel, the Turkish-American Clubs Project quickly collapsed. Funding was still provided by Nash to construct the building in Ankara for the Turkish Hearths, but the YMCA was no longer involved, neither directly nor indirectly. There had been plans at the time to build on the proposed Turkish-American Clubs Project and form a Turkish-American Friendship Association. This association would have promoted cooperation on social, economic, financial, scientific and agricultural matters as well as youth work. It had been suggested that Ahmet Robenson should serve on the administrative committee of this association.[35] With the abandoning of the Turkish-American Clubs Project, plans to establish the association were quietly dropped. Later, in October 1926, Jennings and Ahmet Robenson encountered Tanrıöver by chance while passing through Ankara, and, as if to show that there were no hard feelings, the three had tea together.[36]

Briefly president of Galatasaray Sports Club, and a figure entrusted by the Americans to engage in high-level discussions with the Turks on sensitive cultural issues, by the mid-1920s Ahmet Robenson was clearly prominently involved in Turkish politics. The health minister of the time, Refik Saydam, sent complimentary tickets to Jennings and Ahmet Robenson for them to attend the opening ceremony of the Turkish Grand National Assembly in Ankara on 1 November 1926. The two were allocated prized seats behind the parliamentary deputies and in front the leading government bureaucrats.[37] They would have heard Atatürk's opening speech for the new session of parliament, in which he gave a personal account of how he had survived an assassination attempt against him only months earlier.

Ahmet may well have maintained contact with Refik Saydam, who later became the general secretary of the CHP in 1938 before becoming the fourth prime minister of the Republic of Turkey one year later.

The Smyrna Welfare Council Project

The collaboration between Ahmet Robenson and Asa Jennings did not end with the initial failure of the Turkish-American Clubs Project. The two were soon working together again to promote the Smyrna Welfare Council Project. This was another American-backed scheme to set up a social welfare programme for the city of Izmir and was effectively a relaunch of work previously planned in 1923. The project had the backing of Hüseyin Aziz (Akyürek), the mayor of Izmir, and a member of the Izmir branch of the Turkish Hearths. Previously the Governor of the Izmir region, Aziz was heavily involved in plans to modernise and reconstruct Izmir. Large parts of the city had been destroyed in 1922 by a great fire when Turkish nationalist forces were wreaking revenge on locals who had supported the Greek invasion and occupation of Anatolia. Aziz had given his backing to open the first automatic telephone exchange in Izmir, had initiated works to upgrade the city's sewerage system, and, with French urban design experts, had drawn up plans to reconstruct large areas of Izmir with new residential quarters and business districts.

Upon the invitation of Aziz, Jennings led an American delegation to Izmir on 1 December 1926 to discuss the establishment of the Smyrna Welfare Council. Ahmet Robenson was present again as an interpreter and also, it seems, as a key adviser.[38] A decision was taken to set up the council. One of its principal stated objectives was to provide assistance and education to children from socially deprived backgrounds. Campaigns were to be organised to raise funding. Ahmet was swiftly appointed head of the council's Physical Education Committee. The committee was tasked with the responsibility to cooperate with various federated sports clubs to set up a programme of physical education. Employing a gang of sixty prisoners from the city jail, Ahmet was placed in charge of a scheme to prepare a modern sports field with full amenities. It seems that he succeeded in quickly establishing a rapport with the convicts. They were happy enough to work outside the prison and were even financially rewarded for their efforts.[39] An orphanage was also established, and the first public playground in Turkey was built. Modern apparatus was imported from the US to equip the playground.[40]

The Smyrna Welfare Council delegated authority to Ahmet Robenson to organise festivities and amusements for the national holiday, known as Children's Day, on 23 April 1928. This turned out to be a celebration on a grand scale. Three hydroplanes and three aeroplanes flew over the city dropping toys and also leaflets on which local children had written messages and sayings. Bands played music, cinemas were opened, street parties prepared, buffet spreads laid out, and a special playground was erected.[41] This was a party Spencer Robinson himself would have been proud of organising.

Ahmet Robenson also exploited the occasion to promote a public health campaign in which he had become very closely involved. Through his work with the Smyrna Welfare Council, he played an important role in the Committee of the Society for the Protection of Children of Smyrna. This committee was lobbying to improve the distribution of sterile milk for children in the city. Many infants in the area had died during the First World War because of the lack of clean milk. The Smyrna Welfare Council was keen to manage the milk drop station which had been set up by the committee, and Ahmet seems to have played a pivotal role here. On 23 April 1928, the children marched through the streets of Izmir carrying posters demanding the right to have pure milk.

However, Ahmet Robenson faced criticism for printing and distributing letters in both French and Turkish. These letters had asked residents how much pasteurised milk they needed. Hikmet Bey, one of the directors of the CHP's Izmir branch, and another member of the Turkish Hearths, criticised the Smyrna Welfare Council for using the French language when issuing a proclamation with regard to the milk drop station. A visibly angry Ahmet Robenson responded by saying that French was only used for the publication of a relatively small number of letters, with many more letters written in Turkish. He then added that he was the only person back in 1908 'to take a brush and paint in my hands and go out in Constantinople to paint over foreign languages and write "here is Turkey, write in Turkish". It is nothing great to talk of patriotism; it is necessary to act.'[42] Ahmet's frustration was obvious. It seems that certain diehard Turkish nationalist groups were quick to cast suspicion on his activities and question his work solely because of his family background.

Shortly after the Children's Day celebrations, the Smyrna Welfare Council was dissolved. A meeting had taken place back in January 1928 to discuss the council's future work. At the time, Asa Jennings was in the US seeking to raise further funds. The meeting soon turned into a heated discussion when Hikmet Bey and others rejected a proposal to turn the council into an association. Acting as a broker, Ahmet Robenson had once more attempted – this time without success – to bring calm to the proceedings. According to Ahmet, the new mayor of Izmir, Hulusi Bey (Hulusi Alataş), had influenced other participants at the meeting to press for the council's dissolution. Hulusi Bey was apparently furious that Jennings had turned down his offer of depositing 60,000 Turkish liras into a bank account in the council's name.[43] The failure to reach an agreement led to the eventual winding up of the Smyrna Welfare Council in the summer of 1928. Yet again, Ahmet was powerless to stop the forces of Turkish nationalism, represented by the Turkish Hearths, ruining an American backed and funded social welfare project. The Americans decided instead to launch a similar welfare project in Ankara and this paved the way for the establishment of the American Friends of Turkey in 1930 to coordinate a range of social assistance programmes.

Working for the Smyrna Welfare Council may well have forced Ahmet Robenson to move to Izmir with his wife and also mother. In a letter posted to his half-sister Gertrude in April 1928, the day before he organised the Children's Day festivities, he explained how they had moved 'from Constantinople to Smyrna a year and half ago'.[44] It is not clear what Nina Robenson was doing in this period. Apparently much to their disappointment, Ahmet and Nina failed to have children of their own.

Family rumours that Nina may have been 'a Russian princess' should not be taken seriously. It seems that she was actually proud of her Polish identity. This was the nationality she chose to use in her identification records. Grodno, now a part of Belarus, had formerly been part of the Polish–Lithuanian Commonwealth. After the partition of Poland in the late eighteenth century, Grodno was part of Tsarist Russia until the First World War. Nina may have had a close relative (brother?) who helped look after Ahmet's mother in her later years. The family have a photograph of a 'Pierre Jankovsky', who was training to be a civil engineer in the Russian-language section of the Ecole Du Genie Civil in Paris in November 1928. The photograph reveals a quite confident, serious-looking, balding young man.

What is known for certain is that on 5 February 1930, Nina was a passenger on the ship *Mauretania*, which set sail from Cherbourg and arrived in New York six days later. The passenger manifest noted that 'Fatma Robinson' was aged thirty-one years, born in Grodno of Polish nationality, and was employed as a secretary. Her permanent address was recorded as 19 Leloi Sokak, Smyrna, Turkey. This may well have been Lale Sokak, which was located in Balcova, one of the districts of Izmir popular with foreigners at the time. Nina's physical characteristics were also given. She was 5 feet 6 inches tall, with a dark complexion, dark hair, green eyes and no obvious marks of identification. Immediately below her name was the text 'Russia League of Nations'. Did this mean that Nina worked as a secretary for an organisation connected with Russia and the League of Nations (the predecessor, as it were, of the later United Nations)? Russia was not admitted to the League of Nations until September 1934. But, how could Nina be working for the Russians while living in Izmir? Nina's known anti-Bolshevik sentiments suggest that she was unlikely to have been in the employ of the Stalinist regime in Moscow, and records do not indicate any important meeting held in New York in early 1930 to discuss issues relating to the League of Nations or Russia's possible membership.

It seems that Ahmet was already in New York when Nina arrived. He had decided to leave Turkey and emigrate to the US. Why had he chosen to make such a life-changing decision? Family members suggest that he had become disillusioned with living in Turkey and that his work had not been fully acknowledged by the Turks. Certainly, Turkey was experiencing a surge in xenophobia in this period. Still apparently looked upon as a foreigner by some Turks, Ahmet may have felt excluded and unappreciated. He must have been frustrated by the obstacles placed before him in his attempts to work together with the Americans on social welfare projects. In particular, he must have been exasperated by the mounting opposition and suspicion from the Turkish Hearths. Probably feeling increasingly disenchanted, and perhaps fatigued, Ahmet took what must have been a painful decision, leaving his mother behind to embark on a new life with his wife outside of Turkey.

Why had Ahmet Robenson not chosen to return to Britain? One may speculate that he felt few ties with the land of his ancestors. He had been born in India and had lived only briefly in Brighton as a very small child. He may not have communicated much with his mother's immediate family circle living in England, although he does seem to have maintained some contact with the relatives of his half-brother Minick Robinson. There are significant questions here that may never be properly answered. What is clear, however, is that the decision to move to the US marked the definite end of an important phase in the life of Ahmet Robenson.

A Carpet Seller in New York

It has been argued that there were three major waves of migration to the US from the Ottoman Empire and Turkey.[45] The first large-scale movement occurred in the nineteenth century and early twentieth century. This was mostly of uneducated, single, young male peasants, with very little or no knowledge of English, who invariably took up manual labour jobs in factories. A number returned to their homeland and their families when they had accumulated sufficient savings. This first wave, in its later phase, also included non-Muslim minorities who sought to avoid military service. Until the passing of legislation in 1908, these minorities had been exempted from serving in the armed forces.[46] A second wave, after 1945, mostly consisted of professionals, including scientists, physicians and engineers who were seeking new opportunities abroad. The military coup in Turkey in 1980 sparked a third movement of people fleeing to the US to avoid political persecution.

Immigration to the US from Turkey became much more difficult for a period after the US Congress passed the Johnson-Reed National Quota Act in 1924. This followed legislation seven years earlier which insisted that new migrants to the US should pass a literacy test. According to the new regime in place in 1924, only about 100 immigrants were allowed to migrate from Turkey to the US each year, and most of these were actually family members of immigrants who had already settled in the US.[47]

It seems that Ahmet Robenson had migrated to the US some time in 1929. He had paid for his wife's passage to New York in February 1930. Interestingly, though, according to the passenger list of the vessel his wife sailed on, 'Fatma Robinson' was planning to stay with a friend at 295 5th Avenue in New York and not with Ahmet. Most probably, his close work with the Americans in Turkey in the past decade had enabled Ahmet and his wife to be included in the limited quota of migrants coming from Turkey to the US.

According to the family narrative, Ahmet Robenson set up a carpet business in the US and possibly in Canada later. After initial success, his partner (name unknown) in the firm went bankrupt and, as a consequence, Ahmet also suffered financially – in line with the past experiences of several of his family members. He was later employed as a caretaker for a large family estate.

Looking through the available records, this account of Ahmet Robenson's later life was largely accurate. On the register of the *Mauretania*, it was noted that 'Fatma Robinson' did not intend to stay in the US. The address she gave for her supposed visit was that of the well-known Textile Building in New York. This was a showroom building for the home textiles industry, including oriental rugs. At the time, a large number of carpet manufacturers and wholesale dealers operated from the Textile Building. The name of the friend with whom Nina planned to stay was typed in the ship's passenger list as 'Larseekhan Reig'. Unfortunately, this name is not able to be traced, although a number of Poles with the surname Reig were living in New York in the 1930s.

The US census for 1930 listed 'Ahmet' and 'Fatma Robinson' living at 325 W. 71st Street on 1 April of that year. They resided in 'house number' 40. This was a rented property. They were paying a monthly rental of $100. It was noted that the couple possessed a radio. Until recently a luxury item, American business and political leaders had come to regard the ownership of a radio set as a source of cultural 'uplift' for the population as well as being an important tool to advertise products – hence the interest in radio ownership in the census.[48] Surprisingly, in the 1930 census, it was recorded that Ahmet had emigrated to the US in 1920 and his wife had followed one year later. The two were listed as aliens, with Ahmet mistakenly noted as being born in Indiana (rather than India!). According to the census, Ahmet's occupation was 'merchant of oriental rugs'. Fatma did not have an occupation. Their next-door neighbours at the Upper West Side property included 'a buyer for a department store' who had as her lodger 'a model for a department store'. House number 42 was a property with fifteen lodgers of mixed nationality. The occupations ranged from music teacher, merchant, law office clerk and stenographer to librarian, investigator and author.

Clearly, by April 1930, the Robensons had taken up residence in New York. While not exactly living a life of luxury, it seems that Ahmet had been able to quickly start up a business. However, he had no experience in the carpet trade, and this may have forced him to work with a partner. The name of his business is not known. The contemporary telephone and business directories for New York I was able to discover do not refer to any company with the name Robinson working in the carpet business. Competition in the oriental rug trade would have been intense. Armenians, expelled from the Ottoman Empire, had started selling oriental carpets in the early 1900s. By the early 1940s, they were joined by Persian Jews dealing and importing handmade rugs from Iran.[49] The famous oriental rug district in New York was situated in an area between 28th and 33rd Streets.

A photograph of Nina and Ahmet taken at Sea Cliff, New York, dated 28 August 1930, is in the possession of Ahmet's relatives in Turkey. Sea Cliff was a resort town on Long Island's 'Gold Coast' and was famous for its late Victorian summer houses, which were perched on a cliff overlooking a beach. The location had originally been used in the mid-nineteenth century for German Methodist revival meetings. In the early 1930s the first White Russian families began to establish summer houses at Sea Cliff and two Russian Orthodox churches were eventually constructed to serve the community. This may well have been the Robensons' first holiday in the US, and they could have taken the ferry to cross to Long Island from New York. In the photograph, the two are outside in what appears to be a garden, with Ahmet seated and Nina standing close behind him. Scribbled on the back of the photograph in what appears to be Ahmet's handwriting is the comment, 'Do not think it is my stomach sticking out. I was leaning back in a deep chair.'

A glimpse into Nina's seemingly effervescent character and of the life of the Robensons in the US can be gathered from an undated postcard Nina despatched to an Edna Hess in Upper Darby, Pennsylvania. Nina wrote about how their 'experiences' were getting more exciting each passing day in the 'beautiful city' of Istanbul. It seems that the Robensons had travelled back to Turkey to spend vacation there. A 'fierce mix-up over hotels' had finally been satisfactorily resolved and she and Ahmet were relaxing in the roof garden of a Turkish restaurant sipping 'thick, syrupy coffee'. Nina finished her message by noting that there was more to tell when she returned home.

Edna Hess was the wife of the chemical engineer Myron J. Hess. The couple lived in Upper Darby in the 1930s and early 1940s. Before marrying Edna (née Keesey) in 1921, Myron had served in the US Army Coast Artillery Corps in the latter part of the First World War, rising to the rank of first lieutenant. A graduate of the University of Pennsylvania, in 1924 he joined S. Twitchell Company of Camden, New Jersey. In a highly successful career, Myron became president of the National Manufacturers of Beverage Flavors. Myron was following in the footsteps of his father. Known as 'the Syrup Man of Philadelphia', Harry Hess had been connected with the Twitchell Company for over fifty years. Myron died of 'coronary occlusion' in 1958. Edna later remarried, and in 1969 she was the executive vice president of Frostie Enterprises (the successor business to S. Twitchell Company, and famous for its production of root beer).

I struggled to fathom how the Robensons and Hesses had become friends given that they did not live in the same state and there appeared to be no common interest in the oriental rugs business. However, an obituary of Myron Hess which I eventually came across provided me with the answer. Though Myron was known for his active service to the community, the obituary added that much of his off-duty time was spent promoting the Boy Scouts of America.[50] Here, then, was the connection that had enabled the two couples to become close friends. Obviously, Ahmet Robenson was keen to maintain his long-established ties with the Scouting world after his abrupt departure from Turkey.

The US census of April 1940 refers to an 'Ahmed' and 'Nina Robinson' living at 116 W. 76th Street. It was recorded that the fifty-three-year-old 'Ahmed' had been born in England, while his forty-three-year-old wife's birthplace was Poland. Ahmed's occupation was 'manager of imports', so he was still presumably working in the carpet trade. His annual income for 1939 was reported to be around $1,500. Nina was listed again as having no occupation, but had income from other sources. A question on the census inquired about their level of educational attainment. It was noted that both husband and wife had completed the fourth year of college.

The Robensons were two of over twenty lodgers in a house owned by the forty-three-year-old Gertrude Frazer, originally from Wallsend, near Newcastle. Gertrude and her family had arrived in the US in January 1920, a decade before the Robensons emigrated to New York. Living together with Gertrude was her daughter, who worked as a hairdresser, and her two sons, who were shipyard helpers. Gertrude was the daughter of a shipyard's plumber born in Germany but with British nationality. Other lodgers in the house came from England, Germany, France, Russia, Greece and Mexico. They held down jobs such as banking clerk, chauffeur, cook, ironworker and hotel maid.

Although presumably living in relative comfort, and broadening their social contacts, after spending over ten years in the US, the Robensons were still only lodgers. This may have been quite a comedown for a couple who had once held offices of authority and positions of influence. Writing to his half-sister back in 1924, Ahmet had boasted:

> I am one of the leading men of all sports in this country as well as one of the founders, and have some other business. I worked up an outstanding position and am quite pleased of my works which are prospering day by day.[51]

Developing a successful career and a good reputation had clearly been important to Ahmet Robenson. The experience of falling down the social ladder in a country where people would have had little or no knowledge of their past achievements may not have been easy for Ahmet and Nina.

The Robensons were still at the same New York address in 1942 according to the Second World War draft registration card for 'Ahmet Abdullah Robinson'. By the terms of the fourth draft, conducted in the US on 27 April 1942 (the so-called 'Old Man's Draft'), all men born on or after 28 April 1877 and on or before 16 February 1897 were obliged to complete a draft registration card. These men were not expected to perform military service, but the authorities were keen to compile a thorough inventory of the manpower resources that could be exploited for all types of national service in the war.

On the draft registration card, it was noted that Ahmet Abdullah Robinson was 5 feet 11 inches tall and weighed 175 pounds. He had hazel eyes, brown hair and a ruddy complexion. He was registered as self-employed and his listed place of employment was the same as his home address. Interestingly, the card noted that Ahmet Abdullah Robinson was born in Kurseong, India, on 23 February 1884. This was incorrect. Ahmet Robenson (Peel Harold Robinson) had been born in Kalimpong in May 1889. Ahmet's eldest brother, Spencer John Bernard Robinson (Yakup Robenson) was born in Kurseong in February 1884. Why had Ahmet decided at this time to use the birth place *and* date of one of his brothers? Declaring himself five years older than his actual age would not have affected his status with regard to the draft. There does not appear to be any obvious reason for Ahmet to suddenly adopt part of his brother's identity.

The controversy over the draft registration card does not end there. 'Ahmet Abdullah Robinson' also had to give the name and address of a person who could vouch for him and knew his address. Here, the name Mrs N. Stevens of 988 5th Avenue, New York was listed. I now know that this was an alternative name used by Ahmet's wife, Nina. Why would this name and address be used on the draft registration card? According to the US census of 1940, there were a number of occupants living at 988 5th Avenue. These included a fifty-four-year-old widow, a writer of financial articles, and the young executive of a ship repair company. Most interestingly, another resident of the property was Frederic Rene Coudert, who was at the time an influential attorney and a member of the New York State Senate. One of the scions of a well-known family of New York lawyers, in the period 1940–42 Coudert was a key member of the Rapp-Coudert Committee, also known as the Joint Legislative Committee to Investigate the Educational System of the State of New York. This committee sought to identify the extent of Communist influence in the public education system of New York State.

Was Mrs N. Stevens (Nina Robenson) working at the time for Frederic Rene Coudert? Her anti-Bolshevik sympathies have been noted. The work of the Rapp-Coudert Committee has been viewed as a kind of dress rehearsal for the later anti-Communist witch hunt orchestrated by US Senator Joseph McCarthy. In the heyday of McCarthyism, the controversial Immigration and Nationality Act of 1952 (the McCarran-Walter Act) permitted the government to deport immigrants or naturalised citizens who were suspected of engagement in acts of subversion. However, there were also provisions in the act for suspending the deportation of certain deserving aliens. According to the US Congressional Record of 1953, on 27 July of that year the Senate and House of Representatives produced one of several lists of aliens for which the US Attorney General had suspended the deportation for more than six months. This list included 'Nina Yankowsky Robinson', 'Fatima Nina Robinson' and 'Nina Stevens', who were acknowledged to be one and the same person. A 'Spencer John Bernard Robinson', also known as 'Ahmed Beye Abdullah Robinson', was on another list released two days later.[52] If Nina had, indeed, previously worked for Frederic Coudert – although there is no clear evidence that this was the case – this would have worked to her advantage when suspected Communist sympathisers were rounded up and deported in the early 1950s. It would also have ensured that her husband would have been saved from deportation.

The Robensons may have vacated the property at 116 W. 76th Street by 1943. A Mrs Nina Robinson is listed in the 1943 New York City telephone directory as living at 331 West 70th, again in the Upper West Side of the city. This remained the address for this Mrs Nina Robinson throughout the 1940s. In the 1953 telephone directory, a Mrs Nina Robinson was registered as living at 157 W. 130th, which was an address in the Harlem area.

Last Days at Lyndhurst

Ahmet Robenson finally became a US citizen on 9 January 1956, which was not a mandatory process. When petitioning for naturalisation, aliens had to present their immigration record (i.e. a passenger list) and names used in all US official records ostensibly had to tally. The US District Court of New York City accepted the petition for nationalisation of 'Spencer John Bernard Robinson'. The birth date given was again 23 February 1884. Why did Ahmet once more employ the full name of his deceased eldest brother? Did this mean that Ahmet had first entered the US in 1929 using the name of his eldest brother? And, how was Ahmet successful in his petition for naturalisation given the various names he had used in official records? This repeated use of different names by Ahmet Robenson is difficult to comprehend. I have not been able to find any official record of a petition for naturalisation made by Nina.

There are stories within the family that refer to Ahmet Robenson owning and operating gas stations near New York after abandoning the carpet business. These accounts cannot be confirmed. What is definite, though, is that by January 1956 Ahmet was no longer self-employed. He gave an address in Tarrytown, in the Southern District of New York, when he petitioned to be naturalised. The full address – Lyndhurst, 635 So Broadway – was that of the famous Gothic revival mansion known as Castle Lyndhurst on the banks of the Hudson River.

Now used as a museum, film set and site for Halloween-themed tours, the twenty-room crenelated mansion at Lyndhurst with its large, picturesque grounds was originally built in 1838 by the designer Alexander Jackson Davis. The property was occupied first by William Paulding, then mayor of New York City. Later, the property was owned by George Merritt, a Manhattan dry goods tycoon. After this, the reported ninth-richest man in American history, notorious financier and 'robber baron' Jay Gould, bought Lyndhurst in 1880 to use as his summer house. Gould had amassed his personal wealth by buying and selling railroads. Accused of attempting to corner the gold market in New York City through a network of corruption, together with a fellow speculator he played a leading role in the so-called 'Black Friday' panic of 24 September 1869, which almost led to the collapse of the US financial system.[53] Upon Jay Gould's death in 1892, one of his daughters, Helen Gould, inherited the property at Lyndhurst. After Helen passed away, Jay Gould's younger daughter, Anna, acquired the estate in 1938. Following Anna's death in Paris in November 1961, and in the face of complicated litigation with Anna Gould's heirs, the US Congress eventually decided in 1964 to leave most of the estate to the National Trust for Historic Preservation. In her will, Anna had bequeathed the property to them.

Sometime before 1956, Ahmet Robenson had become one of the managers of Lyndhurst under the watch of Anna Gould. Together with Nina, he lived on-site. How had Ahmet secured this post? It is quite possible that Ahmet's earlier sporting exploits in Turkey and his previous work with the Americans in Istanbul, Ankara and Izmir may have helped him to obtain the managerial position.

Making use of her father's accumulated wealth, Helen Gould was famous for her philanthropic works and her acts of charity. A devout Christian who was at one time vice president of the American Bible Society, she had donated $150,000 for the construction of what would become the main hall at Robert College in Istanbul. Known as Gould Hall, the building was completed in 1914 on the site of what was then the American College for Girls – Robert College later relocated to this piece of land. Helen also raised money for the YMCA and at one time served on its national board. In the spring of 1912, she participated in a much-publicised 'coast-to-coast' speaking tour to gather more funding for the YMCA. In 1913, Helen married Finley Johnson Shepherd, who was the Eastern representative of the Missouri Pacific Railroad, a part of the rail system Jay Gould had helped set up.

Helen's sister Anna was a much more controversial figure. A creature of high society, in 1895 Anna had married Paul Ernest Boniface (known as 'Boni'), who held the title Marquis de Castellene. After having five children, Anna divorced the marquis in 1906 on the grounds of infidelity on his part. Two years later, she married his cousin Helie de Talleyrand-Perigord, Duc de Sagan. The duke, with whom Anna had a further two children, was a descendent of Napoleon's famous foreign minister, Talleyrand. Inheriting Lyndhurst in 1938, the 'duchess' continued to spend most of her time either in Paris or in downtown New York on the fourteenth floor of the Plaza Hotel. Known as the 'mystery woman', on her occasional visits to the estate she would sleep in the small tower bedroom she had stayed in as a child.[54] Rumour was that she expected the dining room table to be laid out each evening in case she decided to return to Lyndhurst from the city.[55] Her bodyguard, the well-known detective Raymond C. Schindler, lived on property immediately adjacent to Lyndhurst at Spratt House until his death in 1959. Anna's arrival to take up temporary residence at Lyndhurst was important enough to merit local press attention.[56]

Although Anna was unlikely to have known Ahmet Robenson in person, she may have agreed to employ him given his past links with the YMCA in Istanbul. There would have been much work for the gardeners and caretakers at Lyndhurst. The main building housed numerous art treasures. The gardens were spacious. However, under the duchess parts of the estate had fallen into disrepair. This included a bowling alley, a Roman pool, and a greenhouse which at one time was the largest private greenhouse in the world. Ahmet was present in the period of upheaval at Lyndhurst after the death of the duchess. Concerned that the life and works of the robber baron Jay Gould may be honoured in some way, the Village Board of Trustees in Tarrytown was up in arms in November 1964 at the decision to make the estate a museum. The local residents argued that they had not been properly consulted. Pressing to retain tax income from the estate, they also disapproved of the tax exemption plan approved by Congress.[57]

Richard Miller, the former official historian of Tarrytown, noted that in the early 1960s Ahmet – known then to Richard Miller as Spencer Robinson – was living as a caretaker in the grounds of Lyndhurst in the 'gingerbread' cottage which was situated very close to the Hudson River. At the time, Miller was a young student employed in a summer job that involved the cataloguing of all the books at the Lyndhurst property. According to Miller, Mr Robinson was a 'very gracious man' who always greeted him if they met by chance on the estate. They did not come across each other often, though, as Mr Robinson spent most of his time in the cottage.[58] This was presumably because of Nina's poor health.

Together with his father, mother, and younger brother Hakan, Ahmet Ceylan visited his great-uncle at Lyndhurst in 1964. Unfortunately, at that time Nina was not in a fit state to receive visitors. Ahmet Ceylan's mother, Gülperi, recalls how Ahmet Robenson inquired about where his sister Maud was buried. In an emotional interview with Ahmet Robenson published by a magazine in 1965, he is quoted as saying,

> I left my heart in Üsküdar (a district in Istanbul), because my mother, Fatma, lies on Sultantepe. All my classmates, all my friends, my club, my memories of youth, all are there![59]

The death of 'Spencer Robinson', whose last known residence was in Tarrytown, was registered in the final quarter of 1965. Again, the birth date given was 23 February 1884. Ahmet Robenson seems to have passed away quietly. There does not appear to have been an obituary in the local news. Nina may have passed away over ten years later. A Nina Robinson, born 14 December 1899, died at Orangeburg, Rockland, New York, in December 1975. At the time, the Rockland Psychiatric Center was still in operation in Orangeburg, and Nina may have been a resident there when she died.

After a full and hectic life, in his later years Ahmet Robenson looked to have found tranquillity in the scenic grounds of the Lyndhurst estate. We will never know what may have happened if Ahmet had chosen to remain in Turkey. He and Nina did return to Turkey on at least one occasion, but in their later years it seems that the couple did not make the voyage across the Atlantic. Certainly, Ahmet was not in attendance when his sister Maud was laid to rest.

Spy, information broker or frustrated patriot? Commentators of different political persuasions continue to reassess Ahmet's life and spin stories that serve to reinforce their own personal predilections and ideological viewpoints. Ahmet Robenson himself contributed to the confusion by weaving a story which purportedly linked his family to the descendants of Cecil Rhodes. Perhaps harbouring resentment at his family's treatment at the hands of the authorities of the day, Ahmet may have sought to secure a modicum of revenge by providing a counter-narrative which stressed the ostensible distinguished origins of the Robinson/Robenson household. I cannot help but feel that here was a man who achieved much, but who could have accomplished and contributed far more if the circumstances had allowed.

7

The Robinsons:
Meanwhile, in England...

'Everyone's story matters,' said Morris. And all the books agreed.
William Joyce, *The Fantastic Flying*
Books of Mr Morris Lessmore

Introduction

While different members of the Robinson family were active abroad, the descendants of Spencer and Isabella Robinson based themselves in England. Minick Robinson returned after living and working in India for roughly four years. He most probably did not venture overseas again. It seems that neither Minick nor his offspring attempted to go and seek out their relatives in Germany, Turkey or the US. In contrast, family members living abroad did occasionally visit the Robinsons in England. One wonders how much the Robinsons, residing at the time in Portsmouth, were aware of the successes and achievements of relatives such as Gertrude Eisenmann or Ahmet Robenson.

Finding the last remaining direct descendant of Spencer and Isabella was an exciting major breakthrough in my research. In his work on the Robinsons of Lincolnshire, in the briefest of mentions, Peter Woods noted that a Bernard Spencer Robinson, the sole great-grandson of Spencer Robinson, was born in 1947 (actually August 1946) and was living in Peterborough in 1973.[1] I was later able to track down Bernard via his mother, Margaret. Newspaper articles in a local newspaper celebrating Margaret's birthdays after she reached the age of 100 alerted me to the Bernard's approximate whereabouts.

Previously, I had very quickly established important ties with the branch of the Robinson family in Turkey, through Spencer

Robinson's second wife, Hannah. However, until I was able to contact Bernard, my information about the Robinsons in England had been largely confined to browsing Internet websites and sifting through old newspaper collections. Finally meeting Bernard and exchanging details with him about his family was a pivotal moment. Until then, the Robinsons in England were simply names recorded in data bases. These were names which had little meaning for me. I had known only a little about Minick and May Belle, the two offspring from Spencer Robinson's first marriage. Through my communications with Spencer Robinson's great-grandson, I was also able to get more of a feel of how, and to what extent, different branches of the Robinsons, living in various countries, remained in touch with each other.

Unless otherwise cited, much of the information in this chapter comes from contacts and an interview with Bernard and his wife Becky. Unfortunately, because Bernard's father suffered from serious health problems in his later years, many of the details I have gathered stem from Bernard's own memories and experiences or from the recollections of his mother.

Spencer Robinson's son Minick, and his family, came to regard the island city of Portsmouth as their home. Unlike their relatives living abroad, the Robinsons who remained in England did not become involved in political intrigues, rub shoulders with royalty, or make a name for themselves as famous sporting celebrities. Nevertheless, these Robinsons had their own stories to tell of hardship and tragedy, and of enterprise and wealth.

Continuing urban poverty went hand in hand with the agricultural depression in late nineteenth-century England. Women still laboured in the sweatshops of the overcrowded cities and men toiled for long hours on the factory floor or down the pit. However, better-organised trade unions and the growth of a socialist movement eventually compelled the government to introduce social and economic reforms. The foundations of the welfare state were laid in the first years of the twentieth century. Legislation for old-age pensions and national insurance enabled many to escape the ignominy of seeking poor relief in the workhouse. A second Industrial Revolution based on iron, steel, electrification and engineering was gathering momentum. Gradually, there were improvements in housing and in living and working conditions. The expansion of the transportation system, with the introduction of the internal combustion engine and the further extension of the railway network, enabled more workers to leave slum areas and move to the suburbs. For example, around 700,000 people moved to the outskirts of London between 1901 and 1911.[2] More reforms, though, were required. Women still did not have the vote, and, in the years immediately prior to the First World War, miners, railwaymen, textile workers and dockyard hands went on strike to secure higher wages and improved working conditions.

This was a period when the middle class dramatically expanded in size. The growth of commerce and industry resulted in a demand for clerical jobs. The spread of free education meant that these posts could be filled by a literate workforce.[3] The descendants of Spencer Robinson who stayed in *fin de siècle* England seemed, in effect, to straddle the divide between the upwardly mobile affluent middle class and workers who were still struggling to make ends meet. Spencer's daughter became engaged to the son of a prosperous entrepreneur who lived on a country estate in rural Somerset as well as residing in a fine house in the suburbs of London. Spencer's son, on the other hand, married a young woman who came from a broken family and who had recently worked in conditions akin to those of the sweatshop. This was another example of 'like father like son'. Spencer Robinson's second wife, Hannah, had also come from a troubled and poor background.

The Robinsons came to live and work in the Portsmouth district. They became closely connected with life around the government dockyard and the military encampments in the area. The womenfolk had earlier struggled to earn a living in the harsh conditions of the local corset-making industry. The Robinsons were one of many hard-working families living in Portsmouth. While by no means near the bottom of the social leader, money still had to be earned. Could a case be made, then, that the Robinsons in Portsmouth were caught between what was at the time a comfortable middle class and the struggling working class? Minick's earnings from his labour in the dockyard were quite meagre, and unlike his father, he was not destined to work in a managerial position. There is no evidence that his wife, Emily, had a paid job after they married. On the other hand, as outlined below, it seems that Minick was able to benefit, in part, from money left by his father.

May Belle Robinson
Little has been said about the life of May Belle, the daughter of Spencer and Isabella Robinson. This was another life which was tragically

cut short. At the time of the 1891 census, the twenty-year-old May Belle was living in Peckham Rye, Camberwell, with her grandmother Mary Ann Robinson, her aunt Jessie Clitherow, and Jessie's husband, Robert, the surgeon. No occupation was listed next to May Belle's name. She was eventually engaged to Douglas Andrews Gordon Harding, one of the sons of Douglas H. Harding, a well-known rope, line and twine manufacturer. A reputable company involved in the imports of jute and sisal, Douglas Harding and Sons Ltd had been established in the mid-eighteenth century and by the late 1800s ran its successful business from Whitecross Street in central London. The family firm boasted that the hammocks it produced were 'the best and strongest in the world'.[4]

It seems that May Belle had known the Harding family for some time. In August 1893, she helped out in the bazaar and fete which was traditionally organised by the Hardings at their country seat in Sutton Montis near Yeovil in Somerset. Money was being raised to support the local village church. In the extensive grounds of Sutton Montis House, various amusements were provided, a band played music, maypole dancers offered entertainment and a tea hut was supplying refreshment for the many guests. Playing an active role in the proceedings, May Belle 'enthusiastically presided' over 'a very extensive art gallery' which 'attracted large crowds'.[5]

May Belle died on 11 May 1895 aged only twenty-four. She had been suffering from galloping consumption for five weeks before her death. May Belle passed away at the family home of the Hardings at 'Hurstleigh' in Thurlow Park Road, Dulwich, Surrey, only days before her planned marriage to her fiancé. She was buried in the graveyard of the Holy Trinity Church in Hagworthingham in Lincolnshire by the side of her grandmother, who had died two years earlier.

Understandably, perhaps, May Belle had not prepared a will and so she died intestate. However, a grant of letters of administration was issued in favour of her brother Minick Robinson, the 'only next of kin'. This enabled Minick to access the personal estate of May Belle, which had a gross value of a little over £136. Minick Palmer Robinson remained the only surviving child from the marriage of Spencer and Isabella.

Following the death of May Belle, a visibly distraught Douglas Andrews Gordon Harding lost all interest in the family business and became a missionary. He eventually married ten years later, had children, and travelled to China to carry out his missionary work. Active as a Protestant missionary in Chefoo (now known as Yantai) in Shandong Province in north-eastern China, he died in November 1929.

Minick Palmer Robinson

In contrast to his sister, there is firm evidence that Minick lived and worked in India for a period in the late 1880s. His apprenticeship at the locomotive repair shop at Tindharia provided a useful springboard for securing employment back in England after his father's death. The property at 15 Festing Road, Southsea, which Minick was able to purchase in 1908, was at one time full of Indian furniture, mostly black in colour, which had presumably been crated and transported to England when the Robinsons returned from Bengal.

By the time of the 1891 census, Minick was in lodgings at 45 Over Street in Brighton. This was near to the guesthouse run by his stepmother, and presumably the two kept in close contact during this period. Over Street was situated in the North Laine district of Brighton and was one of the last areas in that neighbourhood to be developed. Sanitary conditions were quite poor. Houses had no inside toilets, and local residents often kept pigs and chickens in open yards. Because of its proximity to the railway terminal, the district was one where railway staff tended to live. Men who worked in the nearby foundries and breweries were also lodgers in North Laine.[6]

Minick worked as an engine fitter and turner for the London, Brighton and South Coast Railway Company. He was registered as a new hand in December 1890, and one year later was reported receiving an income of 4 shillings per day. The company operated the 'Brighton Line', which connected the capital with the south coast. Minick was working at a time when the company's Brighton Railway Engineering Works was at its peak, employing over 2,650 staff to maintain carriages and locomotives. This was arguably the golden age of the London, Brighton and South Coast Railway Company. Under its chief mechanical engineer, Robert J. Billinton, repair facilities in Brighton were expanded and new tank engines designed.[7]

Having started employment on the railways, on 3 July 1891 Minick joined the Royal Engineers for a period of 'short service' – i.e. seven years with the colours and five years with the reserves. Details of Minick's appearance were provided on his enlistment card. He was almost 5 feet 8 inches in height and weighed approximately

10 stones. With medium complexion, he had black hair and hazel-coloured eyes. As distinguishing features, Minick had a scar under his chin and on his left little finger. He joined the Royal Engineers as a sapper (responsible for various military engineering duties). Transferring to the reserve in 1898, he was recalled to active duty in February 1900 at the time of the Boer War. He was finally discharged in July 1903 having not served abroad. While in the armed forces, Minick passed specialised classes in submarine mining and engine driving.

At the end of the nineteenth century, special companies of the Royal Engineers were chiefly responsible for the laying of defensive submarine mines on rivers and coastal estuaries in Britain. These were employed to protect ports and dockyards further upstream. Vessels were used to carefully position the mines in a predetermined pattern on the river or seabed. These fixed mines were connected by cables to the shore. If an enemy boat approached the minefield, observers on land could then electronically detonate the mines. Powerful searchlights were also developed to illuminate the minefields at night. Considerable manpower was needed to monitor the various minefields dotted across the country. The Royal Engineers were therefore assisted by militia divisions or by the Volunteers.

Training to be a submarine miner was quite intense. Recruits only received a higher rate of pay if they could swim at least 100 yards and manage to keep afloat for one minute while fully clothed. In addition to completing a general course on submarine mining, other related courses were offered for trainees. A course on 'engine driving' extended over nine months and was taught 'to selected men only'. Engine driving involved work with engines on vessels and launches and with stationary engines on shore for electric lighting and steam hoists. It entailed the repair of all parts of machinery and included other tasks such as removing and re-tubing boilers.[8] According to his army record, in November 1893 Minick passed a course on engine driving with a 'superior' grade. He received a 'very superior' grade for engine driving in February 1896.

It seems that Minick Robinson acquired a sought-after expertise in submarine mining and engine driving. One of his first military postings was to Fort Monckton in Portsmouth. Named after the late eighteenth-century governor of Portsmouth, Lt-Gen Sir Robert Monckton, the base was the headquarters of the Fourth Company of

Submarine Miners of the Royal Engineers. Exercises in laying naval mines and using searchlights were regularly carried out near the fort.

The vice captain of Minick's company at the time, and the main instructor at the Submarine Mining School, who was responsible for the welfare of his men, was a certain W. Seely Vidal. Vidal has a particular claim to fame: the golfing term 'Colonel Bogey' has been attributed to the captain. In late Victorian England, 'Hush, Hush Here Comes the Bogey Man' was a popular music hall song. One of the lines in the song warned, 'He'll catch you if he can.' In golf, the 'ground score' (today's par for each hole) was looked upon as the minimum number of shots a proficient golfer should take for each hole. When they were not able to outplay the ground score, golfers started to say that they were getting 'caught' by the ground score, as if they were being caught by 'Mister Bogey', the 'Bogey Man'. The so-called 'bogey score' thus began to be employed in place of the ground score. In 1892, Vidal, then the honorary secretary of the United Services Club at Gosport, helped work out the bogey score for each hole for his golf course. Playing with colleagues, Vidal joked that as members of the military they could not compare themselves against a mere 'Mister Bogey'. He suggested that their imaginary rival should be a commanding officer and should have at least have the rank of colonel. Vidal then saluted the fantasy and expressed delight to be playing against him. Thus, the term 'Colonel Bogey' was created. Vidal then wrote to *The Field and Gold* magazine describing the system of playing against the mythical Colonel Bogey.[9] The term proved to be a popular one and was quickly adopted by the golfing fraternity. Later, somewhat confusingly, 'bogey' was used for a score of one above par for a hole. I do not know if Minick Robinson himself played golf.

While serving at Fort Monckton, Minick married Emily Frances Jones at St James Church, Portsea, on 25 May 1893. The couple would have one child, Spencer Palmer, born at 42 Harold Road in nearby Southsea on 6 January 1897. Portsea and Southsea were both districts within the city of Portsmouth.

Before the birth of his child, Minick was stationed for a period in Renfrewshire at Gourock on the River Clyde. There, he worked together with the Clyde Volunteer Division of Submarine Miners which was based at Fort Matilda. Constructed in the early nineteenth century, the fort was initially the site of a coastal battery. The headquarters of the Clyde Volunteer Division was expanded and renovated in the early 1890s to accommodate a submarine mining unit. The division was responsible for maintaining the minefield laid across the Clyde between Greenock and Kilcreggin. As a Royal Engineer trained in submarine mining, Minick's presence would have been appreciated by the Clyde Volunteers. A local newspaper at the time reported how 'a small force of Royal Engineers' supervised the work of the Volunteer submarine miners.[10] Emily perhaps accompanied Minick to Scotland given that he did not stay in the barracks at Fort Matilda. Instead, in 1895 and 1896, he lived at two nearby addresses on Cardwell Road overlooking Cardwell Bay.[11]

After completing his seven years' service with the colours, Minick and his family moved to Essex. For a period, Minick worked as an engine fitter in Chelmsford. According to the census of 1901, Minick and his family were living at 6 Cooper's Row, off Broomfield Road. A number of neighbours of the Robinsons on Cooper's Row were also engine fitters; there were also mechanical engineers, iron moulders and an engineer's labourer. Chelmsford had become an important centre for industrial and electrical engineering in Britain's second Industrial Revolution. Guglielmo Marconi opened the world's first radio wireless factory in Hall Street, Chelmsford in 1899, and the town came to be known as the birthplace of radio. Hoffmann Manufacturing Company founded the world's first ball-bearing plant in Chelmsford. Unfortunately, I do not know for which company Minick was employed, but it was quite possible that he worked for the firm Christy & Norris, which operated an iron foundry at the end of Broomfield Road. The business produced manufacturing machinery for the food and agricultural industries. One of Minick's neighbours, Albert Harris, who lived in 1901 at 1 Cooper's Row, certainly earned his living as an engine fitter at Messrs Christy & Norris.[12] Charles Dickens was not one of Chelmsford's admirers. Back in 1835, when working for the *Morning Chronicle* in the East Anglia area, Dickens referred to Chelmsford as 'the dullest and most stupid spot on the face of the earth'.[13]

In early 1900, presumably while living in Chelmsford, Minick was recalled to active military duty as war had broken out with the Boers in southern Africa. Because of their skills in the use of searchlights and the telegraph, a number of submarine miners served in the conflict. This meant that those in the reserve were called up to fill positions vacated at home.[14] It is quite possible, given his location, that Minick served for a period with the submarine mining station at Landguard Fort in nearby Harwich on the River Orwell. Alternatively, he may have worked with the Royal Engineers garrisoned in Colchester. It is perhaps surprising, therefore, that he was registered as an engine fitter living in Chelmsford at the time of the 1901 census. What is clear is that Minick was granted a working furlough by the military between the period 1 September 1901 and 31 March 1902. This would have enabled him to resume his employment as an engine fitter.

By 1905, Minick had returned to the Portsmouth area and was working as a hired fitter at the government's naval dockyard. Records show that he was employed at the dockyard until his death in 1923. In the period known as the 'Great Extension', between 1867 and 1881, the dockyard had almost trebled in size from 99 to 261 acres to enable work to be carried out on the new iron-hulled warships. Shipbuilding was a labour-intensive industry. The workforce employed at the dockyard soared from a total of 6,300 in 1881 to 15,000 by 1914. In the years immediately before the outbreak of the First World War, the naval dockyard in Portsmouth was a buzz of activity. In October 1905, the construction of the world's first dreadnought battleship at Dock Number 13 formally commenced. With its long-range 12-inch guns, and its top speed of 21 knots, the dreadnought made all other forms of battleship obsolete. However, this also meant that the numerical superiority of Britain's fleet had become irrelevant. The firepower and fighting effectiveness of a country's navy became primarily dependent on the number of dreadnoughts available in the fleet. Within five months of its keel being laid down, HMS *Dreadnought* was launched by King Edward VII in February 1906. Germany soon launched its own programme to build the new battleship, and, in what became a naval-arms race between the two rival powers, the Portsmouth dockyard scrambled to build ten dreadnoughts by 1915. Each year the dockyard produced larger and faster dreadnoughts.[15]

I do not know if Minick himself was directly employed in the dreadnought-building programme, although he had commenced work at the dockyard in the same year that it began. The work of a fitter was technical and highly skilled. It was a new, specialist trade in shipbuilding, and there was a fierce rivalry between the fitters and shipwrights. The latter were traditionally involved with the manufacture and repair of the structure of the ship. Engine fitters were tasked with working on the ship's main engines, its gas turbines, and the internal combustion engines. With technological developments and their specialised skills, fitters threatened to upstage the shipwrights in the established hierarchy of labour at the Portsmouth dockyard. The two sets of workers clashed over the allocation of specific tasks. Fitters complained that the shipwrights were determined to exclude them from work concerning the valves, pumps, gun mountings and the watertight doors.[16]

Very few fitters were engaged on an established basis, and those who were believed themselves superior to the rest on account of their guaranteed job security and pension. Hired fitters received a slightly greater wage, but did not have such job security. By the late nineteenth century, the practice was to employ more hired than established men, which provided management with more flexibility with regard to hiring and firing staff.[17] However, jobs in government dockyards were generally more secure than their equivalents in the private shipyards. Moreover, given the expansion of the government dockyard in Portsmouth, the position of hired fitters there was particularly secure.

According to Minick's paybook, in his first two years of employment at the dockyard as a hired engine fitter he received 34 shillings per week. This was at the very bottom of the pay scale for a hired fitter in Portsmouth at the time. Over the following years his pay gradually increased so that in the period between June 1918 and September 1923 he was earning 44 shillings each week. He was also fortunate enough to benefit from Admiralty pension schemes introduced in 1913 and then in 1920. Contracts for hired fitters were renewed annually, usually around Christmas.

There is no evidence that Minick took an active part in industrial unrest in the Portsmouth dockyard in 1913 over worker dissatisfaction with regard to wage levels and long overtime hours. Strike action was threatened as the workforce were feeling the effects of a prolonged period of inflation. The consequences of such industrial action could have been serious given the ongoing naval arms race with Germany. The Admiralty eventually decided to increase pay on average by around 2 shillings per week and the dockyard workers ended their protest.[18] However, this did not have immediate impact on Minick's earnings. Receiving 38 shillings per week since September 1911, his wage packet only increased to 39 shillings per week in September 1914.

In spite of relatively paltry earnings, at the time of the 1911 census Minick and his family were able to live in a seven-roomed house on St Augustine Road in Eastney, a neighbourhood of Southsea in Portsmouth. This was quite a large property for a dockyard worker in an area which was only recently developed following the construction of barracks for the Royal Marine Artillery. Three years earlier he had bought property at Festing Road in Southsea. Was Minick, here, perhaps benefiting from some of the money bequeathed by his father?

Minick passed away in Portsmouth on 24 September 1923. The fifty-four-year-old had died of heart failure, pleurisy and pneumonia. His son, Spencer Palmer, was present at his death. Minick had not prepared a will, but, through letters of administration, he left all his effects of over £2,315 – a very respectable sum of money – to his widow, Emily.

Emily Frances Newell

Minick's future wife was baptised at St Nicholas Church in Brighton on 3 December 1865. Emily was one of six children – four girls and two boys – raised by Mary Newell. Mary lived most of her life estranged from her husband, Stephen. Emily was previously married to Arthur Jones. However, Arthur died only six months after their wedding. Less than five months after the death of her first husband, Emily married Minick. It seems that attempts were made to cover up Emily's previous marriage to Arthur Jones.

The Newells were a relatively poor Sussex-based family. They can be traced back to the early eighteenth century when Emily's great-great-grandfather Will lived in the village of Easebourne. The Newells remained in West Sussex for the next few generations, living in the nearby settlements of Easebourne, Trotton and Midhurst. Emily's grandfather worked at one time in a paper mill and he was also an agricultural labourer.

Born in Stedham in Sussex sometime in the 1830s, Emily's father, Stephen Newell, was employed as a baker. Marrying Mary Boxall in 1861, he ran a grocer's shop and bakery with her at Trotton. One worker helped them run the business. Although Stephen and Mary had six children, by 1871 the career of Emily's father had taken a turn for the worse. Separated by this time from his wife and children, Stephen was working in Bramley in Surrey as a 'servant' for a William J. Major, baker and grocer. Major was several years younger than Stephen. Confusingly, the census records refer to a Henry S. Newell – but the place and year of birth correspond with Stephen's details. Ten years later, Stephen's circumstances had improved somewhat. He was working as the head baker at St John's College at Hurstpierpoint in West Sussex. This job must have entailed certain responsibilities. St John's College was a Church of England school which provided instruction for 800 boys. Only affluent families could afford to pay the fees to secure an education for their child in what was a collegiate setting. A Stephen Newell died in Havant in Hampshire in 1903. This was presumably Emily's father.

Emily's mother, Mary Boxall, born in Trotton in 1832, appears to have been quite a character. Her father, Thomas, was a carpenter. After Thomas died, his wife, Hannah, evidently an enterprising and independent woman, continued to run the carpentry business in Trotton, employing one worker. After having separated from Stephen, for some unknown reason Mary continued to refer to herself as being married to a seaman rather than a baker. An ostensible partnership with a sailor could have been exploited to account for her husband's continued absence from the family household. Mary and her children moved and lived in different towns in 1871 and 1881. By 1901, Mary was presenting herself as a widow, although it seems that Stephen was still alive. She is last recorded in 1911 as living with her daughter Eva Ellen Barr and her son-in-law, the naval commander Ernest Barr, in Bobbing, Kent. Again, the information provided by Mary did not appear to be accurate. In the 1911 census, she referred to herself as sixty-eight years of age, although it seems that she was actually eleven years older.

Together with her five siblings, Emily was brought up by her mother. In 1871, she was a young child living in Godalming, Surrey. Ten years later, the teenage Emily, living at 18 Arnaud Street in Portsea, was already working as a stay-maker (corsetmaker) together with her elder sister Louisa. In late Victorian England, Portsmouth was a key centre for the corset industry. This labour-intensive industry perhaps originated from earlier sail making. Women, working as dressmakers, seamstresses and stay-makers, accounted for 21–33 per cent of industrial employment in Portsmouth in the period from 1841 to 1901.[19] Between 1861 and 1901, the number of stay-makers in the Portsmouth district increased from

597 to 2,288.[20] Many women in the area were married to seamen who received inadequate salaries. These women, in particular, were forced to seek a supplementary source of income while their husbands were at sea for prolonged periods. Given the hazards of sailing, there was no guarantee that their men would return home. A large pool of cheap labour could thus be exploited with women working as corsetmakers either in small factories, which were basically sweatshops, or at home. Through the 'putting out' system favoured by manufacturers, women could collect materials from warehouses and then produce garments by working on them at home. Entrepreneurs had the added advantage of being able to select households which had sewing machines, thereby further cutting back on the capital they needed to run a business.[21] In a Portsmouth newspaper of February 1883, the situations vacant column had seventeen separate postings where local manufacturers were seeking indoor or outdoor stay-makers. Firms such as Leethem Reynolds, Totterdell Son, and Royal, and E. Izod and Son were looking to hire machine hands.[22] This work was poorly paid and women and young girls were obliged to work long hours.[23]

The Portsea district itself at the time was an area full of dilapidated buildings near to the dockside. Closed courts and narrow alleyways meant that air could not circulate. The overcrowded site, with its lack of drainage and proper sanitation, had suffered especially in the cholera epidemic of 1848. Notorious for its many brothels, grog shops and bawdy houses catering for the maritime community, by the 1890s the vicinity around Portsea was infamously known as 'The Devil's Acre'.[24]

By 1891, Emily had left her mother and had taken up lodgings at 65 Goodwood Road in Southsea. In contrast to Portsea, Southsea was a well-heeled neighbourhood of handsome residences and shops catering for naval officers and their families, although Goodwood Road itself was still some distance from the attractions of the esplanade and Southsea's two piers. Emily was living with her sister Edith Kate, who had recently married Harry Ferguson, a driver in the Army Service Corps (responsible for army transport). No longer involved in sweated labour, Emily was employed as a shop woman in one of the large number of confectioneries in the Portsmouth district. At the time, confectioners sold bread as well as biscuits and other sweets. Emily's choice of profession may have been influenced by her father's calling.

Most probably via Harry Ferguson, Emily was introduced to Arthur Henry Jones, who also worked in the Army Service Corps. Emily and Arthur were married on 30 June 1892 in Portsea. The two witnesses were Edith Kate and Henry Newell, one of Emily's brothers. Arthur Jones came from another broken family. In 1881, he had been living in Colchester with his sister and brother and his unmarried mother, Emma, who was employed as a charwoman. No father was listed in the household. The sixteen-year-old Arthur was recorded as working as a foundry labourer. On the marriage certificate, Arthur described himself as a turner. A father, also called Arthur and a turner, was mentioned on the certificate.

The military record of Arthur Jones included a long list of misdemeanours. There were numerous charges of being drunk and disorderly, of being absent from barracks without leave, and assaulting police officers while inebriated. Discharged from active service on 20 June 1892, Arthur was given a clean bill of health, although he had earlier suffered from a bout of bronchitis and had spent twenty-two days in hospital in February and March 1892. In July, the newly wed Arthur had placed a notice in a local newspaper seeking employment as a groom or coachman.[25] However, only six months later the twenty-six-year-old army pensioner and groom died of chronic wasting away. There are rumours that in his brief marriage Arthur had been unfaithful to Emily.

Emily swiftly remarried. On 25 May 1893, Emily and Minick were married at St James Church in Portsea. On the marriage certificate, it was recorded that 'Emily Frances Jones' was a spinster. Emily's father was registered as 'Stephen Jones', a baker. Clearly, the intention here was to give the impression that Emily had not been previously married. Why would the Newells have decided to conceal Emily's marriage to Arthur? How did Minick react to such turn of events? The military in Portsmouth were a tight-knit community and so it would have been very surprising if Minick had not known of the previous marriage.

In Victorian England, widows were expected to go through an extended period of mourning before possibly considering a second marriage. After the death in 1861 of her husband, Prince Albert, Queen Victoria had continued to wear her 'widow's weeds' until her own passing. While this was an exception, widows from the upper and middle classes were expected to mourn for at least two years, wearing black clothing initially (for the first year and a day) before gradually dressing in muted colours. Working-class widows, however, could not afford the outlay on mourning clothing and often made do by simply wearing black trimming on a hat.[26]

If widows did remarry, the ceremony was usually a low-key affair with a modest reception and few guests invited. Many widows either decided not to remarry or found it exceedingly difficult to find a new partner. In the Victorian era, only 11–12 per cent of widows remarried. For many bereaved women, widowhood was seen as 'a final destiny'. There were also various stigmas associated with widowhood. Spinsters, especially, regarded the widow as a 'formidable foe'. Viewing widows as 'predators', spinsters were afraid that these unscrupulous women could use their experience, wiles and charms to catch a man.[27]

With regard to the case of Emily, her first marriage had been very brief and her husband may have been unfaithful. She was still young and was not burdened with any children. In these circumstances, a second marriage would likely have been less controversial. Pressing financial concerns may also have compelled Emily to attach herself quickly to a new partner. Nevertheless, the time period between Arthur's death and Emily's marriage to Minick was admittedly rather short.

Unfortunately, we know little of Emily's later life, although she maintained contacts with other members of the Robinson family in Turkey and in Germany. She became interested in spiritualism and clairvoyance, the former having developed a significant following in Portsmouth as the superstitious beliefs of many sailors led to fortune tellers and mediums setting up shop in the port. The wives of mariners turned to fortune tellers for reassurance that their husbands were safe on ship. If their loved ones had perished at sea, women then sought out local mediums to seek guarantees that the spirits of those who had drowned had been able to return home. In late Victorian England, Portsmouth became notorious for its so-called 'port heathenism'.[28]

Interest in the supernatural in Portsmouth was revived after the First World War, when parents were eager to make contact with their sons who had been victims of the conflict. The famous novelist Sir Arthur Conan Doyle is said to have contacted his dead son, Kingsley, in a séance. Doyle had openly declared himself to be a spiritualist in 1916. Setting up a medical practice in Southsea back in 1882, Doyle had quickly established ties with local practising psychics many years before he became a leading proponent of the spiritualist movement. His second wife, Jean, was a medium.

Catering for the interest in the supernatural, the Temple of Spiritualism had been founded in 1905 on Victoria Road South in Southsea. Doyle donated money to the temple. Services were held regularly at the temple, and lectures and performances were given by guest speakers. Details of activities organised at the centre were regularly publicised in the local newspapers.

It seems that Emily did not go public with her interest in spiritualism and clairvoyance. There is no record of her being elected to any office in the Temple of Spiritualism or of her performing in front of an audience, but her grandson has mentioned one anecdote in which Emily told the wardens who came around to provide gas masks for the family that she would not be needing one. Indeed, Emily died immediately before the outbreak of the Second World War.

Emily suffered from eye problems in her final years. She passed away in Southsea on 29 June 1939. In her will, almost all her effects, totalling over £3,682, were left to her son, Spencer Palmer. A small amount was also bequeathed to one of her brothers, Albert Ernest Newell.

Spencer Palmer Robinson

England, in the inter-war period, consolidated and expanded the social and political gains that had been secured for the less advantaged in the years immediately before 1914. Women acquired the right to vote, and a Labour Party more representative of the workers replaced the Liberals as the chief opposition to the Tories. The Victorian era had long since ended and had been replaced by a new age of opportunity. Campaigning for the general election at the end the First World War, British Prime Minister David Lloyd George had promised 'homes fit for heroes'. The Housing and Town Planning Act of 1919 made local authorities responsible for the provision of council housing. Slums were replaced with new properties, and a further housing boom followed in the 1930s. This was made possible by the availability of land, the fall in the price of raw materials, low interest rates, and a marked reduction in the amount that needed to be deposited to secure a home. Society did suffer from bouts of high unemployment, but the Great Depression of the 1930s had a much more negative impact on the economies of the US and Germany.

'Robbie', Minick and Emily's only child, married twice and was the father of three children. In contrast to his father, his working life did not follow an obvious trajectory. Initially employed as a fitter in the Portsmouth dockyard, in the inter-war period Spencer Palmer worked as a commercial traveller (salesman) for the confectionery business George W. Horner and Company. After the Second World War, he was surprisingly involved in 'top-secret' projects working for the Admiralty.

According to his son, Spencer Palmer had a bit of a reputation as a ladies' man. Handsome in appearance, he cut a figure very much like Cary Grant. He had the habit of saying that he was much younger than his real age. Spencer Palmer evidently flourished in the period between the two world wars. A clever investor in property, he had the foresight to purchase a number of terraced houses in the Portsmouth area in the housing boom of the 1930s when prices were falling. In line with the emerging and developing middle class, he also had the free time to enjoy sports and recreation. Much of his leisure time was spent at the Wimbledon Park Tennis Club in Southsea, which opened its doors in 1928. Successful in various tennis competitions, he served as chairman and treasurer of the club; it had struggled financially before he took over as chairman, but under his stewardship its fortunes greatly improved. He was also a responsible family man. Living together with his ailing mother, he single-handedly brought up his two daughters after he divorced his first wife.

Frustratingly, I have not been able to find evidence which proves that Spencer Palmer fought in the First World War – the war which resulted in the deaths of two of his close relatives. A lot of the British war records have been damaged or destroyed by fire. At the outbreak of the war Spencer Palmer was a mere seventeen years of age. It is quite possible, though, that he was called up or volunteered for duty as the war continued over the next four years.

In a sense following in the footsteps of his mother, who had at one time been employed in the confectionery business, Spencer Palmer started work with George W. Horner and Company, the well-known confectionery manufacturers based in Chester-le-Street in Durham. The business had been established in October 1910 by George William Horner, an entrepreneur from Norfolk. Horner took over the premises of what was then a jam factory. At the Stag Works, he quickly built up a sweets company which became famous for its international brands – 'Boy Blue' and 'Dainty Dinah' toffees. The Dainty Dinah products displayed a young, dark-haired Edwardian lady dressed in a bonnet. This colourful image soon grabbed the public's attention and became a popular trademark. Factory girls on occasion posed in Dainty Dinah costumes to advertise the firm. George Horner's chauffeuse, Alice Scott, became a local celebrity for modelling in promotions dressed as Dinah. Dainty Dinah became such an important symbol of the company that a 300-kilogram painted Dainty Dinah bust was designed and positioned on the outside of the works close to the factory's chimney. The grounds around the factory were known as 'the five acres of sweetness'. Stories were told of how women working in the factory tossed sweets out of the windows to children passing on their way to school. In its hey-day the factory employed 770 women and more than 100 men.[29] Up to 2 million sweets a day were produced. Colourful, vintage sweet tins produced by the company are now prized as valuable collectors' items.

As George W. Horner and Company expanded, with the opening of a plant in London, salespeople were required in different parts of the country to promote its products. As early as the 1920s, the confectionery business had acquired a reputation for its well-planned use of a road fleet which operated to collect orders over a wide area. In the 1939 national register – prepared at the outbreak of the Second World War to collect the personal details of every citizen and to issue identity cards – Spencer Palmer, living in Portsmouth, was listed as a commercial traveller for the confectionery manufacturers. A car came with the job, and Spencer Palmer enjoyed travelling extensively around the country.

In the first quarter of 1923, Spencer Palmer married Miriam G. Prosser (b. 1900). Miriam's father, Ivor, had worked in the navy at Portsmouth as a naval signalman. Her mother, Louisa, as in the case of Spencer Palmer's mother, Emily, had been employed as a corsetmaker in her youth. Miriam appeared to come from a textbook family living in the Portsmouth area. Interestingly, however, Louisa also had connections with India as in the case of Spencer Palmer's father, Minick. Louisa Florence Wight was baptised in April 1870 at Jubbulpore in Bengal. Her father, William, had been an armourer sergeant based at the military cantonment in Jubbulpore. Armourer sergeants were responsible for the upkeep of rifles and other mechanical equipment.

Spencer Palmer and Miriam had two daughters, Kathlyn Patricia – 'Pat' – (b. 1923) and Pamela (b. 1925). However, in 1927, Spencer Palmer petitioned for divorce on the grounds that his wife had been unfaithful. After their separation, Miriam ran her own business as a ladies' hairdresser in Portsmouth while Spencer Palmer continued to look after the children as well as work.

According to the 1939 register, Pat was living with a dairy farmer's family on Bossington Farm near Romsey in Hampshire. She was one of the many children evacuated from urban areas to rural communities at the start of the Second World War. Operation Pied Piper commenced on 1 September 1939, upon the outbreak of war, and within three days around 1.5 million children had been resettled in a massive and coordinated operation. Many children were moved from the areas around the docks in Portsmouth and Southampton. Both ports would soon be the target of German bomber attacks.

At the start of hostilities, Spencer Palmer was serving as a part-time member of the Auxiliary Fire Service (AFS). Formed in 1938 as a part of the Civil Defence Service to provide back-up support to the regular fire service, the AFS was staffed by unpaid volunteers. By September 1939, the AFS had recruited over 200,000 members.

The AFS was forced to play an active front-line role in the Blitz of Portsmouth. The first German attack on the port on 11 July 1940 killed eighteen residents. One month later, over 200 enemy planes targeted the dockyards. The Portsmouth Blitz refers to the three deadly and sustained waves of attacks in January, March and April 1941. According to the local press, the evening raid on 10 January 1941 became known as the 'Night of Terror'. Over 300 aircraft dropped 25,000 incendiaries and hundreds of high-explosive bombs. Six churches and three major shopping centres were destroyed and 170 people were killed. The city was ablaze, and the blood-red glow could be seen as far away as on the French coast.[30] Spencer Palmer would have been on the front line struggling to save lives and property.

The Portsmouth members of the AFS also attempted to lend assistance to firefighting crews at the time of the Southampton blitz at the end of November 1940. This was the first time Spencer Palmer was at the wheel of one of the fire engines, and he drove the whole of the journey from Portsmouth to Southampton in first gear. The trip would be a wasted one: the two services had different equipment, with the Portsmouth firemen's hose couplings incompatible with the hydrants of Southampton. An exasperated Spencer Palmer and his colleagues could only stand and watch as parts of Southampton were engulfed.

Little is known of what happened to Spencer Palmer's two daughters. Pat often babysat her half-brother Bernard, and taught him how to play the piano. She died in Southampton in the third quarter of 1982. Her younger sister, Pamela, married a Charles W. Clarke in Portsmouth in the third quarter of 1947. The following year they had a son, Leonard. The marriage was an unhappy one, and, after a divorce, Pamela emigrated to Australia.

In the third quarter of 1935, in Portsmouth, Spencer Palmer married Margaret Mary Hall. At the time of the marriage, Margaret was in her mid-twenties. She was ten years younger than Spencer Palmer's first wife. A state-registered nurse and midwife, Margaret was forced to curtail her career following her marriage. At the time, as a condition of their work, hospital nurses were required to live on-site. It was therefore impossible for a nurse to continue in her profession if she married.

Margaret was a Catholic and had been educated at a convent school. Spencer Palmer was a Protestant. Religious differences were not important. However, it appears that until their marriage Margaret had not known that Spencer Palmer was divorced, had two daughters and lived with his mother.

Spencer Palmer's second wife came from a very different family background. Her great-great-great-grandfather was James Smith (1762–1818), the world-famous shoemaker. Originally a travelling leather salesman, in 1792 Smith opened a small shop behind Norwich market and began to make and sell shoes. His claim to fame was that he was the first shoemaker to offer a cheap alternative to expensively produced bespoke footwear. He realised that most feet were of a similar size, and so there was no need to produce shoes which were all made-to-measure. This realisation enabled Smith to mass-manufacture shoes and thereby gain a decisive edge over his competitors. Smith died in 1818 and his son Charles passed away shortly after, but the shoe business was maintained by trustees for James's grandson Charles Smith Winter.[31]

Charles Smith Winter (1806–67), the well-known Norwich-based wholesale manufacturer of light footwear for women and children, was one of the first businessmen in England to employ the Singer Sewing Machine in 1856. This revolutionised the production of shoes, although the introduction of the machine was at first highly unpopular. Fearful of losing their jobs, protesting workers vented their opposition by going on strike.[32] Winter also held high public office in his native Norwich, serving as magistrate, sheriff and mayor. Known for his enthusiasm for civic duty, he was President of the Benevolent Association for the Relief of Decayed Tradesmen, their Widows and Orphans. His residence was at Heigham Grove House – a large, impressive Gothic Revival mansion situated amid extensive gardens. After Winter's death, the shoe business was transferred into the hands of James Southall, who later became identified with the 'Start Rite' footwear. Originally, the plan had been for one of the sons, Charles Smith Winter Junior, to inherit the family business, but he had died at the age of twenty-seven, shortly before his father passed away.

The descendants of Charles Smith Winter benefitted from the wealth accumulated from the shoemaking business. His granddaughter Edith Laurette Winter, raised in a boarding school in England and in a convent in France, married Francis Joseph Hall, an insurance clerk, in the late 1890s. Their fourth child, Margaret, was born at the end of 1910. With the outbreak of the Second World War, Margaret Robinson was able to join the ambulance service and make use of her medical training. After the war, she gave birth to a son, Bernard Spencer, in 1946. In her final years, Margaret became somewhat of a local celebrity in the Leicester area, having re-located to the East Midlands to be near her son. Living until the grand old age of 106, her last birthdays were a cause for celebration in the local media, and overviews of Margaret's life were published by the press.

Spencer Palmer Robinson himself had passed away in Southsea many years earlier in March 1963. Although he had recovered from a stroke in October 1946, he had spent the last ten years of his life practically bedridden. After the Second World War, Spencer Palmer had been involved for a period in confidential work for the Admiralty Signal Establishment at Haslemere in Surrey, and then for the Admiralty Signal and Radar Establishment which was established at Portsdown Hill in Portsmouth in 1948. He may have been involved in projects concerning the advancement of radar systems. If this was the case, his work in military technology bore some resemblance to that of his father, who, fifty years earlier, was engaged in work to develop naval mines. It is far from clear, though, how Spencer Palmer was recruited by these institutions given that he seems to have had no background in military research and technology.

Until he went to Sheffield University to study Civil and Structural Engineering, Bernard Spencer Robinson had continued to live at the family home at 15 Festing Road. The family's long association with Portsmouth came to an end in 1977. Bernard's mother had moved out of Festing Road to return to Norfolk, the county of her birth, in 1973, although it would take another four years for the Portsmouth property to be sold. Bernard worked first as a civil engineer in Peterborough, and he held a number of other posts before later completing a master's degree in Transport and Traffic Engineering, again at Sheffield University. He retired in 2011 after working as a traffic engineer and a civil engineer manager involved in highway development. In 1984, Bernard had married Rebecca McGloin from Sheffield.

Ties that Bind or Loosen?

Given the contrasting fortunes of the Robinsons in England, the Ottoman Empire/Turkey, Germany and the US, to what extent did family members maintain ties with one another? Did certain individuals play any role in attempting to keep the family connected, or did the family gradually fragment? In an age before the internet, and with telephone connections still rudimentary, communications would have relied largely on the postal system. The immediate problem here, though, is that so little correspondence between family members has been preserved.

I know from Ahmet Robenson's correspondence in January 1924 with his half-sister Gertrude that Emily Robinson was in contact with her relatives in Turkey. Ahmet wrote that about two weeks ago he had received a letter from Mrs Palmer Robinson (i.e. Emily) letting him know that 'poor Palmer' (i.e. Minick) had died, and that her son, Spencer Palmer, had lately married and was living at Portsmouth with her.[33]

Surprisingly, perhaps, Emily appears to have played a central role in helping to keep together the different branches of the Robinson family. In January 1933 she was still in contact with Ahmet Robenson's sister Maud, who was living in Turkey. Emily wrote how she was 'so very pleased' to have received a letter from Maud after such a long time. She noted that her son, Spencer, would write to Maud himself and 'send the photos'. Emily described how she had 'several letters from the brother Harold' but she had 'not heard from him for years'. She was delighted to hear that Maud had become a mother again to a little girl and that her husband was treating her well. In a very affectionate, sisterly tone, Emily added, 'Poor Maud you have suffered as we all do.' This may have been a reference to the difficulties caused by Maud's separation from her first husband. Emily shared Maud's wishes for them both to meet up some time – sadly, this would never come to pass. Emily also noted that Gerty (Gertrude) had visited her in England a couple of years ago.[34]

Ahmet Robenson actually did maintain ties with Emily's son, Spencer Palmer, and with Spencer Palmer's second wife, Margaret. Throughout the Second World War and the years after, when England was in the grip of food rations, Ahmet despatched food parcels, stockings and toys 'in a large box' to the Robinson household at Southsea. Later, there were also letters sent by airmail to England from Tarrytown in New York State. One of the young Bernard Spencer Robinson's favourite toys was the china model of a Donald Duck money box sent to him by Ahmet. Bernard's mother had to place an elastic plaster over the slot on the money box to prevent her son from continually inserting coins. The treasured Donald Duck remains in Bernard's possession. In the early 1960s, Bernard and his mother prepared a small recording about what life was like in England on a Grundig TK5 reel-to-reel domestic tape recorder. The tape was then sent by airmail to 'Uncle Bernard and Nina'.

Ahmet Robenson was known affectionately to Bernard Spencer Robinson as 'Uncle Bernard'. Ahmet was one of Bernard's godfathers, although it is not known if Ahmet himself made the trip to England for the boy's christening. The name Bernard Spencer Robinson comes from Ahmet and from Bernard's father, Spencer Palmer. Clearly, in spite of the physical distance and the passage of time, the bonds between Ahmet Robenson and Bernard and his family remained close.

Gertrude's grandson Alfred apparently visited Southsea as a boy in the early 1950s on occasion. It would have been quite unusual for a German youth to be travelling around England so soon after the war. Bernard recalls how Alfred usually wore braces. Alfred was given permission to take the young Bernard for rides on Spencer Palmer's bicycle. He cycled 30 to 40 miles each day.

There were also visitors to Southsea from Turkey. In the early 1960s, two young Turkish women stayed in Southsea for several days. And, in the late 1960s, a Turkish lady with her husband were received as guests. The lady in question was a granddaughter of Maud from her first marriage.

Perhaps, it would be an exaggeration to say that Portsmouth served at one time as a hub for members of the Robinson family who lived overseas. It seems highly unlikely that Hannah visited Festing Road. With the possible exception of visiting London in 1900 to contact her solicitor over the money that had been originally left intestate by Spencer's first wife, Isabella, Hannah may have never returned to England after her departure to Constantinople in late 1891. Nevertheless, relatives did come to stay with the Robinsons in Southsea until at least the late 1960s. When the Robinsons eventually left the Portsmouth area in the mid-1970s, this could have made it more difficult for ties to be maintained between family members in England and abroad. It seems that different branches of the family then became further separated. They had, anyway, long since established homes in their various places of residence. England no longer appeared to be a magnet attracting visits from the Robinsons based overseas. Perhaps Alfred's unfortunate death had already resulted in the curtailment of the German connection – with the subsequent passing of Ahmet Robenson, contacts with the US would have automatically come to an end.

Issues over money and inheritance may have caused some tensions within the family before and after the First World War. Gertrude's concerns over this matter, and Hannah's interest in acquiring access to Isabella Robinson's assets, have been previously noted. Ironically, concerns over family inheritance may have been an important contributory factor in holding the family together for a period. It seems, though, that we will never know the full details of how Spencer Robinson's assets and estate were distributed.

I have concentrated on following the footsteps of the immediate descendants of Spencer Robinson from both his first and second wives. But what of the offspring of Spencer Robinson's several brothers and sisters? It would not have been possible for me to attempt to trace the lives of all these many individuals in any meaningful way. Still, one is left to wonder if these other Robinsons established any close ties, for instance with Minick or with Ahmet Robenson. I did not come across any information to suggest that they did. And what of the Rodda and Lintott families? I have no evidence that Hannah maintained any contact with her relatives in the London area and beyond, but was this really the case? No living relatives of Hannah's in Turkey appear to have been aware of the activities of the Roddas in England. In my communications with the German branch of the family there was no mention of the Lintotts, even though Ida Lintott seemed to have been so close to Gertrude Rodda/Eisenmann. Again, a reader may be able to shed more light on these matters.

The story of the Robinsons unfolded in eighteenth-century rural Lincolnshire. By the first decades of the twentieth century, many in the family had severed their ties with the county. None of Spencer Robinson's immediate family now live in East Keal. The Robinsons appear to have been long forgotten in the village. Certainly, the local historian Kit Lawie was not aware of Spencer Robinson's past contributions to social life in East Keal. In search of work and new opportunities, some Robinsons had relocated away from the area while others had tried their luck overseas. Having served his initial apprenticeship in a railway workshop, upon his return to England Minick Robinson sought employment in Brighton at one of the busiest railway companies in the country. For Minick, with no experience in the farming sector, Lincolnshire would have held little attraction. For Spencer Robinson's immediate descendants, Lincolnshire was no longer home.

Before I started this research, two living members of the Robinson family – Bernard Robinson, the great-grandson of Spencer Robinson, and Ahmet Ceylan, Spencer's great-great-grandson – had not been aware of each other's existence. Both relatives had been vaguely aware of Spencer. However, the one character in the family with whom both had felt a connection was Ahmet Robenson. 'Uncle Bernard' may never have seen Bernard Robinson in person, but both Bernard Robinson and Ahmet Ceylan had fond memories of their relative and the two were the recipients of gifts from him.

In my opinion, Ahmet Robenson was a key figure in the family. A connecting agent, it was he who built bridges between family members who were geographically dispersed and then helped sustain them. Literally a man of many names – 'brother Harold', 'Uncle Bernard', and 'Ahmet *dayı*' (i.e. 'Uncle Ahmet', according to Ahmet Ceylan's mother, Gülperi), as well as the various names he used when in the US – Ahmet Robenson was a figure known by the various branches of the family. Among the host of colourful and eye-catching individuals in the Robinson family, Ahmet Robenson was the one with whom I could most relate. He lived and worked for many years in the Ottoman Empire and Turkey, but, because of his background, was viewed as a foreigner by some people in positions of authority. Perhaps without Ahmet Robenson's zest and enthusiasm to maintain ties with his relatives it would have been much more difficult for the Robinson family as a whole to preserve some form of unity. Indeed, without the presence of Ahmet Robenson, it may not have been possible to produce this book.

Postscript

If history were taught in the form of stories,
it would never be forgotten.
Rudyard Kipling, *The Collected Works*

When I started researching the Robinson family I had little idea of what I might stumble across. There was talk among family members in Turkey of connections to India. Some of Ahmet Robenson's exploits were quite well known. Hannah Rodda/Robinson also loomed large in the family narrative. Spencer Robinson appeared to be a more peripheral yet nevertheless important figure. Delving into records and archival materials, I soon encountered characters whose place in the annals of the Robinson family had been forgotten or somehow overlooked. In particular, the discovery – or, in truth, rediscovery – of Gertrude Rodda/Eisenmann, with her fame and sporting achievements, came as a surprise and was a revelation. An unexpected addition to the family story, here was an intriguing character whose individual foibles and personal adventures further enriched the Robinsons' history.

Learning more about Hannah's life and her torrid affair with the so-called Dr Gholab Shah was especially illuminating. This was a story locked away in some unremembered drawer and the key then thrown away. I was aware for some time of a 'Goolab Shah' living in London in 1891 as an Indian oculist, but there did not seem to be any connection between this Goolab Shah and the 'Dr Gholab Shah' who was the supposed famous Afghan warlord, and whose marriage to Hannah was extensively reported in the national and local press. Hours of research into the literature of the Second Anglo-Afghan War failed to unearth a leader of the *Ghazis* named Gholab Shah. Another key to unlock this particular drawer was only discovered almost by chance after painstakingly browsing through diplomatic correspondence in the National Archives. Reading, and indeed touching, Hannah's voluminous letters addressed to the Office of the Prime Minister was an experience in itself. It also proved very helpful as the letters enabled me to gain much more of an insight into Hannah's character and personality.

Searching to learn more about the Robinsons, my journey steered me along roads which compelled me to cross the paths of other noteworthy individuals. Family histories do not make sense and cannot be complete without taking into consideration the stories of other people with whom family members interacted. For example, 'Abdullah' Quilliam seemed to play a significant role in the lives of Hannah and her son Ahmet, while Mustafa Zeki Pasha's important place in the history of the Robinson family should also not be overlooked.

Researching the Robinsons offered many rewards. As well as face-to-face interviews with family members, I also struck up conversations via e-mail with other relatives of the Robinsons and distant cousins of other characters whom the Robinsons encountered. These were fellow explorers who were also seeking to learn more about their family roots. By chance, I came across one member of the Newell family who had extensive knowledge of several generations of the Newells and was willing to share what data he had with me. In e-mail messages posted as far back as the early 2000s, this relative had appealed for any news and information on Emily Frances Newell. For some reason, he had completely lost track of Emily after the 1891 census. In his communications, he expressed concern that he would never discover what happened to his long-lost cousin. Establishing contact and exchanging details with this relative of Emily's was particularly satisfying.

A distant relative of Amy Roberts Lillicrap – the unfortunate lady who ended up in a lunatic asylum in Devon as a result of her liaisons with Eliahie Bosche – was especially eager to learn more from me about the rogue Indian oculist. Another relative of the Robinsons of Lincolnshire informed me of how a branch of the family in the distant past was directly connected to nobility. In the late eighteenth century, a Susanna Southwell of the village of Hemingby in Lincolnshire had married William Robinson, one of the sons of Samuel Robinson and Lydia Brocklesby. This relative of the Robinsons had been able to trace the Southwell family as far back as the mid-twelfth century. In the fourteenth and fifteenth centuries, the 'Southills' were well-known landowners. They were also titled. For example, there was a Sir Henry Southill who was born in Southill, West Riding, Yorkshire, in 1310. One of his descendants had three sons from a relationship with a member of the Percy household, at the time one of the most powerful families in northern England. Clearly, there are other stories connected to the Robinson family that warrant closer investigation.

History is full of what-ifs, and the example of the Robinson family is another case in point. There are many pivotal moments in the history of the Robinsons. To list but a few: What would have happened if Spencer Robinson had remained a tenant farmer in Lincolnshire? How would the future have unfolded if Hannah Robinson had not met Eliahie Bosche and had stayed in her guesthouse in Brighton? What would have become of Ahmet Robenson if he had decided to remain in Turkey instead of emigrating to the US? Such questions offer endless possible scenarios and countless permutations.

In practice, it is the choices we make that really matter. As agents, we are able to choose to some extent what courses of action we wish to follow. In the example of the Robinsons, social, political and economic circumstances inevitably set bounds and limits on what they could accomplish. Nevertheless, within these restrictions, there was still scope for individual family members to make key decisions.

This book started with an open-ended inquiry: Who were the Robinsons? The more I learned, the greater my appetite became and the more I needed to discover. One story led to another. Matryoshka-like, a box was opened to reveal within itself other hidden boxes which in turn demanded to be accessed. The answers to certain questions often led to the prompting of further questions whose answers were not immediately forthcoming. Conspiracy theories, misinformation and distortions of the truth, including by family members themselves, made the task at hand that much more difficult.

Through archival research, newspaper records, personal correspondence and the like, it has been possible to capture what a member of the Robinson family was doing at a given location at a fixed moment in time. But, chinks and more significant breaks in the narrative remain. Attempting to follow the Robinsons, the trail may disappear for a while only to be picked up again later. Sometimes, one can almost hear loud and clear the voices of family members. Ahmet Robenson can be heard forcefully expressing his views on the activities of the Smyrna Welfare District Council. Hannah's entreaties to the British prime minister's office continue to reverberate. Often, though, the voices of family members are drowned out by the cacophony of other speakers or by the incessant background chatter and gossip that comes with the repeated enactment of daily routines. At such times we might not hear from the Robinsons for several months, if not years. Or, like a radio station, reception could be weak and intermittent – but background whispers may still occasionally be picked up over the static if we become attuned and listen carefully and intently.

Perhaps readers will be able to address some of the unresolved questions raised in this book. The relationship between the Rodda and Lintott families continues to baffle me. I also still want to learn more about the connections between the Quilliams and Hannah and her sons, and about Martha May Thompson's interest in Ahmet Robenson and to what extent it was reciprocated. Stories are not necessarily closed chapters. They can be further developed and reinterpreted if new information comes to light.

Tracing the lives of ancestors, one is struck by the ephemeral nature of one's existence. We can follow to some extent the life of a particular relative from the date of their birth to the day on which they passed away. Significant milestones can be identified and observed – marriage, the births of children, new careers, moving home, periods of incarceration, the loss of a loved one. We are all leading transient lives as we pass through our allotted time in history. But, arguably, many of us would like to leave our mark on history in some way, or at least to be remembered by our friends and relatives.

With regard to the Robinsons, their impact, whether on the history of Lincolnshire, the British Raj, the Ottoman Empire/ Turkey or Germany, cannot be disputed. However, history is not solely comprised of the events that have been recorded and have left an impression at the national or local level. The histories of individuals and families are themselves worthy of attention. All history is constantly being added to and reshaped as further details are unearthed.

Families also live on, as in the example of the Robinsons. One branch of a family may be extinguished, but there are invariably other offshoots to trace and follow. As family historians, we seek to establish connections with our ancestors. Through our research, we may reconnect with long-lost, forgotten or hitherto unknown cousins. In our efforts to investigate and unravel the past, we might therefore learn much more about our present. As Shakespeare succinctly observed, 'What's past is prologue.'

Notes

Introduction
1. Marchand and Lindenfeld, 'Germany at the *Fin de Siècle*', in Marchand and Lindenfeld (eds), p.5.
2. For a good overview of the Robinsons of Lincolnshire, see, Woods, *A Short History*.
3. *Dünden Bügüne İstanbul Ansiklopedesi, Cilt 1*, p.132.
4. Bali, *From Anatolia to the New World*, p.363.

1 Spencer Robinson I: Lincolnshire Roots
1. Woods, *A Short History*, p.1.
2. *Lincolnshire Chronicle*, 15 September 1837, p.3.
3. Woods, *A Short History*, pp.2, 4–5, 34 and 35.
4. Lincolnshire County Archives, Misc. Dep. 17/2.
5. Woods, *A Short History*, p.33.
6. Haggard, *Rural England, Volume 2*, p.144.
7. McQuiston, 'Tenant Right', *Agricultural History*, p.109.
8. Holderness, 'The Victorian Farmer', in Mingay (ed.), p.228.
9. *Ibid.*, p.242.
10. McQuiston, 'Tenant Right', *Agricultural History*, p.95.
11. Perkins, 'Tenure, Tenant Right', *The Agricultural History Review*, p.18.
12. Rawding, *The Lincolnshire Wolds*, pp.104–5.
13. Brown, *Farming in Lincolnshire*, pp.119 and 123.
14. *Ibid.*, p.128.
15. *Ibid.*, pp.69–70, and Rawding, *The Lincolnshire Wolds*, pp.23–5.

16. Offer, 'Farm Tenure and Land Values', *The Economic History Review*, pp.11–2.
17. Brown, *Farming in Lincolnshire*, p.26.
18. Stead, 'The Mobility of English Tenant Farmers', *The Agricultural History Review*, p.174.
19. Much of the detail about East Keal is taken from Lawie and Richardson (eds), *East Keal*.
20. 'Disused Stations: Spilsby', http://www.disused-stations.org.uk/s/ spilsby/ (accessed 15 August 2018).
21. *Commercial Directory and Gazetteer of Lincolnshire*, pp.298–9.
22. Macaulay, *The History of England*, pp.32–3.
23. Balfour, 'Legends of the Cars', *Folklore*, pp.149–56.
24. Brown, *Farming in Lincolnshire*, pp.10 and 59.
25. Woods, *A Short History*, p.12.
26. *Stamford Mercury*, 25 January 1833, p.3.
27. Lincolnshire County Archives, Misc. Dep. 17/2.
28. *Stamford Mercury*, 21 November 1845, p.3.
29. Fricker (ed.), *The North Lincolnshire Poll Book 1852*, p.204.
30. *Stamford Mercury*, 5 May 1865, p.2.
31. *Lincolnshire Chronicle*, 17 June 1853, p.4.
32. Lincolnshire County Archives, Misc. Dep. 17/11.
33. Woods, *A Short History*, p.14.
34. *Stamford Mercury*, 1 July 1892, p.2.
35. *The Gazette*, 2 December 1881, no. 25044, p.6520.
36. Woods, *A Short History*, pp.16, 26 and 33.
37. Elizabeth's sister, Mary Florence, after the death of her first husband married in 1906 the much younger George Gordon, Lord Haddo. Gordon was the son of the Earl of Aberdeen and could trace back his descent to Henry VIII. In 1934, three years before her death, Mary assumed the title of the Marchioness of Aberdeen and Temair.
38. *Nottinghamshire Guardian*, 12 April 1878, p.8.
39. *Market Rasen Weekly Mail and Lincolnshire Advertiser*, 5 April 1879, p.4.
40. Woods, *A Short History*, p.15. Woods quoted Miss Nancy Neave, whose father took over the running of Saxby Manor in 1885.
41. *Yorkshire Post and Leeds Intelligencer*, 14 November 1884, p.5.
42. *Yorkshire Post and Leeds Intelligencer*, 20 February 1885, p.2.

43. *The Colonies and India*, 23 January 1885, p.34.
44. Woods, *A Short History*, p.15 – quoting Nancy Neave.
45. *The Colonies and India*, 24 April 1885, p.28.
46. Woods, *A Short History*, p.15 – quoting Enid Pater, a granddaughter of Peele Robinson.
47. http://www.southafricansettlers.com/?p=36756 (accessed 22 March 2018)
48. Woods, *A Short History*, pp.16–7.
49. Lincolnshire County Archives, Misc. Dep. 17/1.
50. *Stamford Mercury*, 28 January 1887, p.2.
51. *Lincolnshire Echo*, 21 February 1899, p.4.
52. Sparrow, *Frank Brangwyn and His Work*, p.62.
53. Woods, *A Short History*, pp.19–21.
54. Michael B. Goodrick (ed.), 'East Kirkby 16th May 1719, 250th Anniversary', http://www.goodrickfamilyhistory.co.uk/419741414 (accessed 1 August 2016); and *Lincolnshire Standard and Boston Guardian*, 3 September 1938, p.10.
55. Woods, *A Short History*, p.41.
56. *Lincolnshire Chronicle*, 24 November 1865, p.7.
57. *Stamford Mercury*, 6 April 1860, p.5.
58. *Stamford Mercury*, 20 July 1860, pp.4–5.
59. *Stamford Mercury*, 28 September 1860, p.5.
60. *Lincolnshire Chronicle*, 24 January 1862, p.8.
61. *Lincolnshire Chronicle*, 11 July 1862, p.7.
62. *Stamford Mercury*, 26 January 1866, p.7.
63. *Stamford Mercury*, 17 January 1868, p.7.
64. *Stamford Mercury*, 9 December 1864, p.7.
65. Lincolnshire County Archives, Misc. Dep. 17/11.
66. *Stamford Mercury*, 21 October 1870, p.7.
67. Lincolnshire County Archives, Misc. Dep. 17/2.
68. *Stamford Mercury*, 22 September 1871, p.7.
69. *Stamford Mercury*, 25 August 1871, p.7.
70. *Stamford Mercury*, 10 November 1871, p.7, and 1 September 1871, p.7.
71. *Stamford Mercury*, 10 November 1871, p.7.
72. *Stamford Mercury*, 1 September 1871, p.7.
73. *Kelly's Post Office Directory of Essex, Herts, Middlesex, Kent, Surrey and Sussex, 1867*, http://www.genuki.org.uk/big/eng/SSX/WestFirle (accessed 7 August 2016).

74. http://firle.com/house-visits/the-family/ (accessed 7 August 2016).
75. *Ibid.*
76. Howkins, 'Types of Rural Communities', in Thirsk (gen. ed.), p.1320.
77. Brandon and Short, *The South East*, p.317.
78. Short, 'The Evolution of Contrasting Communities', in Short (ed.), pp.31–2.
79. Howkins, 'Types of Rural Communities', in Thirsk (gen. ed.), p.1320.
80. *Sussex Advertiser*, 19 December 1871, p.6.
81. *Commercial Gazette*, 28 August 1873, p.564.

2 Spencer Robinson II: A Life in India

1. *Derby Mercury*, 3 October 1888, p.8.
2. Alkış, *Çanakkale'de Şehit Düşen Futbolcular*, pp.53–6.
3. 'Ahmet Robenson', https://tr.wikipedia.org/wiki/Ahmet_Robenson (accessed 17 December 2016).
4. Dozey, *A Concise History*, p.53.
5. Details of the various occupations of Spencer Robinson in India are collected from the annual editions of the *Bengal Directory*, renamed the *India Directory* in 1885.
6. Kennedy, *The Magic Mountains*, p.226.
7. *Ibid.*, p.118.
8. Kenny, 'Climate, Race and Imperial Authority', *Annals of the Association of American Geographers*, pp.699–700.
9. Lama, *Through the Mists of Time*, pp.46–57.
10. O'Malley, *Bengal District Gazetteers*, p.22.
11. Dozey, *A Concise History*, pp.48, 49, 57 and 102.
12. O'Malley, *Bengal District Gazetteers*, p.37.
13. Dozey, *A Concise History*, pp.171 and 173.
14. *Ibid.*, p.174.
15. Kling, 'The Origin of the Managing Agency System', *The Journal of Asian Studies*, p.38.
16. Misra, *Business, Race and Politics*, pp.23–4.
17. Harrison, *Bird and Company*.
18. *Ibid.*, p.16.
19. *Darjeeling Himalayan Railway: Illustrated Guide*, p.7.
20. Harrison, *Bird and Company*, pp.16–7.
21. Donaldson, 'Railroads of the Raj', *LSE Asia Research Centre*, pp.6–7.

22. Wallace, *The Darjeeling Himalayan Railway*, p.40.
23. Bhanja, *Darjeeling at a Glance*, p.18.
24. Martin, *The Iron Sherpa ... Vol.1*, pp.25–6.
25. Mazuchelli, *The Indian Alps*, pp.20–5.
26. Harrison, *Bird and Company*, pp.17–8.
27. Macpherson, 'Investment in Indian Railways', *The Economic History Review*, pp.177–80.
28. For full details of the DHR, see Martin, *The Iron Sherpa ... Vols I and 2*.
29. 'A Brief History of the Darjeeling Himalayan Railway', http:// www.dhrs.org/page16.html (accessed 18 August 2018).
30. 'Darjeeling Himalayan Railway: A UNESCO World Heritage Site', http://dhr.indianrailways.gov.in (accessed 18 August 2018).
31. Rai, *History of the Darjeeling Himalayan Railway*, p.243.
32. Macgeorge, *Ways and Works*, p.310.
33. Martin, *The Iron Sherpa ... Vol.2*, pp.319–22 and 329.
34. 'Darjeeling's Little Train – Steaming since 1881', http://www. the-south-asian.com/Nov2000/Darjeeling_train2.htm (accessed 18 August 2018).
35. *Flag of Ireland*, 24 January 1885, p.1, and 28 March 1885, p.6.
36. Letter of Hannah Robinson to G. M. Reily of the Land Mortgage Bank of India, 4 October 1885. For this and other correspondence in India from and to Hannah and Spencer Robinson, see, University of Glasgow Archive Services, GB 248 UGD 091/2/5/2/1/48 (36).
37. Letter of Spencer Robinson to G. M. Reily, 25 September 1885.
38. *The Gazette*, 17 July 1885, no. 25491, p.3319.
39. *The Gazette*, 27 January 1891, no. 26129, p.509.
40. Letter of Spencer Robinson to G. M. Reily, 16 October 1885.
41. Letter of Spencer Robinson to G. M. Reily, 18 September 1885.
42. Letter of Hannah Robinson to G. M. Reily, 4 October 1885.
43. Letter of Spencer Robinson to G. M. Reily, 13 November 1885.
44. Letter of Spencer Robinson to G. M. Reily, 23 November 1885.
45. Letter of Spencer Robinson to G. M. Reily, 2 December 1885, and 9 December 1885.
46. Letter of Spencer Robinson to G. M. Reily, 6 January 1886.
47. University of Glasgow Archive Services, GB 248 UGD 091/2/5/2/1/48 (19).
48. Letter from the Planters Stores and Agency Company Limited to Spencer Robinson, (?) January 1886.

49. Letter of Spencer Robinson to G. M. Reily, 2 December 1885.
50. Details of 1889 are sketchy. Unfortunately, the British Library does not hold the *India Directory* for that year.
51. Koehler, *Darjeeling*, pp.68–9.
52. O'Malley, *Bengal District Gazetteers*, p.105.
53. Lama, *Through the Mists of Time*, p.130.
54. Griffiths, *The History of the Indian Tea Industry*, pp.96–7.
55. Koehler, *Darjeeling*, p.118.
56. *Ibid.*, pp.133 and 141.
57. O'Malley, *Bengal District Gazetteers*, pp.78–86.
58. Koehler, *Darjeeling*, pp.117–8.
59. Dozey, *A Concise History*, p.88.
60. Lethbridge, *The Golden Book of India*, p.91.
61. Hirschmann, *Robert Knight*, no page numbers given.
62. Martin, *The Iron Sherpa … Vol.1*, p.293.
63. *Ibid.*, p.291, and Rai, *History of the Darjeeling Himalayan Railway*, pp.36–7 and 161.
64. Frankopan, *The Silk Roads*.
65. Letter of Spencer Robinson to M. Finucane, Teendaria, 17 July 1887 in Watt, *Selections from the Records*, p.34.
66. Watt, *Selections from the Records*, pp.16–7, 49 and 50.
67. Harris, 'Silk Roads and Wool Routes', *India Review*, p.207.
68. Addy, *Tibet on the Imperial Chessboard*, p.46.
69. For details of the 1888 Sikkim Expedition, see, Paget, *Frontiers and Overseas Expeditions from India*, pp.50–8; Iggulden, *The 2nd Battalion Derbyshire Regiment*; and Markham, *The Sikkim Expedition*.
70. Iggulden, *The 2nd Battalion Derbyshire Regiment*, p.58.
71. Letter of Spencer Robinson to G. M. Reily, 2 November 1885.
72. '100 Years of Tindharia Workshop – DHR, Darjeeling Himalayan Railway', http://www.indiangorkhas.in/2015/08/100-years-of-tindharia-workshop-dhr.html (accessed 18 November 2016).
73. *Homeward Mail from India, China and the East*, 18 February 1880, p.196, and 12 May 1880, p.539.
74. *Homeward Mail from India, China and the East*, 6 June 1889, p.732.
75. Letter of Spencer Robinson to G. M. Reily, 16 October 1885.
76. Hawson, *Darjeeling and the Dooars*, p.23.
77. *The Englishman (Calcutta)*, 22 November 1889, p.6.

78. Burton, 'Making a Spectacle of Empire', *History Workshop Journal*, p.127, and 'On the 1886 Colonial and Indian Exhibition', http://www.branchcollective.org/?ps_articles=aviva-briefel-on-the-1886-colonial-and-indian-exhibition (accessed 19 August 2018).
79. Tharoor, *Inglorious Empire*, and Wilson, *India Conquered*.

3 Hannah Rodda: From Bethnal Green to Constantinople
1. Bali, *The Saga of a Friendship*, note 259, p.175.
2. Bali, *From Anatolia to the New World*, p.363.
3. 'The History of Benenden', http://www.benenden.history.pollardweb.com (accessed 20 August 2018).
4. Baker (ed.), *A History of the County of Middlesex*, pp.120–32.
5. 'From "Marghas Yow" to Marazion, Jewish Rumours in Cornwall?' https://ashtronort.wordpress.com/2013/07/10/from-marghas-yow-to-marazion/ (accessed 20 August 2018).
6. Deacon, *The Cornish Family*, p.80.
7. Gavin, *Sanitary Ramblings*, no page numbers given.
8. *Shipping and Mercantile Gazette*, 2 September 1857, p.5.
9. 'Merchant Seamen's Orphan Asylum, London/Wokingham', http://www.childrenshomes.org.uk/SnaresbrookSeamen/ (accessed 20 August 2018).
10. 'A Flax Mill in Romsey', https://www.hampshiremills.org/Newsletters/91%20Winter%2010%20Newsletter/91%20Page%206.htm (accessed 20 August 2018).
11. *The Gazette*, 13 February 1855, no.21662, p.588, and 19 August 1862, no.22654, p.4412.
12. *The Era*, 11 April 1885, p.9.
13. *The Era*, 24 May 1884, p.14.
14. *The Stage*, 27 August 1903, p.11.
15. *Brighton Herald*, 30 April 1881, p.2.
16. *The Court, Lady's Magazine, Monthly Critic and Museum*, Vol. 24 (March 1844), p.49.
17. *Windsor and Eton Express*, 23 August 1884, p.4.
18. Kotar and Gessler, *Cholera: A Worldwide History*, p.166.
19. *Windsor and Eton Express*, 12 February 1876, p.4.
20. *Reading Mercury*, 31 January 1885, p.5.
21. *The Weekly Chronicle*, 4 October 1845, p.4.

22. Knox, *Boom: The Underground History of Australia*, no page numbers given.
23. *The Gazette*, 17 November 1865, no. 23038, p.5406.
24. *Hampshire Telegraph*, 4 August 1877, p.4.
25. *The Era*, 15 April 1877, p.20.
26. Stuart and Park, *The Variety Stage*, p.131.
27. McLaren, *A Prescription for Murder*, p.11.
28. Robinson, *Chaplin*, no page numbers given.
29. *Homeward Mail from India, China and the East*, 17 November 1880, p.1306.
30. Kennedy, *The Magic Mountains*, p.122.
31. MacMillan, *Women of the Raj*, pp.39–40.
32. Procida, *Married to the Empire*, pp.40–1.
33. MacMillan, *Women of the Raj*, pp.167–78.
34. *Ibid.*, pp.152–4.
35. Kennedy, *The Magic Mountains*, p.132.
36. Letter of Spencer Robinson to G. M. Reily, 2 December 1885.
37. Letter of Hannah Robinson to G. M. Reily, 13 October 1885, and 24 November 1885.
38. Letter of Spencer Robinson to G. M. Reily, 16 October 1885.
39. Chaudhuri, 'Memsahibs and Motherhood', *Victorian Studies*, p.530.
40. MacMillan, *Women of the Raj*, p.149.
41. Walton, *The English Seaside Resort*, pp.88–9.
42. Geaves, *Islam in Victorian Britain*, pp.71–2.
43. Pool, *Studies in Mohammedanism*, p.404.
44. Gilham, *Loyal Enemies*, p.110, and *Whitstable Times*, 2 November 1891, p.3.
45. Geaves, *Islam in Victorian Britain*, pp.69–71.
46. *Ibid.*, p.65.
47. *Ibid.*, pp.71–2 and 223.
48. *Ibid.*, pp.75–6.
49. *Liverpool Mercury*, 20 April 1891, p.6.
50. National Archives, Kew, General Registry Office, RG48/310.
51. *The Crescent*, 11 May 1898, p.299.
52. Gilham, *Loyal Enemies*, p.54.
53. *Ibid.*, n.135, p.265.
54. *Glasgow Herald*, 1 November 1890, p.7.
55. National Archives, Kew, FO 800/32/37 and FO 800/32/38.

56. *Ibid.*
57. Mukherjee, 'A Warning against Quack Doctors', *Historical Research*, pp.76–91.
58. *Sussex Agricultural Express*, 31 October 1891, p.2.
59. *Pall Mall Gazette*, 27 November 1891, p.6.
60. *Liverpool Mercury*, 27 November 1891, p.6.
61. *Cambridge Independent Press*, 4 December 1891, p.6.
62. *Dublin Evening Telegraph*, 30 November 1891, p.2.
63. National Archives, Kew, FO 78/4416, no.280.
64. 'Fake "Indian Doctors" in Australia: A Brief History', https://www.sbs.com.au/yourlanguage/hindi/en/article/2017/04/20/fake-indian-doctors-australia-brief-history (accessed 21 August 2018).
65. National Archives, Kew, FO 1951/1743 and FO 1951/1747.
66. Güçlü, *Zeki Kuneralp*, pp.66–7.
67. Daunt, *The Palace Lady's Summerhouse*, p.99.
68. *Freeman's Journal*, 1 November 1894, p.4.
69. National Archives, Kew, FO 372/11/29 File 23639.
70. *The Graphic*, 7 April 1906, p.431.
71. *London Evening News*, 28 May 1908, p.3, and 2 June 1908, p.3.
72. *Cambridge Independent Press*, 18 June 1909, p.7.
73. *The Evening News*, 8 March 1909, p.7.
74. Kamberidou, 'The East in the Eyes of Western Women', *Proceedings of the East in the Eyes of the West.*
75. *The Crescent*, 6 March 1895, p.73.
76. Güner, 'Akaretler Sıra Evleri', in Kaya (ed.), p.238.
77. *The Crescent*, 11 May 1898, p.299.
78. Geaves, *Islam in Victorian Britain*, pp.225–6.
79. *Ibid.*, p.72.
80. Findley, *Ottoman Civil Officialdom*, p.200.
81. 'On the Trail of the Elusive Admiral', http://www.levantineheritage.com/testi39.htm (accessed 24 August 2018).
82. Woods, *Spunyarn*, p.121.
83. *The Crescent*, 11 May 1898, p.299, and 25 May 1898, p.331.
84. 'Mehmed Raif, Davutpaşalı', https://islamansiklopedisi.org.tr/mehmed-raif-davutpasali (accessed 24 August 2018).
85. Letter of Peel Harold Robinson to Gertrude Eisenmann, 22 January 1924.
86. Letter of Peel Harold Robinson to Gertrude Eisenmann, 22 April 1928.

87. Letters of Hannah Robinson to her daughter, Maud, 23 July 1943, and 26 July 1943.
88. Mansel, *Levant*, for full details of the British community in Izmir.
89. Letter of Hannah Robinson to her daughter, Maud, 26 July 1943.
90. Letter of Peel Harold Robinson to Gertrude Eisenmann, 22 April 1928.
91. *Vakit-Yeni Gazete*, 23 May 1948.

4 Gertrude Rodda/Eisenmann: A Racing Amazon

1. *Die Groene Amsterdammer*, 3 April 1904, p.5.
2. 'England's Star Women Motorists', *The Motor Way*, Vol.14 (1905), p.11.
3. *East Anglian Daily Times*, 22 October 1887, p.5; and *Evening Star*, 24 August 1889, p.3.
4. Letter of Peel Harold Robinson to Gertrude Eisenmann, 22 January 1924.
5. *Ibid.*
6. 'England's Star Women Motorists', p.10.
7. *Hamburger Nachrichten*, 15 December 1931, p.13.
8. 'Der Weg zum Global Player: Die Internationalisierung der Bosch-Gruppe,' https://amicale-citroen.de/wp-content/uploads/2012/09/journal-bosch-geschichte-teil-2.pdf (accessed 24 August 2018).
9. *Hamburger Nachrichten*, 29 August 1900, p.12.
10. *The Sporting Life*, 30 May 1900, p.21.
11. *Neue Hamburger Zeitung*, 7 January 1902, p.11.
12. Grand, 'The New Aspect', *The North American Review*, pp.271 and 274.
13. Ledger, 'The New Woman', in Ledger and McCraken (eds), pp.23–4.
14. 'August 1888: Bertha Benz takes World's First Long-Distance Trip in an Automobile', https://media.daimler.com/marsMediaSite/en/instance/ko/August-1888-Bertha-Benz-takes-worlds-first-long-distance-trip-in-an-automobile.xhtml?oid=9361401 (accessed 24 August 2018).
15. O'Connell, 'Motorising and Modernity', in Carnevali and Strange (eds), p.113.
16. Disko, *The Devil's Wheels*, pp.253–4 and 268.
17. *Ibid.*, p.284.

18. Shepherd, 'The British Press', *Victorian Periodicals Review*, p.384.
19. Scharff, *Taking the Wheel*, pp.36–7.
20. Clarsen, *Eat my Dust*, pp.14–5.
21. O'Connell, *The Car and British Society*, pp.47–8.
22. *Ibid.*, p.48.
23. Fraunholz, *Motorphobia*, p.49.
24. Merriman, *Mobility, Space and Culture*, p.99.
25. Clarsen, *Eat my Dust*, pp.2–8 and 24.
26. 'England's Star Women Motorists', p.11.
27. 'NSU', http://fleshandrelics.com/2014/03/nsu.html (accessed 25 August 2018)
28. 'England's Star Women Motorists', p.11.
29. *The Graphic*, 26 August 1905, p.32.
30. 'England's Star Women Motorists', p.11.
31. 'Frauen in Rennsport: Über frühe Rennfahrerinnen und Sozias', https://www.motorradonline.de/motorradsport/frauen-im-rennsport-ueber-fruehe-rennfahrerinnen-und-sozias.466476.html (accessed 25 August 2018).
32. *The Sphere*, 20 June 1908, p.12.
33. *Berliner Tageblatt*, 25 August 1906, p.7.
34. 'England's Star Women Motorists', p.11.
35. Koshar, 'Organic Machines', in Lekan and Zeller (eds), pp.117–22.
36. Fack, 'Die Veränderung des Mobiltätsverhaltens von Frauen', in Flade and Limbourg (eds), pp.41–2.
37. 'Some Famous Motor Dogs', *The Lady's Realm*, Vol. 20 (1906), pp.321–3.
38. *Ibid.*, pp.325–6.
39. 'Meine Ausfahrt von Hamburg nach Frankfurt und Zurück', *Allgemeine Automobil-Zeitung*, 40 (1903), pp.9–14.
40. *Beverley and East Riding Recorder*, 14 November 1903, p.8.
41. *The Globe*, 26 October 1903, p.2.
42. Alfred Fuhr, 'The Institute of Traffic Sociology at AVD and its Work', https://www.academia.edu/33905589/The_Institute_of_Traffic_Sociology_at_AvD_and_its_work_the (accessed 26 August 2018).
43. Letter of Peel Harold Robinson to Gertrude Eisenmann, 22 April 1928.
44. Letter of Emily Frances Robinson to Maud (daughter of Hannah Robinson), 6 January 1933.

45. *Hamburger Nachrichten*, 15 January 1933, p.11.
46. Bahr and Erker, *Bosch*, p.92.
47. '...erlaubt sich, seine wesentlich erweiterte Wirkungstätte zu zeigen', *Wirtschaft in Bremen*, 9 (2012), https://www.handelskammer-bremen.de/blob/hbihk24/Presse/Magazin_WiBB/Wirtschaft_in_Bremen_2012/1299570/f22aa9e7f3b18123e7f7de847a71945a/Wirtschaft_in_Bremen_09_2012-data.pdf (accessed 26 August 2018).
48. *Hamburger Nachrichten*, 14 January 1930, p.18.
49. Liedtke, 'Germany's Door to the World', in Cesarani (ed.), p.82.
50. Grenville, *The Jews and Germans of Hamburg*, pp. 44 and 47–8.
51. Bajohr, *'Aryanisation' in Hamburg*, pp.28–31.
52. Grenville, *The Jews and Germans of Hamburg*, p.174.
53. Bajohr, *'Aryanisation' in Hamburg*, p.230.
54. Bahr and Erker, *Bosch*, pp.184–5.
55. '...erlaubt sich...', *Wirtschaft in Bremen*, 9 (2012).
56. Bahr and Erker, *Bosch*, p.185.
57. *The Canadian Patent Office*, p.5685.

5 The Robenson Brothers: In Peace and at War

1. Ahmad, *From Empire to Republic*, p.144.
2. Zürcher, *The Young Turk Legacy*, p.81.
3. Ahmad, *From Empire to Republic*, p.170.
4. Zürcher, *The Young Turk Legacy*, p.215.
5. *Ibid.*, pp.68–72.
6. Çalışlar, *The 150 Years of the Galatasaray Lycée*, pp.190–4.
7. Ünaydın, *Galatasaray ve Futbol*, pp.61–71.
8. 'Galatasaray Tarihi – Yönetim Kurulu', https://www.extraloob.com/forums/threads/galatasaray-tarihi-yonetim-kurulu.144299/ (accessed 27 August 2018).
9. Sunata, *İstibdattan Meşrutiyete*, p.331.
10. 'Tanıdığım eski Sporcular', http://earsiv.sehir.edu.tr:8080/xmlui/bitstream/handle/11498/32794/001517597006.pdf?sequence=1&isAllowed=y (accessed 27 August 2018).
11. Bali, *From Anatolia to the New World*, p.363.
12. Yıldız, *Strengthening Male Bodies*, pp.36–40.
13. Gurbetoğlu, 'II Meşrutiyet Dönemi', *Ankara Üniversitesi Eğitim Bilimleri Fakültesi Dergisi*, pp.86–7.

14. Goldblatt, *The Ball is Round*, pp. 162 and 168–70; and Okay, 'The Introduction, Early Development', *Soccer and Society*, pp.3 and 6.
15. Okay, 'The Introduction, Early Development', *Soccer and Society*, p.4.
16. 'İlk Yıllar', https://galatasaraydakurek.com/2013/05/01/ilk-yillar/ (accessed 27 August 2018).
17. 'Türkiye'de Basketball', *Cumhuriyet*, 14 May 1959, p.6.
18. Ünaydın, *Galatasaray ve Futbol*, pp.119–20.
19. 'The Story of Barry Family: A Selection from the Protected Family Archives by Cengiz Kahraman', http://levantineheritage.com/note94.htm (accessed 27 August 2018).
20. 'Ahmet Robenson', http://www.biyografya.com/biyografi/1037 (accessed 27 August 2018).
21. 'Galatasaray Tarihi…'
22. Yüce, *Ale'l-ıtlak Baldırı Çıplak*, p.284.
23. Appiah, 'Cosmopolitan Patriots', *Cultural Inquiry*, p.622.
24. Halliday, 'Three Concepts', *International Affairs*, pp.187–8.
25. Gunesch, 'Education for Cosmopolitanism', *Journal of Research in International Education*, p.256.
26. 'Scouting History Around the Globe', http://usscouts.org/usscouts/history/brownsea.asp (accessed 28 August 2018).
27. Warren, 'Sir Robert Baden-Powell', *The English Historical Review*, pp.376, 385 and 387.
28. Proctor, 'Introduction: Building an Empire of Youth', in Block and Proctor (eds), p.30.
29. Akmese, *The Birth of Modern Turkey*, p.168.
30. Tuğluoğlu, 'II. Meşrutiyet Döneminde Milliyetçi', *Cağdaş Türkiye Tarihi Araştırmaları Dergisi*, p.123.
31. Ünaydın, *Galatasaray ve Futbol*, pp.130–1.
32. Sunata, *İstibdattan Meşrutiyete*, pp.331 and 337.
33. Toprak, 'Meşrutiyet ve Mütareke Yıllarında', *Toplumsal Tarih*, p.15.
34. Akmese, *The Birth of Modern Turkey*, p.168.
35. Besikci, *The Ottoman Mobilization of Manpower*, p.208.
36. Akmese, *The Birth of Modern Turkey*, p.170.
37. Besikci, *The Ottoman Mobilization of Manpower*, p.211.
38. Turnaoğlu, *The Formation of Turkish Republicanism*, n.126, p.162.

39. Besikci, *The Ottoman Mobilization of Manpower*, pp. 212 and 220–3.
40. Toprak, 'Meşrutiyet ve Mütareke Yıllarında', *Toplumsal Tarih*, p.15.
41. 'Sakarya İzci Oymağı'na Tarihçe', http://www.sakaryaizcigrubu. org/hakkimizda/tarihce/ayrintilitarihce.html (accessed 28 August 2018).
42. Uzgören, *Türk İzcilik Tarihi*, p.15.
43. 'Ata ve Ahmet Robenson', http://girgin.org/galatasaray-lisesi-ve-spor-kulubunden-kesitler/ata-ve-ahmet-robenson/ (accessed 28 August 2018).
44. *The New York Times*, 25 July 1909, p.3.
45. National Archives, Kew, FO 383/345.
46. 'Bisiklet ve Derrace-i Süvaran Cavit Cav', http://informadik. blogspot.com/2015/03/bisiklet-sporu-ve-derrace-i-suvaran.html (accessed 28 August 2018).
47. Süme and Özsoy, 'Osmanlı'dan Günümüze', *Selçuk Üniversitesi Sosyal Bilimler Enstitüsü Dergisi*, p.353.
48. Geaves, *Islam in Victorian Britain*, pp.253–6.
49. *Swindon Advertiser and North Wilts. Chronicle*, 27 November 1908, p.9.
50. Gilham, *Loyal Enemies*, p.76.
51. Geaves, *Islam in Victorian Britain*, p.258.
52. *Greenock Telegraph and Clyde Shipping Gazette*, 25 November 1908, p.3.
53. *London Standard*, 25 November 1908, p.10.
54. Yüce, *Ale'l-ıtlak Baldırı Çıplak*, p.224.
55. 'Ahmet Robenson', https://eksisozluk.com/ahmet-robenson--296636 (accessed 28 August 2018).
56. Alkış, *Çanakkale'de Şehit Düşen Futbolcular*, pp.61–4.
57. 'Çanakkale'de bile konuşulan Goller', http://www.tribundergi. com/haber/canakkale-de-bile-konusulan-goller (accessed 28 August 2018).
58. Sunata, *Gelibolu'dan Kafkaslara*, pp.31 and 49.
59. Letter of Abdurrahman Robenson to Ali Sami, 21 January 1915. Text provided by Dr Gün Kut, Associate Professor, Bosphorus University, Istanbul.
60. 'Abdurrahman Robenson', https://rerererarara.net/abdurrahman-robenson--24475 (accessed 28 August 2018).

61. Sunata, *Gelibolu'dan Kafkaslara*, p.50.
62. Yüce, *Ale'l ıtlak Baldırı Çıplak*, p.280.
63. 'Çanakkale Türkiye Cumhuriyeti'nin Önsözüdür', https://www.ureticihaber.com/kose-yazisi/386/canakkale-turkiye-cumhuriyetinin-onsozudur.html (accessed 28 August 2018).
64. 'English Brothers in Turkish Service', https://forum.axishistory.com/viewtopic.php?t=116481 (accessed 28 August 2018).
65. Woodfin, *Camp and Combat*, p.40.
66. Hadaway, *Blood on the Sand*, p.7.
67. 'English Brothers in Turkish Service.'
68. 'Galatasaray', https://forum.axishistory.com/viewtopic.php?t=100306 (accessed 28 August 2018).
69. 'Gayrimüslim Vatan Şehitlerimez, Ruhlarınız Şad olsun', http://www.basyaylahaber.com/yazar-gayrimuslim-vatan-sehitlerimiz-ruhlariniz-sad-olsun-95.html (accessed 28 August 2018).
70. Anglesey, *A History of the British Cavalry*, p.41.
71. Macmunn and Falls, *Military Operations*, p.169.
72. Rogan, *The Fall of the Ottomans*, p.313.
73. Massey, *The Desert Campaigns*, p.46.
74. Hadaway, *Blood on the Sand*, pp.14–5.
75. Massey, *The Desert Campaigns*, p.48.
76. 'Sina Çölünde Bir Şövalye – Galatasaraylı Halet', https://canakkalemuharebeleri1915.com/makale-ler/iclal-tunca-orses/397-sina-colunde-bir-sovalye-galatasarayli-halet (accessed 28 August 2018).
77. Massey, *The Desert Campaigns*, p.49.
78. Bozkurt, '1. Dünya Savaşı'nda', *Atatürk Araştırma Merkezi Dergisi*, p.108; interview with Mehmet Yüce and others on *Açık Radyo*, 2 February 2018, http://acikradyo.com.tr/spor/alel-itlak-baldiri-ciplak (accessed 7 November 2018); and correspondence with Mehmet Yüce.
79. Yıldız, *Strengthening Male Bodies*, p.67.

6 *Ahmet Robenson: A Man of Many Names*

1. For a detailed account of the occupation of Istanbul, see Criss, *Istanbul under Allied Occupation*.
2. *Ibid.*, p.109.
3. Mango, *Ataturk*, pp.202 and 246.

Notes

4. For negotiations in 1919 and 1920 over the future of Istanbul, see, Helmreich, *From Paris to Sevres*.
5. For details of the complicated politics of the Caucasus in 1918 and 1919, see, Zürcher, *The Unionist Factor*; Hovannisian, *The Republic of Armenia*; and, Allen and Muratoff, *Caucasian Battlefields*.
6. Sürmeli, 'Güneybatı Kafkas Hükümeti', *Atatürk Dergisi*, p.91.
7. *Ibid.*
8. 'Mütareke ve Mahallı Teşkilatlanma', http://oltulu.net/Forum.asp?forum=oku&msgid=146&alfom=&alfomad= (accessed 30 August 2018).
9. Sürmeli, 'Güneybatı Kafkas Hükümeti', *Atatürk Dergisi*, p.93.
10. Küçükuğurlu, 'Cihangiroğlu İbrahım Bey'in', *Atatürk Dergisi*, p.258.
11. Sürmeli, 'Güneybatı Kafkas Hükümeti', *Atatürk Dergisi*, p.94.
12. *Ibid.*, pp.94–5; and Karabekir, *İstiklal Harbimiz*, p.355.
13. Yenigazi, 'Kars, Sarıkamış ve Oltu'nun', *Bizim Ahıska*, p.37.
14. Dadrian and Akcam (eds), *Judgment at Istanbul*, n.27, p.185.
15. Anon, 'A Side-Show', *The Journal of the United Service Institution of India*, pp.103–9.
16. National Archives, Kew, FO 371/3658.
17. Karagöz, *Güneybatı Kafkasya*, pp.95–6, 98 and 123.
18. Letter of Peel Harold Robinson to Gertrude Eisenmann, 22 January 1924.
19. Gür, 'Robert College', in Criss, Esenbel, Greenwood and Mazzari (eds), p.48.
20. 'Introduction', in *ibid*, p.3.
21. DeNovo, *American Interests and Policies*, p.266.
22. *Ibid.*, p.270.
23. *The Orient*, 8, 23 (8 June 1921), p.226.
24. *Dünden Bügüne İstanbul Ansiklopedisi, Cilt 7*, p.532.
25. Kuran and Hiçyılmaz, *Osmanli'dan Günümüze*, p.22.
26. Much of the following on the story of the Taksim Stadium is from, Yüce, *Ale'l-ıtlak Baldırı Çıplak*, pp.237–55.
27. *Cumhuriyet*, 5 September 1925. This piece was drawn to my attention by Mehmet Yüce.
28. Bali, *The Saga of a Friendship*, pp.140–1.
29. *Ibid.*, p.175.

261

30. Üngör, *The Making of Modern Turkey*, pp.180 and 182.
31. Bali, *The Saga of a Friendship*, p.154.
32. *Ibid.*, p.175.
33. *Ibid.*, pp.178–81.
34. Szurek, 'The Linguist and the Politician', in Aymes, Gourise and Massicard (eds), pp.83–4.
35. Bali, *The Saga of a Friendship*, p.424.
36. *Ibid.*, p.201.
37. *Ibid.*, p.202.
38. *Ibid.*, p.204.
39. *Ibid.*, p.228.
40. *American Friends of Turkey*, p.8.
41. Bali, *The Saga of a Friendship*, pp.220–7.
42. *Ibid.*, p.227.
43. *Ibid.*, p.234.
44. Letter of Peel Harold Robinson to Gertrude Eisenmann, 22 April 1928.
45. Kaya, 'Comparing and Contrasting Turkish Immigration', *International Journal of Turkish Studies*, p.78.
46. Bali, *From Anatolia to the New World*, pp.34–5.
47. Kaya, 'Immigration and Struggle for Integration', in Kucukcan and Gungor (eds), pp.274–5.
48. 'The 1930 Census in Perspective', https://www.archives.gov/publications/prologue/2002/summer/1930-census-perspective.html (accessed 1 September 2018).
49. 'Oriental Rugs: The Art Maker's Sleeping Beauty', *The Epoch Times*, 23 April 2013.
50. *Ice Cream Review*, Vol. 41 (1958), p.84.
51. Letter of Peel Harold Robinson to Gertrude Eisenmann, 22 January 1924.
52. *Journal of the Senate*, pp.344 and 364.
53. 'The "Black Friday" Gold Scandal', https://www.history.com/news/the-black-friday-gold-scandal-145-years-ago (accessed 1 September 2018).
54. 'The Realms of Gould', *American Heritage*, 21, 3 (1970); and 'Big Old Houses – Bread upon the Hudson', *New York Social Diary*, 2 June 2015.
55. 'Lyndhurst … the Duchess's Gift', *River Journal*, 15 December 2013.

56. *Wellsville Daily Report*, 7 July 1958, p.2.
57. *Kingston Daily Freeman*, 19 November 1964, p.42.
58. Information from correspondence with Richard Miller.
59. Bali, *From Anatolia to the New World*, p.364.

7 *The Robinsons: Meanwhile, in England...*
 1. Woods, *A Short History*, pp.26 and 29.
 2. Heffer, *The Age of Decadence*, p.443.
 3. *Ibid.*, p.118.
 4. *Morning Post*, 7 August 1889, p.1.
 5. *Bridport News*, 8 September 1893, p.6.
 6. 'Street History: Over Street', http://mhms.org.uk/content/street-history-over-street (accessed 3 September 2018).
 7. 'Brighton Railway Engineering Works', http://www.mybrightonandhove.org.uk/page_id__8572.aspx (accessed 3 September 2018).
 8. Brown, *History of Submarine Mining*, pp.53 and 132–3. Brown served as an assistant instructor at Portsmouth when Minick trained at the submarine mining school there.
 9. 'Col. Bogey's Birthplace', http://www.gosportheritage.co.uk/col-bogey/ (accessed 3 September 2018).
10. *The Greenock Telegraph and Clyde Shipping Gazette*, 23 January 1896, p.2.
11. *Scottish Post Office, 1895–1896*, p.160, and *Scottish Post Office, 1896–1897*, p.163.
12. *The Newsman*, 2 October 1909, p.2. This article refers to Albert's unfortunate death in an accident outside a public house in Chelmsford.
13. Wreyford, *The Secret History of Chelmsford*, no page numbers given.
14. Brown, *History of Submarine Mining*, pp.90–1.
15. Quail, *Portsmouth in the Great War*, pp.15–7.
16. Galliver, *The Portsmouth Dockyard Force*, p.65.
17. *Ibid.*, pp.15–6.
18. Galliver, 'Trade Unionism in Portsmouth Dockyard', in Lunn and Day (eds), pp.119–20.
19. Quail, *Portsmouth in the Great War*, p.35.
20. Riley, 'The Industries of Portsmouth', *Portsmouth Papers*, p.16.
21. *Ibid.*, p.15.
22. *Portsmouth Evening News*, 9 February 1883, p.4.

23. Bell, *The Magical Imagination*, p.42.
24. Beaven, 'Slum Priests as Missionaries', *Forum Navale*, p.62.
25. *Portsmouth Evening News*, 15 July 1892, p.4.
26. Higgs, *A Visitor's Guide*, p.174.
27. Phegley, *Courtship and Marriage*, pp.158–9.
28. Bell, '"They are Without Christ and Without Hope"', in Beaven, Bell and James (eds), pp.49–68.
29. 'Boom and Bust Revealed the Fall of Sweet Company's Fortunes', http://www2.newsquest.co.uk/the_north_east/history/echomemories/durham/306/230806.html (accessed 3 September 2018).
30. 'Portsmouth and the Blitz', http://portsmouthblitz.co.uk/?page=raids/blitz (accessed 3 September 2018).
31. Holmes, *Two Centuries of Shoemaking*, pp.13 and 27.
32. Church, 'Labour Supply and Innovation', in Davenport-Hines (ed.), pp.95–6.
33. Letter of Peel Harold Robinson to Gertrude Eisenmann, 22 January 1924.
34. Letter of Emily Frances Robinson to Maud (daughter of Hannah Robinson), 6 January 1933.

Select Bibliography

Archives and On-line Sources
Ancestry (ancestry.co.uk)
Findmypast (findmypast.co.uk)
Forces War Records (forces-war-records.co.uk)
General Register Office (gro.gov.uk)
NewspaperArchive (newspaperarchive.com)
The British Newspaper Archive (britishnewspaperarchive.co.uk)
The Gazette (thegazette.co.uk)

Lincolnshire County Archives, Lincoln.
*East Keal and Stickford Estates of the Property of J. H. Short Esq. –
1835*, Misc. Dep. 17/2.
*East Keale Sale Receipts and Expenses on Account of the East Keale
Estate up to 4 April 1864 – Short Papers*, Misc. Dep. 17/11.
J. H. Short – Edlington and Thimbleby Rental Account, Misc. Dep.
17/1.

National Archives, Kew
*Consul Gurney at Marseilles asks if he can issue a Passport to Goolab
Shah...*, 13 July 1906, FO 372/11/29 File 23639.
*Correspondence between Arminius Vambery and the British Foreign
Office*, FO 800/32/37 and FO 800/32/38.
*"G.H.Q. General Staff – Intelligence – no.3640 "I" – Report on the
Self-Styled 'SW Caucasus State'"*, FO 371/3658.
Letter of Hannah Robinson to the Office of the Prime Minister,
20 June 1892, FO 1951/1743.

Letter of Hannah Robinson to the Office of the Prime Minister, 10 September 1892, FO 1951/1747.

Memo by Mr Adam Bloch, Dragoman, Pera, 5 September 1892, FO 78/4416 no.280.

Message of Mrs M. M. Thompson to her Fiancee – Ahmed Robinson Bey, 6 November 1917, FO 383/345.

The Quilliam Case (1905): Moslem Marriage in Mosque, General Registry Office, RG/48/310.

University of Glasgow Archive Services

A Bundle of Correspondence Relating to Sub-Lease of Land at Kurseong by Spencer Robinson to the Land Mortgage Bank of India Limited – C. H. Barnes, GB 248 UGD 091/2/5/2/1/48 (36).

Sub-Lease of the Undernoted Lands at Kurseong Granted by Spencer Robinson, Esq. to the Land Mortgage Bank of India Limited ... with Annexed Receipts from the Manager, Burdwan Raj Estate to Spencer Robinson, Esq..., GB 248 UGD 091/2/5/2/1/48 (19).

Directories, Encyclopaedias and Gazetteers

Bengal Directory (Calcutta: Thacker, Spink and Company, various years)

Commercial Directory and Gazetteer of Lincolnshire (Nottingham: Morris & Co., 1863)

Dünden Bügüne İstanbul Ansiklopedesi, Cilt 1 (Istanbul: Tarih Vakfı Yayınları, 1993)

Dünden Bügüne İstanbul Ansiklopedesi, Cilt 7 (Istanbul: Tarih Vakfı Yayınları, 1994)

India Directory (Calcutta: Thacker, Spink and Company, various years)

Journal of the Senate of the United States of America, 1st Session of the Eighty-Third Congress (Washington DC: US GPO, 1953)

Kelly's Post Office Directory of Essex, Herts, Middlesex, Kent, Surrey and Sussex, 1867, http://www.genuki.org.uk/big/eng/SSX/WestFirle (accessed 4 September 2018)

O' Malley, L. S. S., *Bengal District Gazetteers: Darjeeling* (Calcutta: The Bengal Secretariat Book Depot, 1907)

Scottish Post Office, Gourock Directory, 1895–1896, and 1896–1897.

The Canadian Patent Office Record and Register of Copyrights, Vol.85, 7–9 (Ottawa: Edward Cloutier, 1957)

Watt, George, *Selections from the Records of the Government of India, Revenue and Agriculture Department, Vol. 1, pt. 1, 1888–1889* (Calcutta: The Superintendent of Government Printing, India, 1889)

Theses

Galliver, Peter W., *The Portsmouth Dockyard Workforce 1880-1914*, University of Southampton, Faculty of Arts, M.Phil. thesis, 1987.

Rai, Bhawna, *History of the Darjeeling Himalayan Railway and its Socio-Economic Impact on Darjeeling 1880-1899*, University of North Bengal, Department of History, Ph.D. thesis, 2014.

Yıldız, Murat Cihan, *Strengthening Male Bodies and Building Robust Communities: Physical Culture in the Late Ottoman Empire*, University of California, Los Angeles, Department of History, Ph.D. thesis, 2015.

Books and Monographs

Addy, Premen, *Tibet on the Imperial Chessboard: The Making of British Policy towards Lhasa, 1899–1925* (Calcutta and New Delhi: Academic Publishers, 1984)

Ahmad, Feroz, *From Empire to Republic: Essays on the Late Ottoman Empire and Modern Turkey, Volume One* (Istanbul: Istanbul Bilgi University Press, 2nd ed., 2014)

Akmese, Handan Nezir, *The Birth of Modern Turkey: The Ottoman Military and the March to World War One* (London and New York: I. B. Tauris, 2005)

Alkış, Ali Sami, *Çanakkale'de Şehit Düşen Futbolcular: Yedi Kandilli Avize* (Istanbul: Yarımada Yayınları, 2008)

Allen, William Edward David, and Muratoff, Paul, *Caucasian Battlefields: A History of the Wars on the Turco-Caucasian Border 1828–1921* (Cambridge: Cambridge University Press, 1953)

American Friends of Turkey, Inc. (New York, 1931)

Anglesey, The Marquess of, *A History of the British Cavalry 1816-1919, Volume 5: Egypt, Palestine and Syria, 1914 to 1919* (Barnsley: Leo Cooper, 1998)

Bahr, Johannes, and Erker, Paul, *Bosch: History of a Global Enterprise* (Munich: C. H. Beck, 2015)

Bajohr, Frank, *'Aryanisation' in Hamburg: The Economic Exclusion of Jews and the Confiscation of their Property in Nazi Germany* (New York and Oxford: Berghahn Books, 2002)

Baker, T. F. T. (ed.), *A History of the County of Middlesex: Volume 11. Stepney, Bethnal Green* (London: Victoria County History, 1998)

Bali, Rıfat N., *The Saga of a Friendship: Asia Kent Jennings and the American Friends of Turkey* (Istanbul: Libra Kitapçılık ve Yayınçılık, 2009)

Bali, Rıfat N., *From Anatolia to the New World: Life Stories of the First Turkish Immigrants to America* (Istanbul: Libra Kitapçılık ve Yayınçılık, 2013)

Bell, Karl, *The Magical Imagination: Magic and Modernity in Urban England, 1780–1914* (Cambridge: Cambridge University Press, 2012)

Bell, Karl, '"They are Without Christ and Without Hope": Heathenism, Popular Religion and Supernatural Belief in Portsmouth's Maritime Community, c. 1851-1901', in Brad Beaven, Karl Bell and Robert James (eds), *Port Towns and Urban Cultures: International Histories of the Waterfront, c. 1700–2000* (London: Palgrave MacMillan, 2016), pp.49–68.

Besikci, Mehmet, *The Ottoman Mobilization of Manpower in the First World War: Between Voluntarism and Resistance* (Leiden and Boston: Brill, 2012)

Bhanja, K. C., *Darjeeling at a Glance* (Darjeeling: Oxford Book & Stationery Co., 4th ed., 1944)

Brandon, Peter, and Short, Brian, *The South East from AD 1000* (London and New York: Routledge, 1990)

Brown, Jonathan, *Farming in Lincolnshire 1850–1945* (Lincoln: History of Lincolnshire Committee, 2005)

Brown, William Baker, *History of Submarine Mining in the British Army* (Chatham: W. & J. Mackay, 1910)

Church, R. A., 'Labour Supply and Innovation 1800–1860: The Boot and Shoe Industry', in R. P. T. Davenport-Hines (ed.), *Capital, Entrepreneurs and Profits* (Oxford and New York: Frank Cass, 2006), pp.89–109.

Clarsen, Georgina, *Eat my Dust: Early Women Motorists* (Baltimore: The Johns Hopkins University Press, 2008)

Criss, Nur Bilge, *Istanbul under Allied Occupation, 1918–1923* (Leiden: Brill, 1999)

Çalışlar, İzzeddin, *The 150 Years of the Galatasaray Lycée: A Window to the West* (Istanbul: Istanbul Research Institute Publications, 2018)

Dadrian, Vahakn N., and Akcam, Taner (eds), *Judgment at Istanbul: The Armenian Genocide Trials* (Oxford: Berghahn Books, 2011)

Darjeeling Himalayan Railway: Illustrated Guide for Tourists (London: McCorquodale & Co., 1896)

Daunt, Patricia, *The Palace Lady's Summerhouse: And Other Inside Stories from a Vanishing Turkey* (Edinburgh: Caique Publishing, 2017)

Deacon, Bernard, *The Cornish Family: The Roots of our Future* (Fowey: Cornwall Editions, 2003)

DeNovo, John A., *American Interests and Policies in the Middle East 1900–1939* (Minneapolis: University of Minnesota Press, 1963)

Disko, Sasha, *The Devil's Wheels: Men and Motorcycling in the Weimar Republic* (Oxford and New York: Berghahn Books, 2016)

Donaldson, Dave, 'Railroads of the Raj: Estimating the Impact of Transportation Infrastructure', *LSE Asia Research Centre, Working Papers, 41* (March 2010)

Dozey, E. C., *A Concise History of the Darjeeling District since 1835 with a Complete Itinerary of Tours in Sikkim and the District* (Calcutta: N. Mukherjee, 2nd ed., 1922)

Fack, Dietmar, 'Die Veränderung des Mobilitätsverhaltens von Frauen im Übergang zur Moderne', in Antje Flade and Maria Limbourg (eds), *Frauen und Männer in der Mobilen Gesellschaft* (Opladen: Leske & Budrich, 1999), pp.33-48.

Findley, Carter Vaughn, *Ottoman Civil Officialdom: A Social History* (Princeton: Princeton University Press, 1989)

Frankopan, Peter, *The Silk Roads: A New History of the World* (London and New York: Bloomsbury, 2015)

Fraunholz, Uwe, *Motorphobia: Anti-automobiler Protest in Kaiserreich und Weimarer Republik* (Göttingen: Vandenbroeck & Ruprecht, 2002)

Fricker, Thomas (ed.), *The North Lincolnshire Poll Book 1852* (London: J. Morton and Simpson, Marshal and Co., 1852)

Galliver, Peter, 'Trade Unionism in Portsmouth Dockyard, 1880-1914: Change and Continuity', in Kenneth Lunn and Ann Day (eds), *History of Work and Labour Relations in the Royal Dockyards* (London and New York: Mansell, 1999), pp.99-126.

Gavin, Hector, *Sanitary Ramblings: Being Sketches and Illustrations of Bethnal Green: A Type of the Condition of the Metropolis and Other Large Towns* (London: John Churchill, 1848)

Geaves, Ron, *Islam in Victorian Britain: The Life and Times of Abdullah Quilliam* (Markfield, Leics.: Kube Publishing, 2013)

Gilham, Jamie, *Loyal Enemies: British Converts to Islam, 1850-1950* (London: Hurst & Company, 2014)

Goldblatt, David, *The Ball is Round: A Global History of Football* (London: Penguin, 2007)

Grenville, J. A. S., *The Jews and Germans of Hamburg: The Destruction of a Civilization, 1790-1945* (Abingdon: Routledge, 2012)

Griffiths, Percival, *The History of the Indian Tea Industry* (London: Weidenfeld and Nicolson, 1967)

Güçlü, Yücel, *Zeki Kuneralp and the Turkish Foreign Service* (Newcastle-upon-Tyne: Cambridge Scholars Publishing, 2015)

Güner, Deniz, 'Akaretler Sıra Evleri: Bir Multigrafik Okuma Denemesi', in Bahar Kaya (ed.), *Dolmabahçe Mekanın Hafızası* (Istanbul: Istanbul Bilgi Üniversitesi Yayınları, 2005), pp.207–48.

Gür, Aslı, 'Robert College; Laboratory for Religion, Shrine for Science – Transformation of Evangelical College Model in Constantinople', in Nur Bilge Criss, Selçuk Esenbel, Tony Greenwood and Louis Mazzari (eds), *American Turkish Encounters: Politics and Culture, 1830-1989* (Newcastle-upon-Tyne: Cambridge Scholars Publishing, 2011), pp.48–60.

Hadaway, Stuart, *Blood on the Sand: The Affair at Qatia, Sinai Desert, 23 April 1916* (Hythe, Kent: OGB Publishing, 2nd ed., 2017)

Haggard, H. Rider, *Rural England, Volume 2* (London, New York and Bombay: Longmans, Green and Co., 1902)

Harrison, Godfrey, *Bird and Company of Calcutta* (Calcutta: Anna Art Press, 1964)

Hawson, Eileen, *Darjeeling & the Dooars: Christian Cemeteries and Memorials 1842–1995* (London: British Association for Cemeteries in South Asia, 2006)

Heffer, Simon, *The Age of Decadence: Britain 1880–1914* (London: Penguin Random House, 2017)

Helmreich, Paul C., *From Paris to Sevres – The Partition of the Ottoman Empire at the Peace Conference of 1919–1920* (Columbus: Ohio State University Press, 1974)

Higgs, Michelle, *A Visitor's Guide to Victorian England* (Barnsley: Pen & Sword Military, 2014)

Hirschmann, Edwin, *Robert Knight: Reforming Editor in Victorian India* (Oxford: Oxford University Press, 2008)

Holderness, B. A., 'The Victorian Farmer', in G. E. Mingay (ed.), *The Victorian Countryside, Volume 1* (London: Routledge & Kegan Paul, 1981), pp.227–44.

Holmes, Ken, *Two Centuries of Shoemaking: Start-Rite, 1792-1992* (Norwich: Start-Rite Shoes Ltd., 1992)

Hovannisian, Richard G., *The Republic of Armenia, Vol.1. The First Year, 1918–1919* (Berkeley: University of California Press, 1971)

Howkins, Alan, 'Types of Rural Communities', in Joan Thirsk (gen. ed.), *The Agrarian History of England and Wales Vol. VII, 1850-1914, pt.2*, edited by E. J. T. Collins (Cambridge: Cambridge University Press, 2000), pp.1297–353.

Iggulden, H. A., *The 2nd Battalion Derbyshire Regiment in the Sikkim Expedition* (London: Swan Sonnenschein & Co., 1900)

Karabekir, Kazım, *İstiklal Harbimiz, Cilt 1* (Istanbul: Yapi Kredi Yayınları, 3rd ed., 2010)

Karagöz, Erkan, *Güneybatı Kafkasya: Siyasal ve Sosyal Mücadeleler Tarihi* (Istanbul: Park Kitap Yayınları, 2010)

Kaya, Ilhan, 'Immigration and Struggle for Integration: The Case of Turkish Americans', in Talip Kucukcan and Veyis Gungor (eds), *Turks in Europe: Culture, Identity, Integration* (Den Haag: Turkevi Research Centre, 2009), pp.271–86.

Kennedy, Dane, *The Magic Mountains: Hill Stations and the British Raj* (Berkeley, Los Angeles and London: University of California Press, 1996)

Knox, Malcolm, *Boom: The Underground History of Australia from Gold Rush to GFC* (London: Viking, 2013)

Koehler, Jeff, *Darjeeling: A History of the World's Greatest Tea* (London and New York: Bloomsbury, 2015)

Koshar, Rudy, 'Organic Machines: Cars, Drivers and Nature from Imperial to Nazi Germany', in Thomas Lekan and Thomas Zeller (eds), *Germany's Nature: Cultural Landscape and Environmental History* (New Brunswick, New Jersey and London: Rutgers University Press, 2005), pp.111–39.

Kotar, S. L., and Gessler, J. E., *Cholera: A Worldwide History* (Jefferson, Nc.: McFarland & Company Inc., 2014)

Kuran, Aram, and Hiçyılmaz, Ergun, *Osmanlı'dan Günümüze – Ermeni-Rum-Musevi Külüpleri ve Sporcuları* (Poseidon Yayıncılık: no place or date of publication given)

Lama, Basant P., *Through the Mists of Time: The Story of Darjeeling* (Kurseong: Bhawani Offset Printing and Publication, 2008)

Lawie, Kit, and Richardson, Michael (eds), *East Keal: The Story of a Village* (East Keal: Marden Hill Press, 2000)

Ledger, Sally, 'The New Woman and the Crisis of Victorianism', in Sally Ledger and Scott McCraken (eds), *Cultural Politics at the Fin de Siècle* (Cambridge: Cambridge University Press, 1995), pp.22-44.

Lethbridge, Roper, *The Golden Book of India: A Genealogical and Biographical Dictionary of the Ruling Princes, Chiefs, Nobles and Other Personages, Titled or Decorated, of the Indian Empire* (Delhi: Aakar Books, 2005 – first published in 1893)

Liedtke, Rainer, 'Germany's Door to the World: A Haven for the Jews? Hamburg, 1590–1933', in David Cesarini (ed.), *Port Jews: Jewish Communities in Cosmopolitan Maritime Trading Centres, 1550-1950* (London and Portland, Or.: Frank Cass, 2002), pp.75–86.

Macaulay, Thomas Babington, *The History of England from the Accession of James II, Volume III* (New York: Cosmo Classics, 2009)

Macgeorge, G. W., *Ways and Works in India* (Westminster: Archibald Constable and Co., 1894)

MacMillan, Margaret, *Women of the Raj: The Mothers, Wives and Daughters of the British Empire in India* (New York: Random House, 1988)

Macmunn, George, and Falls, Cyril, *Military Operations: Egypt and Palestine: From the Outbreak of War with Germany to June 1917* (London: HMSO, 1928)

Mango, Andrew, *Ataturk* (London: John Murray, 1999)

Mansel, Philip, *Levant: Splendour and Catastrophe on the Mediterranean* (London: John Murray, 2010)

Marchand, Suzanne, and Lindenfeld, David, 'Germany at the Fin de Siècle: An Introduction', in Suzanne Marchand and David Lindenfeld (eds), *Germany at the Fin de Siècle: Culture, Politics and Ideas* (Baton Rouge: Louisiana State University Press, 2004), pp.1–32.

Markham, Lt C. J., *The Sikkim Expedition from January 1888 to January 1890* (Calcutta: The Superintendent of Government Printing, 1890)

Martin, Terry, *The Iron Sherpa: The Story of the Darjeeling Himalayan Railway, 1879–2006: Volume 1* (Chester: RailRomances, 2006)

Martin, Terry, *The Iron Sherpa: The Story of the Darjeeling Himalayan Railway, 1879–2006: Volume 2: The Route, Locomotives, Railway Stock and Infrastructure* (Chester: RailRomances, 2010)

Massey, W. T., *The Desert Campaigns* (New York and London: G. P. Putnam's Sons, 1918)

Mazuchelli, Nina Elizabeth, *The Indian Alps and how we crossed them: Being a Narrative of Two Years' Residence in the Eastern Himalayas and Two Months' Tour of the Interior, By a Lady Pioneer* (New York: Dodd, Mead and Co., 1876)

McLaren, Angus, *A Prescription for Murder: The Victorian Serial Killings of Dr Thomas Neill Cream* (Chicago: University of Chicago Press, 1993)

Merriman, Peter, *Mobility, Space and Culture* (London and New York: Routledge, 2012)

Misra, Maria, *Business, Race and Politics in British India, c. 1850–1960* (Oxford: Clarendon Press, 1999)

O'Connell, Sean, *The Car and British Society: Class, Gender and Motoring, 1896–1939* (Manchester and New York: Manchester University Press, 1998)

O'Connell, Sean, 'Motoring and Modernity', in Francesca Carnevali and Julie-Marie Strange (eds), *20th Century Britain: Economic, Cultural and Social Change* (Harlow: Pearson Education, 2nd ed., 2007), pp.111–26.

Paget, William Henry, *Frontiers and Overseas Expeditions from India. Vol. IV. North and North-Eastern Frontier Tribes* (Simla: Government Monotype Press, 1907)

Phegley, Jennifer, *Courtship and Marriage in Victorian England* (Santa Barbara, Denver and Oxford: Praeger, 2012)

Pool, John J., *Studies in Mohammedanism, Historical and Doctrinal, with a Chapter on Islam in England* (Westminster: Archibald Constable and Co., 1892)

Procida, Mary A., *Married to the Empire: Gender, Politics and Imperialism in India, 1883-1947* (Manchester: Manchester University Press, 2002)

Proctor, Tammy M., 'Introduction: Building an Empire of Youth: Scout and Guide History in Perspective', in Nelson R. Block and Tammy M. Proctor (eds), *Scouting Frontiers: Youth and the Scout Movement's First Century* (Newcastle-upon-Tyne: Cambridge Scholars Publishing, 2009), pp.26–38.

Quail, Sarah, *Portsmouth in the Great War* (Barnsley: Pen & Sword Military, 2014)

Rawding, Charles K., *The Lincolnshire Wolds in the Nineteenth Century* (Lincoln: History of Lincolnshire Committee, 2001)

Riley, R. C., 'The Industries of Portsmouth in the Nineteenth Century', *Portsmouth Papers, 25* (1976)

Robinson, David, *Chaplin: His Life and Art* (London: Penguin, 2nd ed., 2001)

Rogan, Eugene, *The Fall of the Ottomans: The Great War in the Middle East, 1914–1920* (London: Allen Lane, 2015)

Scharff, Virginia, *Taking the Wheel: Women and the Coming of the Motor Age* (Albuquerque: University of New Mexico Press, 2nd ed., 1999)

Short, Brian, 'The Evolution of Contrasting Communities within Rural England', in Brian Short (ed.), *The English Rural Community: Image and Analysis* (Cambridge: Cambridge University Press, 1992), pp.19–43.

Sparrow, Walter Shaw, *Frank Brangwyn and His Work* (Boston: Dana Estes, 1911)

Stuart, Charles Douglas, and Park, A. J., *The Variety Stage: A History of the Music Halls from the Earliest Period to the Present Times* (London: T. Fisher Unwin, 1895)

Sunata, İ. Hakkı, *İstibdattan Meşrutiyete Çocukluktan Gençliğe* (Istanbul: Türkiye İş Bankası Kültür Yayınları, 2006)

Sunata, İ. Hakkı, *Gelibolu'dan Kafkaslara: Birinci Dünya Savaşı Anılarım* (Istanbul: Türkiye İş Bankası Kültür Yayınları, no date given)

Szurek, Emmanuel, 'The Linguist and the Politician: The Türk Dil Kurumu and the Field of Power in the 1930s-40s', in Marc Aymes, Benjamin Gourise and Elise Massicard (eds), *Order and Compromise: Government Practices in Turkey from the Late Ottoman Empire to the Early 21st Century* (Leiden: Brill, 2015), pp.68–96.

Tharoor, Shashi, *Inglorious Empire: What the British did to India* (London: C. Hurst & Co., 2017)

Turnağlu, Banu, *The Formation of Turkish Republicanism* (Princeton: Princeton University Press, 2017)

Uzgören, Gökhan, *Türk İzcilik Tarihi* (Istanbul: Papatya Yayıncılık, 2000)

Ünaydın, Ruşen Eşref, *Galatasaray ve Futbol: Türkiye'de Futbol, İstanbul'da Spor Nasıl Başladı, Neler Yaşandı* (Istanbul: Kakitap, 2014)

Üngör, Uğur Ümit, *The Making of Modern Turkey: Nation and State in Eastern Anatolia, 1913–1950* (Oxford: Oxford University Press, 2011)

Wallace, Richard, *The Darjeeling Himalayan Railway* (Doncaster: Darjeeling Himalayan Railway Society, 2nd ed., 2009)

Walton, John K., *The English Seaside Resort: A Social History, 1750–1914* (Leicester: Leicester University Press, 1983)

Wilson, Jon, *India Conquered: Britain's Raj and the Chaos of Empire* (London: Simon & Schuster UK, 2017)

Woodfin, Edward C., *Camp and Combat on the Sinai and Palestine Front: The Experience of the British Empire Soldier, 1916–1918* (Houndmills, Basingstoke: Palgrave MacMillan, 2012)

Woods, Henry F., *Spunyarn: From the Strands of a Sailor's Life Afloat and Ashore, Volume 2* (London: Hutchinson, 1924)

Woods, Peter, *A Short History of the Robinson Family of Bishop Norton, West Torrington, South Ormsby, Asgarby, East Keal and Authorpe in the County of Lincoln* (2002)

Wreyford, Paul, *The Secret History of Chelmsford* (Stroud: The History Press, 2014)

Yüce, Mehmet, *Ale'l-ıtlak Baldırı Çıplak: Hatırat, Makalat, Mulakat* (Istanbul: İletişim Yayıncılık, 2018)

Zürcher, Erik J., *The Unionist Factor – The Role of the Committee of Union and Progress in the Turkish National Movement, 1905–1926* (Leiden: Brill, 1984)

Zürcher, Erik J., *The Young Turk Legacy and Nation Building: From the Ottoman Empire to Ataturk's Turkey* (London and New York: I. B. Tauris, 2012)

Articles and Conference Proceedings

Anon., 'A Side-Show in the Aftermath of the World War', *The Journal of the United Service Institution of India*, 55, 241 (October 1925), pp.95–110.

Appiah, Kwame Anthony, 'Cosmopolitan Patriots', *Cultural Inquiry*, 23, 3 (Spring 1997), pp.617–39.

Balfour, M. C., 'Legends of the Cars', *Folklore*, 2, 2 (June 1891), pp.145–70.

Beaven, Brad, 'Slum Priests as Missionaries of Empire in a British Naval Port Town, Portsmouth c.1850–1900', *Forum Navale*, 72, 2 (March 2016), pp.54–77.

Bozkurt, Celil, '1. Dünya Savaşı'nda Filistin Suriye Cephesi'nde Nili Casusluk Örgütünün Faaliyetleri', *Atatürk Araştırma Merkezi Dergisi*', 30, 88 (March 2014), pp.89–114.

Burton, Antoinette, 'Making a Spectacle of Empire: Indian Travellers in Fin de Siècle London', *History Workshop Journal*, 42 (Autumn 1996), pp.126–46.

Chaudhuri, Nupur, 'Memsahibs and Motherhood in Nineteenth-Century Colonial India', *Victorian Studies*, 31, 4 (Summer 1988), pp.517–35.

Grand, Sarah, 'The New Aspect of the Woman Question', *The North American Review*, 158, 448 (March 1894), pp.270–6.

Gunesch, Konrad, 'Education for Cosmopolitanism; Cosmopolitanism as a Personal Cultural Identity Model for and within International Relations', *Journal of Research in International Education*, 3, 3 (2004), pp.251–75.

Gurbetoğlu, Ali, 'II Meşrutiyet Dönemi Çocuk Dergilerinde Çocukluk Anlayışı', *Ankara Üniversitesi Eğitim Bilimleri Fakültesi Dergisi*, 40, 2 (2007), pp.63–92.

Halliday, Fred, 'Three Concepts of Internationalism', *International Affairs*, 64, 2 (Spring 1988), pp.187–98.

Harris, Tina, 'Silk Roads and Wool Routes: Contemporary Geographies of Trade between Lhasa and Kalimpong', *India Review*, 7, 3 (2008), pp.200–22.

Kamberidou, Irene, 'The East in the Eyes of Western Women Travellers of the 18th and 19th Centuries: Solidarity and Understanding the Past', *Proceedings of the East in the Eyes of the West*, International Conference of the Faculty of Arts, Kuwait University, 26–28 November 2013.

Kaya, Ilhan, 'Comparing and Contrasting Turkish Immigration to the United States and Europe', *International Journal of Turkish Studies*, 19, 1–2 (2013), pp.75–93.

Kenny, Judith T., 'Climate, Race and Imperial Authority: The Symbolic Landscape of the British Hill Stations in India', *Annals of the Association of American Geographers*, 85, 4 (December 1995), pp.694–714.

Kling, Blair B., 'The Origin of the Managing Agency System in India', *The Journal of Asian Studies*, 26, 1 (November 1966), pp.37–47.

Küçükuğurlu, Murat, 'Cihangiroğlu İbrahim Bey'in 93 Harbi'nden Kurtuluş Savaşı'na kadar Kars ve Çevresindeki Teşkilatanmada Oynadığı Rol', *Atatürk Dergisi*, 3, 2 (2002), pp.249–60.

Macpherson, W. J., 'Investment in Indian Railways, 1845–1875', *The Economic History Review*, 8, 2 (December 1955), pp.177–86.

McQuiston, Julian R., 'Tenant Right: Farmer Against Landlord in Victorian England 1847–1883', *Agricultural History*, 47, 2 (April 1973), pp.95–113.

Mukherjee, Sumita, 'A Warning Against Quack Doctors: The Old Bailey Trial of Indian Oculists, 1893', *Historical Research*, 86, 231 (February 2013), pp.76–91.

Offer, Avner, 'Farm Tenure and Land Values in England c.1750–1950', *The Economic History Review*, 44, 1 (February 1991), pp.1–20.

Okay, Cüneyd, 'The Introduction, Early Development and Historiography of Soccer in Turkey: 1890-1914', *Soccer and Society*, 3, 3 (2002), pp.1–10.

Perkins, J. A., 'Tenure, Tenant Right and Agricultural Process in Lindsay, 1780–1950', *The Agricultural History Review*, 23, 1 (1975), pp.1–22.

Shepherd, Jennifer, 'The British Press and Turn-of-the-Century Developments in the Motoring Movement', *Victorian Periodicals Review*, 38, 4 (Winter 2005), pp.379–91.

Stead, David R., 'The Mobility of English Tenant Farmers c.1700–1850', *The Agricultural History Review*, 51, 2 (2003), pp.173–89.

Süme, Mehmet, and Özsoy, Selami, 'Osmanlı'dan Günümüze Türkiye'de Bisiklet Sporu', *Selçuk Üniversitesi Sosyal Bilimler Enstitüsü Dergisi*, 24 (2010), pp.345–60.

Sürmeli, Serpil, 'Güneybatı Kafkas Hükümeti Tercümanı Ahmed (Robenson)', *Atatürk Dergisi*, 3, 2 (2002), pp.89–96.

Toprak, Zafer, 'Meşrutiyet ve Mütareke Yıllarında Türkiye'de İzcilik', *Toplumsal Tarih*, 52 (April 1998), pp.13–20.

Tuğluoğlu, Fatih, 'II Meşrutiyet Döneminde Milliyetçi Bir Çocuk Dergisi: Talebe Defteri (1913-1919)', *Cağdaş Türkiye Tarihi Araştırmaları Dergisi*, 15, 30 (Spring 2015), pp.99–139.

Warren, Allen, 'Sir Robert Baden-Powell, the Scout Movement and Citizen Training in Great Britain, 1900–1920', *The English Historical Review*, 101, 399 (April 1986), pp.376–98.

Yenigazi, Mehmet Sungur, 'Kars, Sarıkarmış ve Oltu'nun yakın Tarihinden Sayfalar: Mehmet Sungur'un Hatıraları-II', *Bizim Ahıska*, 41 (Winter 2016), pp.34–9.

Acknowledgements

First of all, I would like to thank all the staff at Amberley who helped in the production and publicity of the book. In particular, my thanks go to Connor Stait, Shaun Barrington, Alex Bennett, Nikki Embery and Phillip James Dean. Connor and his colleagues were willing to take a punt on the book at a time when other publishers and agents showed little interest.

Staff at the National Archives, the archives in Lincoln and at the University of Glasgow were very helpful in tracing documents and correspondence. I am also grateful to the Portsmouth Royal Dockyard Historical Trust for providing data.

Special thanks go to Kit Lawie for her kind hospitality and for driving me and my wife through the farmsteads and villages around East Keal. Her knowledge of Lincolnshire, and of East Keal especially, proved to be invaluable. With Anup Saha as our personal guide, we had a fascinating tour of 'colonial Calcutta' and the side streets of modern Kolkata, which lay off the usual tourist trail. Manoj Giri accompanied us on an exciting trip taking in the hill stations of Bengal and Sikkim. Our driver, Uttam, rescued us on several occasions from near impassable roads and potentially treacherous landslides. We will never forget the warm welcome of Tendup Lama in Darjeeling.

I am grateful to Alison Light for her words of advice on finding a publisher. Mehmet Yüce was extremely helpful in digging out details buried in the Ottoman archives and in providing insights into the life of Ahmet Robenson. My thanks also go to Celia Kerslake for helping me promote the book to the British Association for Turkish Area Studies, and to Selim and Sinan Kuneralp, Richard Miller, Alfred

Acknowledgements

Fuhr, Gayle Steinke, Ebru Akcasu and Bob Newell for their assistance. My former work colleague Dr Gün Kut supplied me with useful information about the Robinsons and Galatasaray Sports Club.

My sincere thanks go to Ülker Sayın for helping me translate some of the texts in German, and to Marc Sinan Winrow, Begum Zorlu and my friends Ahmet and Deniz Ceylan for carefully checking over parts of the manuscript.

Of course, this work would not have been possible without the backing of members of the extended Robinson family. The project would not have got off the ground without the initial encouragement of Gülperi Ceylan. Her fond childhood memories of Hannah Robinson spurred me to explore more deeply the lives of the Robinsons. Here, I must also thank Gayle Irwin, Dickon Hugh Wheelwright Robinson, Zeynep Özbora, Nürperi Süer, Geoffrey and Pelin Wilkes, and Gertrud Parschalk.

Bernard and Becky Robinson provided important materials on the family's connections to India and offered useful insights into the lives of the Robinsons who remained in Portsmouth. Ahmet Ceylan supplied key information about the branch of the Robinson family who settled in Turkey. Ahmet attended a number of public gatherings in Istanbul which focused on the history of Galatasaray and there he bravely challenged the views and findings of some Turkish historians who continued to peddle the traditional Ottoman/Turkish line on the Robinson family. Deniz and Ahmet Ceylan, were a constant source of support and encouragement throughout the project.

Last, but not least, my special and warmest thanks go to Nazan, for her interest and enthusiasm, for turning out to be the most demanding proofreader, and for being there.

Index